On Chance Road

A road is the site of many journeys
Richard Long: *Heaven and Earth*

To Beverlay

Hul the unexpected

Lunvence Shelley

'Where *was* this game of chance leading me?'

Highland View by Jerzy Marek
Private Collection/ The Bridgeman Art Library

On Chance Road

A thumb print of Britain

by

LAURENCE SHELLEY

THETIS

First published by Thetis Publications in 2011

Copyright © Laurence Shelley 2011
The moral right of the author has been asserted

British Library Cataloguing-in-Publication Data
A catalogue record for this book is available
from the British Library

ISBN 978-0-9556750-1-0

Cover and text illustrations by Rob Walker
Design and typesetting by Terence Sackett
Back cover photograph by Lielee Shelley

Printed and bound by
SRP Ltd, Exeter EX2 7LW

Published by
Thetis Publications
60 Bay View Road
Northam Bideford
Devon EX39 1BH
Tel/Fax 01237 424424

email: laurenceshelley@aol.com
www.thetispublications.co.uk

For Elwyn and Lyndsey,
Stuart and Amelia

ACKNOWLEDGEMENTS

First and foremost, an enormous vote of thanks to all those whose journeys I was privileged to share. I trust they will be happy with the space I've made for them. For indulging my wayward tendencies but keeping my words on track, thanks to all my writing friends: the Indian King trail-blazers led by Helen Wood and Karen Hughes; the Hartland Writers' Circle who whittled away any excess fat under the watchful eye of Marian van Eyk McCain; and Bideford writers Pamela Hogan and Terence Sackett always close at hand to coax me in the right direction. Special thanks to Terence for his sureness of touch in designing and typesetting the text, and to Rob Walker for his patient professionalism in honing the cover design and illustrations.

I have never felt such an instant rapport with complete strangers as I did throughout this journey. Some names have been changed to respect confidences but they will recognise who they are and I hope those I haven't been able to contact will get in touch. I owe all my fellow travellers the heartiest hugs and handshakes for their unique contributions. Last but certainly not least, I am eternally grateful for the support of my family. Wherever I am, I know they are there.

CREDITS

Heaven and Earth by Richard Long, Tate Publishing, 2009, extract by permission of the author.

Highland View by Jerzy Marek/Private Collection/The Bridgeman Art Library.

The Power of Now by Eckhart Tolle, Hodder & Stoughton, 2001: permission to use extracts applied for.

Photograph of head sculpture by permission of Simon Ruscoe.

Song for Ronald White Leask and *Mum's Song*, extracts by permission of Brindley Leask.

The Blue Door, Newlyn (1934) by Harold Harvey/Private Collection/Image courtesy of Paisnel Gallery.

Photograph of *Whaligoe Women* with permission of the glassmaker, Gillian Mannings Cox.

5

Beforehand

How do we know what journey we are on and where it will take us?

I hadn't realised how much directions can change until I tried walking Hadrian's Wall Path some years ago. Blisters forced me off course but I learnt far more about myself and my fellow human beings from 'off-the-wall' diversions than from following any single-minded path.

That experience whetted my appetite. What would a more random journey teach me? Hitchhiking came to mind. I thrived on it in my youth: the uncertainty of how I'd get on, who I'd meet and what they'd have to say.

Where would I go? I'd travelled east to west along Hadrian's Wall, so how about south to north? Lizard Point is the southernmost point of mainland Britain, and Dunnet Head – a place I'd never heard of – the northernmost. By chance I found that a papermaker lived there. That clinched it. I could do it to Dunnet – how right that sounded! – and look up the papermaker too.

Did I know what I was doing? Family and friends were right to ask. At sixty-five I'd left it a bit late for a mid-life crisis, but I tried to sound like a thinking man. 'I won't get lifts from lone women. Too risky. And I doubt whether I'll get a look-in from the younger generation. But there must be plenty of generous-minded people still around.'

Honestly, I confided to myself, how viable was it to hitchhike at all in 21st century Britain? And what did I know about the Britain of today? Precious little. This trip would give me a chance to reconnect. Where are we going? I'd ask all those who gave me lifts about their sense of direction. While I worked out mine, I'd discover theirs.

I had learnt something from the previous hike. Not for me the last-minute purchase of bargain-buy boots and the blisters that went with them. I dosed the soles of my feet with surgical spirit for weeks to harden the skin. And I spent days agonising over boots before deciding on a German make with a pedigree stretching back to 1370 at an historically great cost (for me) of £85.

And socks? I struck up serious relationships. My collection included inner ones to wick away the moisture, partnered with outer ones to mop it up, and pairs shamelessly double-looped in smart Merino wool. And I pre-walked the combinations. I was well equipped without a doubt. My windproof, waterproof, die-proof jacket with its fleece lining had so many pockets – eleven at the last count – that I could have passed for a mobile filing cabinet, and just in case I needed overnight storage I packed some camping gear.

I was ready for anything but, when I announced that I'd be setting off in November, my sanity was questioned. Whatever had possessed me? 'It's the wrong time of the year,' I was told. 'You'll be cold, wet and miserable.' But others said, 'It's going to be fascinating' and, 'You get what you expect.' I didn't know what to expect. Something told me this was the right time. I had to take a chance. Chance must have known. It was lying in wait.

Orkney Islands

North Ronaldsay

16. Dunnet Head

15. Lybster

14. Portsoy

Inverness

13. Pitlochry

12. Kinross

11. South Queensferry

Glasgow

10. Burnmouth

9. Newcastle

Carlisle

Bradford

Manchester

8. Chesterfield

7. Derby

Birmingham

Leicester

Hereford

Bristol

6. Bath

Taunton

4. Crockernwell

2. St Enoder

Exeter

5. Honiton

3. Lifton

1. Lizard Point

Day One

Lizard Point to St.Enoder

'I couldn't wait to start practising my swagger'

The Love Story

On my walk down to Lizard Point, I hesitated as I passed the Most Southerly House in Britain. Surely there was no better place to start my search for directions. Who lived in this white bungalow not far from the cliff edge, and why? The gate had one of those guard dog warnings that conjure up shredded trousers. I rattled the gate and, with no sign of a savage lick, reckoned it was safe to proceed.

Was anyone in? One knock and a deep breath.

The door opened. 'Yes?' The elderly lady spoke firmly. I detected a slight accent.

'I'm about to start a long hike and wondered what brought you here.' Amazing how well impertinence can be passed off as an innocent enquiry. She was only too happy to tell me.

Her story began in 1945, when she was fourteen, after Germany was occupied. Having attended a relative's funeral, she – Ingrid – and her mother were desperate for a bus to take them to the railway station. After one going the other way stopped, Ingrid found that it was heading straight back to the station. 'I ran from behind the bus to tell my mother when a car showed up out of the blue. I tried to get out of the way double quick but it caught my hip, like someone had punched me hard.'

She was lying like a stick across the radiator. 'When the car braked, I must have shot off, cracking my head on the road. The road was all dusty, so I slid and the skin was torn off my hands down to the knuckles. When I came to, I saw this big black car with a gleaming radiator and straightaway thought 'Mercedes'.' The next thing she heard was the German driver – 'horrible man, in a grey officer's uniform' – barking out "*Verdammt noch mal lauf*", Walk, damn you, walk. When she didn't walk, couldn't walk, he dragged her into the car.

With him was a sympathetic British colonel who talked to her all the time to stop her losing consciousness while they drove to the British Military Hospital. Ingrid had a fractured skull. 'I was unconscious on and off for months.'

The British officer kept in touch and brought a German Shepherd puppy once. 'He said, "You can have him. He's called Dippy". But we were evacuated in a house with five other families and couldn't keep it. He was so sweet. I'll never forget,' she said with a light-hearted shrug, 'he weed on my bed.'

She was off school for months with memory loss and told to redo the year, but they couldn't afford it. She'd hoped to be a vet but that was out of the question. Instead the British officer helped get her a job as a laboratory assistant at the British Military Hospital. 'I did all the dirty work at first, but my English was improving all the time.'

Seeing me with one hand propped on the door post, she broke off. 'I'd invite you in, but we've only just come back from holiday and the place is in such a mess.'

I was only too keen to hear the next instalment.

After the war British films were screened with sub-titles. One film made a big impression: *Love Story*, dubbed *Cornish Rhapsody*. The rugged coastline with waves crashing in from the Atlantic conjured up distant memories. As a girl, she had the same dream, dozens of times, in which she walked for ages across fields before reaching the sea and a sandy inlet backed by rocky cliffs.

Six or seven years on, a new sergeant was due to take charge of the laboratory. Some of her colleagues knew him as Snowy. They told her he'd got blue eyes, blond hair and was Cornish. 'I pricked up my ears,' she laughed, 'and when we met – in June '53 – I fell for him.' Within months they applied to marry. 'Immediately he was taken miles away to Hanover because they didn't agree with

... you know ... marriages between us and them. But he came back every weekend.' The wedding was a perfunctory business. They exchanged rings in a café under the table.

Both were set on living in Cornwall. They travelled round the county on motorbike trying to find the beach of her childhood dreams. Time and again, Snowy would ask, 'Is it this one?' One day, out walking at the Lizard, they came across this deserted old bungalow in a setting that felt all too familiar to Ingrid. They couldn't forget the bungalow and returned two years later to find it derelict.

'Well,' Ingrid said to Snowy, 'at least let's have a picnic in the grounds. See if you can find a plank to put the Thermos on.' He came across an overgrown board in the top of a hedge. Up-ended, it turned out to be an estate agent's 'For Sale' sign. That was how they came to buy the bungalow back in 1963. It had been on the market for eighteen months. Little wonder there'd been no interest.

What did Ingrid make of all this?

'It's fate,' she said, 'that I was knocked down. To have bought this house is a dream come true.'

A warm handshake with Snowy who'd been clearing up inside and I bade goodbye. Only then did I notice the Mercedes in the drive but I hadn't seen the dog. It had to be a well-contented one – a German Shepherd for sure.

What a start to my journey! Ingrid's story – of a reverse with a real upside – set me thinking. How could I tip fortune in my favour? I sauntered down to the southernmost beach and casually picked up a flat pebble. Yes, this would do it. I skimmed it across the calm stretch of water beyond the lapping waves. Three ... four I counted. Not good enough. One more go. Better. Five ... maybe six bounces.

It was a good luck pointer: reaching beyond to that one more lift. A link with the past too. This skimming game was played back in Roman times. It was a Roman game, *ludus latrunculorum*, the Soldier's game, that helped give direction to my previous journey. This was a new game. I'd better start playing. Except that, in retracing my steps, I was stopped in my tracks.

The Serpentine Symmetry

Outside some wooden buildings, painted a cheerful blue, a man on a stool was chipping away at a block of stone cradled in a thick cloth on his lap. 'P.L.Casley & Son, Local Serpentine Stone Specialists' a sign on the roof read. I watched as flakes fell to the ground from the sharp taps of his hammer.

'What's that about?' I asked. Mr Casley, I presumed.

'It's a lighthouse,' he said, 'or will be.' He'd been working the stone for thirty years, as his father before him. Perhaps not for many more years. Deposits of good quality serpentine, with its subtle green and red colouring, were being exhausted. 'The only other source is in the north-east of Scotland,' he said. 'They call it Portsoy marble.'

I wondered if my path might take me there. A shame that time was running out for this stone and the family tradition, since he still enjoyed the work, especially the contact with people.

'They come from all over the world,' he said. 'Australia yesterday.' Many took away a sample of serpentine as a souvenir of their visit.

I had to follow suit. Among the array of items in his showroom – from lighthouses, lamp bases and bowls to egg shapes and ear rings – one circular brooch caught my eye. Why? The grain of the stone evoked the rippling patterns of water. I'd skimmed a stone on water. Here was water on stone. Symmetry all round: a brooch for my wife and a memento for me whenever she wore it!

The Essential Grandmother

At five to eleven, I started hitching. I thanked the cerulean blue sky for its clarity and the rushes of wind for keeping me cool. I noticed everything that wasn't green: a Red Admiral butterfly, purply pink campion, golden yellow gorse and ragwort, deep red rose hips and a few blackberries for the picking.

Fifteen minutes ticked by and twenty cars with them. Twenty-one ... two ... three ... and at the twenty-fourth thumbing, the moment I'd been waiting for arrived: my thumb came to a halt. So did a Toyota Landcruiser. Any reservation about 4 x 4s was consigned to vanishing point. So was another preconception.

'I'm not going far, only a mile or two before I turn off to Cadgwith. Is that any good to you?' the lone woman driver said.

'Is that any good?' And I repeated with asterisks. 'You've knocked me for six. You're the first person to stop and you're a woman.'

'Yes?' Sally said, indulgently.

'Well, I wasn't expecting it.'

'Oh I used to pick up anyone. But nowadays it would be more of a youngster, or someone your age.' I had to take that as a plus.

'Anyway,' I said, 'anywhere north will do.' Sally used to hitchhike. With sunglasses perched jauntily atop swirls of silvery hair, her adventurousness was still shining. We had little time to chat, enough for her to say that children in these parts miss out on some facilities, but were fortunate to grow up in this environment.

'So what gives you direction in life?' I asked, straight to the point.

'That's easy,' she said. 'Being a grandmother.' She had ten grandchildren. 'When your own children leave home, you feel empty. But when they have their own, you feel tremendously useful.' Sally's grandchildren were lucky to have her signpost pointing in their direction.

The Hitchhiker's Guide

Soon after we parted I thought I'd seen an apparition. A dark figure materialised on my side of the road, maybe a hundred yards behind. And no, I wasn't mistaken: it *was* hitchhiking.

One presence any hitchhiker finds haunting is another thumb, especially to the rear. It was futile marching on when any lift would be gone before I had a look-in. I did the pragmatic thing: slow down. The figure looked less like any archetypal hitchhiker the closer he (it *was* a he) came. The man wore a long, dark trench coat, sported a black and well bushed-out beard, but carried no rucksack. His whole bearing was 'swarthy and swash-buckling'. He had the look of a boarder you'd want to repel.

'How're you doing?' I said limply.

'You're not going right,' he said, unsmiling, and ignoring my pleasantry. 'I've been watching you. You can't thumb while you're

13

walking. That's all wrong.'

'It's just that I like to keep going.'

'But not when you're thumbing. They've got to see you. Face the traffic, mate. Show your face. It's courtesy. Be respectful.'

'That's a good one.'

'Yes. And your thumb ...'

'My thumb?'

'Stick it straight out, not upright. You look as though you're saying hello, but you're asking for a lift. Don't worry about the two fingers. That's recognising your existence. The worst is being ignored. And there's another thing.'

'What's that?'

'Your hips are too square. I can tell you're tense. You want to get more relaxed, more angular. Let your body be loose, mate ... a bit like a swagger, see.' He was demonstrating. 'Use the energy, use the swing of the rucksack as it moves from one buttock to the other' – he had an aggressive way with the word 'buttock' – 'to drive you on. Let your hips get into it. If you walk like that, you won't notice the miles and I'll tell you this,' – he was into full-frontal mode – 'you'll cover more ground. Know what?'

I didn't get a chance to guess.

'It's more like a dance.'

'I never thought,' I said, not knowing what to say.

'Where're you going to stand?' This was turning into an interrogation.

I gave him the screwed-up look.

'Think about it. I mean this corner now. You need to stand back. Why? You don't want to block a driver's view, do you? God, look how he's cut the corner' – he broke off to berate a disrespectful motorist – 'but give them a chance to stop. If it's a fast road with a long lay-by, stand at the start. But on ordinary roads, go to the far end so they can see you and pull in. It's common sense: if you get it wrong, you'll be stuck forever. Look, I've spent six years hitching in this country. Believe me' – and I hadn't even signalled a doubt – 'I know what I'm doing. Get it right, mate. You're at the mercy of time, yes. But you've got freedom. And that's a gift of God.'

By this time I was thinking I must be the greenest-thumbing recidivist he'd ever had the misfortune to meet. But I had one question for this arbiter of hitchhiking etiquette, this proselytizer for the new religion. 'Won't it be difficult,' I said, 'for the two of us to get a lift?'

'Heavens no, man. Three of us and a dog hitched once. No problem,' he said. 'And if there's no joy here, I know the road. There's a junction further on. Or failing that, a pull-in by the holiday park.'

We tried joint thumbing twice, three times and, in between, he started to demonstrate the finer points of legwork. 'Don't walk flat-footed. It's all to do with how far you bring the leg up for the swing you need.' He was about to choreograph the new movements of this hiking ballet when a bus, the *Truronian*, hove into view. This corner must have been the bus stop. It pulled over.

'I'll get on,' he said suddenly.

'Wait a minute,' I said, open-mouthed, 'I don't even know your name.'

'Matthew.'

'D'you have a mobile number?' He was on the bus now, doling out his fare.

'No mate. Sorry. Good luck.'

And he was off. I watched the *Truronian* go. Could I have had a more intensive course in hitchhiking? Or opportunism? Matthew's advice would hardly ever be out of my mind. And I couldn't wait to start practising my swagger.

The Cider Maker

The swagger trials might have progressed had I not been forced on to the verge as cars passed. I felt like a sidestepper's understudy. Practice would have to wait. A little way on, I was presented with a different dilemma. Alongside a junction – Matthew's hitchhiking springboard – was The Lizard Cider Barn. Cider had long had happy vibes for me. I had to live down a ridiculous display of bonhomie once, after being held up at the Highwayman pub on Dartmoor by a pint of the rough stuff. But so soon after starting, ought I to divert? Only one way to find out.

I walked round and came across a youngish chap at a hopper, with a huge mound of apples ready to feed in. 'Enough to keep you going?' I said.

'We've had fourteen tons this year,' he said, 'as much as we can cope with. We've been pressing for three weeks and there's a good way to go yet.'

I wandered over to the shop where I met Sandra, who assisted with sales and Stanley, the quietly spoken man behind this venture. He told me they'd been going seven years and that the fourteen tons of apples would help account for their production capacity of five thousand gallons.

But I wasn't there to find out about the business. I told them where I was heading.

'Scotland?' Sandra queried. 'Well, if you'd left it a month, I could have taken you there. I'll be off to Eyemouth then.'

'Shame,' I said, speculating on the quirk of timing that might have landed me in Scotland in one go, with a woman driver. But now was not the time to be fast forwarding. Looking at the bottled cornucopia on display, I turned to Stanley. 'You must love your work.'

'Oh, I don't drink myself,' he said.

'No? So if I were to ask what sense of direction you get from your work ... ?'

'I'd say it gives me a reason to get up in the morning.'

'Yes? Is that it?'

'That's the truth. I used to work in engineering, then ran a caravan park. I could have retired, but look how many people lose impetus when they give up full-time work. Continue with a routine I say. Keeps me going.'

There was I expecting Stanley to wax lyrical about cider apples, and romance about such deliciously named Cornish varieties as Manaccan Primrose, Ladies Finger, King Byard and Pigs Nose. But in one lift and one diversion, I'd had lessons in life's basics. Keeping it simple was one; suck it and see, another. I didn't come away with a big flagon. 'I'll be happy with a small sample bottle,' I said. 'Make it the Vintage label.'

The Sun Seeker

I waited a while at the junction before itchy feet carried me on. When any car approached, I skipped onto the verge, turned round and fixed a smile to the thumb, but a disarming smile soon seemed at odds with an insistent thumb. I composed a 'wouldn't it be nice if ...' expression instead which appeared to have done the trick when the nicest couple pulled up.

'Very kind of you to stop,' I said. Hard to avoid the unction when faced with yet another woman driver.

'How far are you going?'

'Well, towards Truro. Anywhere that way will help.'

'We've got a bit of a problem,' she said, as I opened the rear door.

Across the back seat was a long parcel shelf, removed to make room for a large and imposing dog. After rearranging the furniture, I introduced myself. Margaret and her husband Keith had been enjoying a short break in their holiday home, oh and Jasper was exasperated that he couldn't get a closer sniff of the newcomer.

'He's got to keep you under surveillance,' Margaret said. Jasper was a Weimeraner, a German breed. With silvery grey coat and an ethereal set to the eyes, it's called the ghost dog. In the deepest wood with owls hooting, branches twitching and (you're not sure whose) heavy breathing, you wouldn't ask this dog the way. Those bluey grey eyes were haunting. It was hard to steer the conversation in any other direction with Jasper peering over my shoulder.

'He's ten years old, but stubborn as ever. He can be insolent sometimes' – I liked that – 'and stare you out. He needs to know who's boss,' she said, 'though you always feel you're one of his pack.' Margaret thought him a dog of little brain, governed by his stomach but Keith demurred, saying he knew how to open the fridge. That did tend to support the stomach hypothesis.

'I'd better tell you what I'm doing.' I handed them one of the cards I'd had printed, styling myself as writer and direction-seeker. 'I'm asking people what gives them a sense of direction.' I thought Jasper might figure in Margaret's answer. Not a bit of it.

'I always think you find your way by the sun,' she said. 'We were driving round Paris once. It was insane. We kept turning off at the wrong junction and the map made no sense. But we wanted to go north. It was about mid-day, so the sun had to be behind us. Amazing how often it comes in useful.'

I'd seen a programme on how homing pigeons navigate. It covered all the theories, like using landmarks, sounds and smells, or plotting the magnetic field through sensors in the eye and beak.

There was a way-out 'morphic resonance' theory which hinged on some paranormal bond between people, place and pigeon. I wouldn't discount any possibility. Neither would I rule out the blindingly obvious and I don't recollect that the sun got much of a mention. But if I had any doubt about where I was going at midday, I knew where to look now ... behind.

'Lucky we picked you up,' Margaret told me. 'It's a bit further this way but Keith said we'd see more of the coast.' Short of Truro, our ways parted and Jasper saw me off with eyes that would surely follow, wherever I went.

The Unbecoming Cauliflower

I'd been dropped off on a hill: not a good launch pad with cars shooting past. At the foot of it though was the Perran ar Worthal Fruit and Vegetable Stall. I fuelled up on an English russet, a Columbian banana, and an apricot yoghurt, after fending off a rapid response unit: a wasp which appeared the instant I peeled the lid.

About to leave, I caught a snatch of a customer's remark: 'I'd have bought that cauliflower if only ...' Why didn't this chap buy it? What I found was bizarre: a cauliflower masquerading as a cluster of limpets, gradated in size with the tiniest ones at the top, and all green. The cauliflower wouldn't have looked amiss in a gallery. 'Limpets Vegetating' sprang to mind.

I've always been taken by trompe l'oeil images. In early childhood, a lion tricked its way into an eiderdown fold. Later, I admired Picasso's vision of an old saddle and handlebars as a bull's head. My all-time favourite is a picture I rescued from the embers of a bonfire. It appears to show a huge tree on fire and, with scorched edges to the paper, the illusion couldn't be more convincing. Actually it's a shot from space of a river's tributaries.

How had these limpet lookalikes come about? The label on the tray identified them as *Romanesco*. Was there a Roman connection? Or were the cauliflowers a freakish accident of nature – the sort of mutant that GM trial objectors warn us about?

I went back to the counter but the assistant's best shot at enlightenment was, 'They came in yesterday and are only available for about two weeks.'

'Perhaps that's why I've never come across them,' I deduced half-wittedly.

She hadn't tasted them but assured me, a little reluctantly, that she'd try one that evening. Then I realised what the customer's 'if only' was about. You'd only buy these cauliflowers if you didn't have to eat them. There'd be another 'if only' in my case: 'if only' it didn't mean sacrificing a work of art. To consume a work of art merely to satisfy culinary curiosity, now that would be ... well, tasteless.

The Converting Pagans

The 'work of art' set me thinking. Why did these visual allusions grab me? I was rebuked in my twenties by an art tutor. Taking the underside of a human skull as my starting point, I turned it into a wild landscape of bare mountains and plunging ravines. 'Can't you do justice to what is?' she admonished.

Perhaps that was it; I was always looking for something beyond present realities. Being where I was wasn't enough. Little wonder I was seeking directions to take me somewhere else. If I looked for guidance now though, it wouldn't be the sun behind that I'd see but Matthew choreographing the hitchhiker's dance.

The road ahead was wider and the verge level enough to get in some good swagger practice. It was as if I'd thrown away the baby walker. Habit is a dullard and a swagger changes everything. The sheer novelty of walking in an angular way puts mileage out of mind. And there's the infectiousness of it.

When your hips are swinging and your feet are springing, it's not long before you're tossing your head back and slicing the air left and right with your nose. The comforting thwack of rucksack on alternate buttock and the bushy-tailed feeling you get from the syncopated rhythm drive you forward hypnotically. Matthew knew what he was talking about. I was enjoying the walk so much that stopping to thumb seemed a sacrifice and, when I did, it was with a certain nonchalance.

Whether it was that or pure luck I don't know, but in no time at all an oldish green car pulled up. Sitting in the driver's seat was a butch and burly-looking chap, complete with earrings – two in one ear – leather shorts and jacket.

'Thanks for stopping,' I said. 'I'm Laurence.'

'And I'm Muggy,' he said, a confidence I felt privileged to share. He introduced me to Helen, his partner sitting in the back, clustered with rings and the daughter alongside. 'She's Shy,' he said, as if it was her name. 'We saw you earlier.'

'Yes, then we turned round and came back,' added Helen.

'You went to that trouble?' I said. 'You shouldn't.' What *was* I saying?

They were off to Tresillian but could take me a good way up the road. Fresh from swaggering and at home with the free-as-air feeling, I asked how they made out.

'We live day to day,' Muggy said.

'What ... round here?'

'Yeah, but not for long. We're buying a bus, travelling. First National is giving away buses. With double deckers you just pay for the tyres but it's a bit more for a single decker. We'll be dishing out fifteen hundred for one: a Mercedes, H reg. My mate who's a fitter works for them. He's sussed it. He's into bikes like me.'

I ought to have known they were bikers. Muggy looked the part.

'We love it,' chimed in Helen. The enthusiasm was breaking out.

'But I've gotta sell a boat and truck first. Shouldn't take long.'

'You can't wait, can you?'

'No. We've had it up to here with rules and regulations. But we've gotta convert the bus first, to live in. Then we'll be off, through Europe and down to Gib. Can't afford to live in England any more. Not when I can go to Gib and live like a king on a hundred quid a week. Look at fags. You pay fifty quid for two hundred here. There it's £8.99. One thing though; you can't take a motorhome into Gib. It's not allowed.'

They were planning to park near the border and walk in. To find work?

'Possibly – my trade's welding – but I may not need to, not for cash. I've got friends there. We live by bartering. Money never changes hands.'

'Are you all going then?' I looked round at Helen and then Shy.

'We teach her at home,' Helen said.

'You won't be shy much longer,' I said. 'Not once you've tasted life on the road. That'll open up a new world. You'll learn so much.' She smiled.

'We'll try it three months at a time,' Helen said.

'We can live off savings,' chipped in Muggy, 'and then it'll be three months back here to earn more dosh.'

'Sounds as though you'll make out fine,' I said.

'Yeah, no trouble. I'm a pagan,' he said, as though that explained it and, just as suddenly, stopped. 'Sorry. We gotta turn off.'

I said, 'No worries', but I was sorry too. I'd enjoyed being an all too brief member of this clan. 'Great to meet you,' I said, shaking hands with them all. 'And you, you won't know yourself,' to Shy who graced me with a wide-mouthed grin.

I headed north towards the A30 and Bodmin beset with one question: what did it mean to be a pagan? The word had a derogatory ring to it, like 'heathen'. In my sketchy picture pagans were Nature worshippers, with 'Swampy' characters battling to the last branch against by-passes. And there'd be an older generation of bearded pagans – Druids celebrating the summer solstice on Salisbury Plain – but with ceremonies I'd think of as weird.

How easy it is to stereotype from ignorance and but a short step to prejudice. Yet meeting this pagan family made me think again. I'd experienced their spontaneous generosity, witnessed their determination to take control of their lives and admired their independent spirit. If being a pagan meant living day to day, that hardly seemed retrograde. It's what I was doing and it was liberating.

The Home-loving Bricklayer

Let loose was how I felt. My feet were well exercised with the new-found manner of propulsion, my eyes soaked up the rich colours of late autumn dressing many trees, while my head still played with the pagan encounter, jumping aboard a converted bus. It took time for this free and easy attitude to be rewarded. But the gods smiled.

A beaming, workmanlike face greeted me from a van. This well-loaded workhorse was possessed by a chap I'd put in his mid-thirties with woolly hat, half-rim specs and tank top. He could take me part way to Bodmin.

I jumped in. 'Have you ever hitchhiked?' I asked.

'Not since I was eighteen.'

'And do you pick up people often?'

'I wouldn't say so. Must be about ten years since I gave anyone a lift.'

'No?' I thought I'd better live up to this singular treatment. I handed him my card and trotted out my mission statement. How did he see his direction?

'Born and bred in Cornwall, man and boy,' he said. 'I'm a grafter, see. I've got mates who've moved on. There's one lives on a yacht off Gran Canaria. He's a chef. Part owns a restaurant on a beach. Nice life if you like it. I've been to Barbados. But tell you what I loved more: coming back.'

'So what do you do then?' I'd glimpsed tools of a trade at the back.

'I'm a bricklayer. But coming from an architectural background, I have to do things right. There's so much crap on those TV makeover programmes.'

'I know, but you're in the trade. Most people wouldn't notice what you pick up on.'

'Probably not. But take bricks: I use reclaimed and handmade when I can, not mass-produced ones. They cost more. That's the trouble. It's all down to price these days.'

I was warming to Paul's ethics. 'And customers don't want to pay?'

'Never as much. Some builders are as bad, pushing up the money by cheapening a job. Roofs for instance. How many new houses d'you see with bigger tiles?'

'Most I would say.'

'Exactly. Why? 'Cause they're a lot quicker to lay. Compare that with houses from the 50s. More common then to use plain Rosemary tiles, smaller so they take a lot longer. But in scale, so much better.'

I knew what Paul meant. Our house was built in the 50s. I was pleased we had to match up to those very tiles when we had an extension.

'I'm lucky,' he said. 'I get work from The National Trust and they mind about these things. And Prince Charles – he's had a big influence in this area. He gets my vote.'

'So you're happy with what you're doing?'

'Where else *would* I be? Bricklaying in Cornwall I'm never far from the sound of the sea. And after a day's work, back home to the family. Can you beat that?'

No, Paul. No. Remarkable to meet a working man so happy with his lot that he wouldn't change a thing. So different to the pagans. But hardly surprising that you'd want to stay put when you believe in what you're doing, and where.

The Trivial Pursuit

Paul had dropped me off on the A30 at ten to three. But the sheer volume of traffic hurtling past on this dual carriageway drained any optimism. Even if I found a suitable lay-by, who would slam on their brakes? I did find a lay-by and no-one answered the question. I trundled on. Cows looked me over but I was an invisible man to drivers hardly a whiff away.

The light was fading when I came to a slip road and crunch time. A signpost pointed down a lane to St.Enoder. Only two letters distinguished it from St.Enodoc, a place familiar from childhood holidays. A story went that St.Enodoc church had once been buried in shifting sands and was only found years later when a golfer's ball struck the steeple. It was a place prized by Sir John Betjeman who lies buried there.

Having nothing better to do while thumbing, I made up nonsensical anagrams from 'Enoder' and attached hypothetical meanings. It's what wayward minds do. 'End Ore' – pot of gold and rainbow came to mind; 'Roe End' – deer's demise … not so promising; 'Rodene' – girls' public school with poor spelling record.

The hitching was no better than my trivial pursuit of the ridiculous so I issued an ultimatum – a lift within five minutes or I'd take evasive action – and carried on with my inanity: 'Er Node' – hesitant at a junction … very relevant; 'Doneer' – doubtful Turkish nosh; 'Dronee' – butt of a dinner party bore. It was then that I came out with the one word, absurd as it was, that made sense: 'Doreen'.

Betjeman had played his part but, at the risk of committal, I'd have to say that 'Doreen' clinched it. I'd make my way to St.Enoder and see if I could fix up some accommodation. Ironic that, while expecting coherent answers from people about their direction, I was taking my cue from a tenuous link with a dead poet and a non-existent woman. Or was she? The half-mile traipse down the lane with my freewheeling mind produced one more impetus for my direction. Wouldn't it be fun to find someone living in a place of which their name was an anagram? Could there possibly be a Doreen in St.Enoder?

The Redeployed Soldier

It was a treat to leave the roar of the traffic behind. How blinkered my vision had been as the hapless observer of a futile race. A short stretch of the legs took me into a different world with open farmland and the distant view of a church. A buzzard suddenly flapped into the skies from a field of stubble.

I coasted down an incline to a terrace of houses but no signs of life. Near the church I glimpsed a plaque on a modern house: 'Dr. Samantha Montague – Homoeopath'. Names must mean something to a 'Samantha'. And she'd know if anyone here did B & B. Perhaps even a 'Doreen'.

I turned back, walked up the drive and was about to knock on the door when I froze. I can't convey my sense of shock at the sight of the brass knocker. This was no ordinary doorknocker. It was in the form of a helmeted figure, a Roman soldier. Only once before had I seen one like this.

In the full battledress of a legionary, this soldier was identical to one I had dug up from the garden of a house we'd lived in at Poole, Dorset. He'd been my buried treasure. I cleaned him up, polished his very boots and he graced our front door for years. He moved with us to North Devon and guarded the terraced house we bought. When we sold it, we left him in charge. Some time later I noticed that the new owners had taken him down to paint the door. I went back. He wasn't there and I was sad he'd been discharged.

Here now was the very same soldier in, for all I knew, the very same doorknocker. I'd hardly believe it if I read it in a book. I knocked once and waited. I knocked again, harder. The sound, as I rapped against the metal back plate, was unmistakably the same. Still no answer. I started off down the lane when something made me turn. Emerging from a bend behind, as from the wings of a stage, was a woman with a lively black terrier. Could this be Samantha? I tracked back, assuming the not-so-innocent expression of a somewhat bemused traveller. We met as she was about to walk up the driveway, looking every inch the professional woman.

I opened up the consultation. 'I suppose you wouldn't happen to know if anyone in the village does B & B?'

She looked blank. 'I'm afraid not. But they may be able to help at the farm.' She gave me directions.

'Thanks. Oh, I knocked earlier, thinking you might be in. I couldn't help noticing your doorknocker. It's remarkably similar to one on a house we used to live in. D'you mind my asking how you came by it?'

'Well, I bought it a few years back.'

'D'you remember where?'

'I can't be sure. At a car boot sale, somewhere near Bude, I think.'

'Really? Our house was at Westward Ho! North Devon, just up the coast from there. It could be the same one.'

'You're not having it back,' she said with a laugh.

'No, no. Of course not. It's just that … I've never seen another one and here it is at St.Enoder.' Her dog was straining and I didn't want to detain her. 'Thanks so much,' I said, and then, 'Oh, I don't suppose you know anyone in the village called Doreen?'

She gave me a distinctly quizzical look. 'Doreen? No. No-one I can think of. Sorry.'

And that was it. I'd asked myself this question before; how is it that when you look for one thing, you often find something else you didn't know you were looking for? I hadn't a clue, except that it seemed I was fated to find it. Past coincidences had helped confirm the rightness of a direction. It took a Roman soldier back on duties to remind me.

The Farmer's Wife

I sallied forth, past the church, and a few bends later reached Glebe Farm. On the other side of a hedge, the head of a woman bobbing up and down caught my eye. She was digging a patch of ground in the corner of a field, with a toddler at her side – a little boy – too young to be her son.

'Sorry to bother you but does anyone do B & B round here?'

'Well, no. No-one I know of. Can't help, I'm afraid.'

I had to resort to my backstop. 'I've a tent, if you know of anywhere suitable.'

'Just a minute.' Harold, her husband, was in the yard beyond. She called him over.

'I'll have to think a minute,' he said. 'You won't want to be troubled by cows.' And, with one finger directing, 'Yes. Go back along the road, over the crossroads, up the hill and a bit beyond you'll see a stack of green bales on the left. There'll do.'

'Great. I'd be happy to pay,' I said, 'or put some work in tomorrow.'

'Any good at milking cows?' he said with a pointed smile.

I backed off. With my accommodation fixed up, rough and ready as might be, I could breathe again. While Harold returned to the yard, I joined his wife in the field. Perhaps she could shed light on where farming was going.

'We've started to go organic,' she said. 'It was a financial decision. You're not pushing your staff or the land to its limits and fertilisers are so expensive. I've just read a fascinating book by Graham Harvey, editor of *The Archers*, called *The Forgiveness of Nature: the Story of Grass*. That convinced me it's the right way to go and everyone seems to want organic now.'

I wondered how they would make out.

'Well, we're starting conversion this month. It takes two years before the milk's organic. We get a grant from DEFRA, though the next three years could be difficult. We've done a lot of ploughing this autumn. The red clover's gone in for nitrogen fixing, to replace the chemical fertiliser. But until that kicks in, it's more difficult. We have to sell some of the cows – there's two hundred at the moment. We can't keep as many to the hectare as we used to.'

'But that'll make life easier, won't it?'

'That was our idea. To make conventional farming pay, you have to get bigger and bigger. And with a big enough milking parlour, you've got to look after that many more animals. They all need care and attention. And then there are the vet bills. But if you're not pushing the cows and yourself so hard, it has to be better.'

The little boy, who'd been helping quite happily, wanted attention himself. Our conversation was punctuated with his cries but I pressed on. 'What about the calves?'

'A calf can only be organic after the conversion period.'

'And the bullocks?'

'I'm not quite sure what we'll do. We might sell on to be beef. But keep the heifers, of course.' She had to break off. The little chap wanted to be heard. I shouldn't have pushed it. She looked me in the face intently, as if passing on a thought that's hit home. 'The world has changed, hasn't it. D'you know, this is the first generation when our age group has to look after grandchildren *and* keep an eye on parents. Mine are in their late eighties.'

'That's a commitment all right.'

'Yes, but what's good is that our son's come back on the farm.'

I glanced at the little boy, her grandson. 'He wants to do his bit. Maybe there'll be a future in it for him too, thanks to the changes you've made.' I said goodbye hurriedly. I had to pitch tent and dusk was in the air.

The Ghastly Night

Not until I'd gone past the church, over the crossroads and up the hill did I realise I'd forgotten 'Doreen'. I never got around to asking the farmer's wife her name. Too late to backtrack now. I'd look her up in the morning. There were those bales to check out. Sidestepping muddy puddles, I spotted a stack in the far corner of a field and trudged across stubble to find about a dozen rolled bales in green and black plastic. Though the location was not good – right next to the A30 with traffic shooting past metres below – it would have to do.

I set up camp straightaway and congratulated myself on one brainwave. Finding the pump nozzle too big for the air bed sockets, I improvised a connection with a bendy drink straw. But I had no control over the drizzle which forced me to peg down for the night, or the thunderous roar from the A30. I hoped to hear the breath of the countryside but the clatter choked it. I thought to mull over the day's events but the din derailed any thinking.

I remembered one thing. My daughter insisted that my movements be tracked by GPS and I had strict instructions to switch on my mobile at a quarter to six each night. Her fiancé had set it up so that my position would be relayed to my wife and the rest of the family. It was a comfort to them and me that they'd know where I was, but a relief that they'd not know where my mind was going.

Pathetic as it was, I tried pinning the sounds down with some judicious onomatopoeia. The culprits fell into different groups. The noisiest I termed the *belters*, blasting my ears with a 'broom-brum', 'bang-blum' or 'boom-bung'. Next were the *slammers*. They tore past with a 'shum, shoom, spoom,' or sometimes 'shurrum'. The last contingent I called the *backstabbers*. Their decibels came back to batter me with sounds like 'bori-mori-brum' and 'beri-merri-broom'. I'd have diagnosed a state of delirium at that stage but there was an epidemic of hurry-sickness down there.

One consolation was the evening meal, a modest affair consisting of one flapjack, swilled down with that sample of vintage Cornish scrumpy. But my night attire wasn't up to the drop in temperature. I put socks on socks and a fleece lining over roll-neck T-shirt over vest. I pulled a woolly hat on and lumped my jacket on top of the sleeping bag. I rubbed the front of one knee against the back of the other again and again to distract myself from the racket and summon oblivion. It didn't work or, if it did, I wasn't aware of it. I hadn't a clue how unconscious I'd been during this ghastly night until the morning when I found the air bed at my side.

Day Two

St. Enoder to Lifton

'The road you travel tells you something about yourself'

The Dead End

The overnight dampness gave way to breaks in the sky. Grey clouds had fingers fringed with pink and a fresh breeze promised a fair weather day. But I'd had to pack up a wet tent before setting off to the farm in a muddle-headed daze after my night's spasms. Questions bugged me. When the wife opened the farmhouse door, I thanked her for the campsite. They couldn't have realised how noisy it would be.

She invited me into the kitchen. 'D'you know,' she said, 'thinking about it, I could have put you up.'

'Very kind,' I said, 'but I managed all right thanks.'

'Would you like some breakfast?'

'Good of you. I have to get on but I meant to ask about the digging.'

She told me she was taking an organic kitchen gardening course and getting the ground ready for broad beans, onions and garlic. She'd bring on some early carrots too with tunnel cloches. 'Are you sure you won't have some breakfast?' she plied.

'Yes really,' I said, thinking 'why not?' Breakfast was crying out for me, but talk of vegetables and I was on another tack. 'I don't suppose you know about a funny cauliflower? Looks a bit like limpets.'

'I think you're talking about a cross between a cauliflower and calabrese,' she said.

Any morsel of enlightenment was welcome. And then there was the business of ... 'I never got around to asking your name.'

'It's ...' The nanosecond gap stretched into an expanding universe of anticipation when the first letter – 'D' – arrived, before 'Denise' dashed it.

'Denise. Yes, oh great ...,' I said,'... to have met you both.' And rabbiting on, 'There's one other thing; St.Enoder. D'you know anything about him?'

'Not much. He came over from Ireland with St.Columb and St.Carantoc, spreading the Christian message, before establishing the church here.'

'Thanks again anyway, and good luck with the organics.'

'And we're diversifying.' She pointed to the buildings at the back of the yard. 'That's our next project: converting the barns to offices for small businesses.'

Good to hear they were turning their lives around. But I had to move on. One thought I couldn't dismiss: what if there once was a 'Doreen'? Where would I find her? There was one obvious place: I searched the churchyard. But lichen infiltrated letters, turning names into multi-coloured jigsaws. Ivy cloaked others while the tentacles of time had loosened the sharp hold of letters on stone.

Along with Fanny, Philippa and an unfamiliar Kezla, I detected a Charlotte, Jane and Nancy. Then one gravestone brought my search to a halt. It read:

In memory of Amelia Ann,
Beloved Wife of John Burt,
who died 23rd November 1871, aged 21
Also of Emma their daughter,
died 4th April 1900, aged 31

It wasn't so much that the mother had died a year or two after giving birth and at such a young age, but that Amelia Ann is the name of my beloved daughter. Yet again I was reminded that what I looked for was not necessarily what I found. Far from home, I needed to know what stared me in the face: nothing is more precious than one's family and no direction worth pursuing without their support. St.Enoder had been good to me. I had 'Doreen' to thank too. In bringing me here, she'd not let me forget where I'd come from.

The day already had a fullness about it, but nearing the gate to my campsite I was rushing. Why? I'd bought into speed too. But time was mine. I'd be ready enough when I arrived and so would a lift. As it happened, a little way on I stopped dead. At the edge of a field right next to the lane – and with the A30 a tolerable background hum away – was a stack of green bales. I walked over to inspect them. I counted. There were 280 and not a black one in sight. So that's what Harold meant when he said 'a stack of green bales'.

The Fast Mover

It was nudging nine o'clock when I reached the approach road to the A30 and started thumbing where a steady curve forced drivers to slow down. Up to now I'd part hitched and part hiked. Here I'd have to stand my ground – there was a wide verge – and face the traffic as Matthew advised. But had I understood what he meant? I'd been facing cars, not drivers. They'd get a good mugshot of me. But what if I looked them straight in the eye?

I looked forward to trialling this tweak of technique. How well it worked. Two vehicles after I began eyeballing, I was on the road again, in another van. Alan, a straight talking guy in his fifties, put me in mind of an older Paul. But Alan's van looked less of a workhorse than Paul's and a lot whiter. Introductions over, I handed him my card, a routine by now.

Quick-firing, Alan quizzed me on whether I'd read about Maslow's theory of motivations. I hadn't but Alan soon put me wise. 'It comes down to basics,' he counselled. 'Cavemen *had* to get out of bed. If they didn't, they went hungry. The trouble today is the toerags swanning around who aren't pulling their fingers out.'

I could see Alan had 'issues'.

'It comes down to this; what's the point of working when the difference between benefit and minimum wage is only something like 50p an hour. Don't get me wrong,' – I hadn't said a thing – 'there are lovely people, 99.9 per cent, who've still got the

Protestant work ethic. But it's too easy to work the system and get by doing nothing.'

'Yes,' I said. 'It's all wrong if there's a disincentive to work for those who can.'

'And what is there to do when you're at home all day? Take my mum.'

Surely she wasn't a toerag.

'She hardly gets out, so my brother and I clubbed together and bought her Sky TV. Worst thing we did. She watches CNN all day. Really. It colours her whole life. We've even talked about taking it away.'

'Gosh, that *would* be something ... I mean to do.' Alan meant business. He could and would. A dog jumped about in the back. I hadn't really taken note of it with Alan holding the stage. 'What breed's that?' I asked, observing its strangely human black beard.

'It's a wire-haired terrier, a Schnauzer.'

Then I spotted Alan's very precise goatee. Snap. 'So what drives you on Alan?'

'I have a lovely family, wife and kids and they're all healthy. What more do I want?' He was sounding like Paul now, if a little less sanguine. 'And I've travelled all over the world. I hitched the whole of France once in twenty-four hours.'

I believed it, implicitly. Alan would always get a move on. I hadn't met anyone quite as dogged. Eyeballing, I had an earful.

The Grateful Carer

Alan had to turn off the dual carriageway before Bodmin which left me stranded on the A30. Long straight stretches and downhill runs made lifts difficult. Alan's hitchhiking through France in twenty-four hours rubbed 'still in Cornwall on day two' in my face. Not that I wanted to burn up the miles but neither did I relish being stuck with the flash and bash of steel.

Alternately pounding the tarmac and pussyfooting tussocks of grass, I felt under siege. Time was an unbroken white line stretching from the edge of my foot to the point where the A30 meets its maker. But salvation comes in many guises – that ought to be an article of hitchhiking faith. This time it took the form of roadworks with a 40 mph speed restriction. Threading my way past traffic cones, I found a convenient place to thumb near a joining road and moments later I was greeted by the cheeriest of saviours.

One look at Judith and the myth that the lone woman driver never picks anyone up was laughable. Judith held open car. Her whole bearing welcomed you. With hair that flounced to her shoulders and a mouth that rose easily to a grin, she'd be a favourite aunt who'd dispense lashings of common sense but be game for a spot of mischief. 'Oh, I don't hitchhike myself,' she said, 'but I'm always giving lifts.'

I gave a brief rundown on why I was thumbing and she pitched in straightaway with her story. 'We moved house twenty-two years ago,' she began, 'from Camborne to Treviscoe when my husband changed jobs. So we had new neighbours – an elderly couple – and got friendly. I did little bits of shopping for them: the Post Office and so on. That's how it all started.' She soon got wrapped up in their lives.

What about her? Did she have children to think about?

'Yes. Fiona would have been about three then, but Richard hadn't been born. Years went by and the couple were getting infirm. I was doing more and more for them till first one had to go into hospital, then the other. Lovely people they were. I visited them off and on before they went into long-term care. The children had left home by then and I'd been wondering what to do with myself when the hospital offered me a job out of the blue.'

'You'd hardly credit where one kind gesture can lead,' I said.

'Well, no. But they needed help on the wards. That was nineteen years ago and, would you believe, I'm still there.'

I wondered how the Health Service had changed in her time.

'I'll tell you. It's respect. People have got no respect for others and they're far too ready to complain. But there's a lot of good about too.' She was quick to paint the other side of the picture. 'It's how you look at it. My Dad's nearly ninety and would have had to wait eighteen months for a prostate operation. We couldn't have him waiting any longer, not at his age, so we paid for a specialist to speed it up and got him into Treliske. He had marvellous treatment.'

That shook me. Here was Judith working for the NHS, paying to speed up treatment – the very person you'd expect to be up in arms – yet more than happy at how her Dad had been treated. Perhaps she appreciated something that many don't: the reality of the day-to-day situations hospitals face. Judith's mindset meant that she would always see things in a positive light. Where did that come from? I'd liked to have talked longer but this was one of my frustrations. Lifts left you when you were just about to get somewhere.

The Impatient Casualty

The moment a road is – in that horrible word – dualled, it's a duel. While drivers jockey for pole position, the humble hitchhiker is a wallflower by the wayside. But on single carriageways I'd felt part of the action. So when Judith dropped me off on a singular section of the A30, I took an optimism with me that bordered on frivolity. What if my next lift was in a BMW or Merc?

The optimism was well founded. The fantasy was not. When Jeremy pulled up, it was not the car that registered – a modest set of wheels – but his age. I never thought an old has-been would get a lift from the be-having younger generation. I bundled myself alongside while we exchanged pleasantries.

'I've only hitchhiked once,' he said.

When I spelt out my mission, Jeremy said simply, 'All I want is to be happy.'

I might have guessed there was something underlying his earnestness.

'I'm on the sick,' he told me. 'Someone ran into my back, hit my towbar and carried me up the road about twenty-five yards.'

The impact damaged a shoulder tendon. It would take a couple of months to mend. He worked in engineering, on maintenance and repair, and loved it. They were keeping the job open. Being off work didn't suit him. But loving it, like Paul the bricklayer did, is all too rare these days. How had he come to do the work he did?

'As a kid I was always taking things apart. Me Dad too.'

'There. He must have got you into it.' If only parents realised how much their actions influence kids.

'The practical subjects at school helped, particularly electronics. It was my hobby anyway. I got City & Guilds and worked as a domestic installer, rewiring sockets, fitting burglar alarms, things like that. Then I branched off into the mechanical side.'

He'd had four jobs so far and turned his hand to kitchen fitting. What experience he'd packed into his twenty-nine years.

'All I want is to be happy though,' he said again. 'The money doesn't matter.'

So what did he do in his spare time?

'Oh, read a *Haynes' Manual*.'

I laughed at the very idea. 'That would do me a serious injury,' I said.

We were nearing Jeremy's turn-off but he wanted to take me to a convenient junction. 'Don't go out of your way,' I insisted. 'Here'll do fine', and I struggled to extricate myself from the seat belt. He watched my efforts without comment. I was pleased he didn't offer to help.

The Big Mouthful

The drop-off point could not have been better; on the outskirts of Bodmin, right outside Roach Foods. Breaking through a peal of sunshine was the tantalising smell of a breakfast foregone. Might this commercial heartland harbour a symbiotic outside caterer? I roamed round an Industrial Park – that euphemism for aesthetic calamity – but spotted my quarry on the approach to a nearby Business Park. 'Snax Bar Open' the sign read. Taking the spelling in my stride, I waltzed up to the van, full of myself. But nothing that a giant beefburger for £2.50 wouldn't make more of.

While I waited for lashings of onion, cheese and brown sauce to envelop the vast landscape of beef sizzling on the hot plate, we – the burger queen and I – chatted. When I told her about my hiking plans, I carried her with me. I knew because she dropped a proverbial bombshell.

'If you wait a minute, Hughy will be over and he's going all the way to Liverpool today. He's a great guy. I'm sure he'll help.'

'What!' I said. 'That would be brilliant.' But where there'd been beefed-up anticipation, there was a fillet of raw fear. I agonised over what news Hughy would bring. 'Going with the flow' had become my rudder – with hitchhiking it has to be – and Liverpool was one of the cities in my sights. It would be only too easy to accept a lift that got me there in no time at all. Faced with what might be the greatest of good fortune, I was reeling. Getting somewhere wasn't the point. A sense of direction was. If I took the easy option and said yes, what would I miss out on? Wouldn't it be all the opportunities to meet other people and discover their directions? Then there was the question I couldn't evade: could I really bring myself to say no?

While I waited, the burger queen told me of her hitchhiking trauma. She and a girl friend were thumbing in the early hours when a campervan stopped. 'He was weird,' she said. 'Once we got in, he kept changing his voice.' Luckily, when he pulled up, they were able to clamber out and take refuge in a nearby house. Seeing their distress, the owner ran them home. 'I'll never hitchhike again,' she said. No wonder that girl hitchhikers are an endangered species.

But I was feeling threatened when she said, 'Here he comes.' The beefburger was ready too. But, preoccupied with the figure heading towards me, I was not. Hughy was a lean-looking chap, in his late fifties probably, with the loose-limbed walk and rush of hair that put me in mind of Stan Laurel. The closeness of any resemblance didn't ease my tension. Nor the imminence of my dilemma.

Our greeting was pally enough and, while the girl explained my hiking plans, Hughy listened sympathetically. Then he straightened himself up, looked me in the eye and delivered his punchline. 'I've got a carful of mates. Sorry.' Whaaa.

'Not to worry,' I said. I wore my disappointment well. Never was I so pleased not to get a lift. I retreated to the end of a wall and perched myself on a coping stone, to take in the enormity of the beefburger. And my escape. On the side of the van, I read 'All Events Catered For'. Thank God that one wasn't.

The 60s Child

By 11.20 I was off again, hopping into the road every so often to sidestep overgrown bushes. But being closer to a possible lift made me feel good … until I reached the junction where Jeremy had offered to take me. You can go off roads. The A30 was back to its dualled worst; a juggernauting beast roaring and rutting its way across all too amenable sloping hills. We wouldn't be subjugated though, my thumb and I. It was a joint decision; we'd stick to the slip road.

I hadn't taken much notice of car models up to now. But twenty minutes on and, with my earlier delusions of grandeur, I couldn't fail to register the approach of a Nissan Micra, a model about which I'd cast many an aspersion. There was a perverse inevitability about its stopping. John might have been manning a steam traction engine, with his peaked cap. It gave him a jovial demeanour, even when he wasn't smiling. Soon we were humming along in the slow lane but the moment I broached my game plan John's concerns surfaced.

'Little England,' he said, 'has lost its identity.'

'Little' sounded affectionate, but small-minded seemed the implication.

'It starts with the children and all that nonsense about not playing conkers. They need challenges, like we had when we were young.'

That took me back. I used to cycle ten miles to and from school. How many kids would be allowed to do that today?

John had something more searching in mind. 'Too many people live in boxes. When I was sixteen or seventeen, the girlfriend and I wanted to go on holiday. Know what I did? Opened a map, closed my eyes and stuck a pin in. "That's the place. Let's go to St.Erth," I said.'

Man after my own heart. I dowsed a map once to find out where we should live.

'We put our luggage on the train at Paddington but when we got to Cornwall it hadn't arrived, so we had to improvise. I knocked on a farmhouse door and when the woman answered, she said, "Oh my dear, you look just like my son." We stayed there a week for next to nothing and that's when our luggage turned up.'

John had learned to get by. He'd been divorced but with a new partner bought some land at Launceston. 'Out of the blue,' he said. Though he wasn't an architect, they'd designed the house themselves and had it built. 'That's another thing,' he said. 'You strive to do something and the bureaucracy kicks in: all the planning regulations for a start, and you get punished right, left and centre with tax on tax.'

Here was the same frustration with the pettifogging and the

punitive as those pagans had felt. With his impulsive streak, John would always find officialdom hard to stomach. But didn't we all have to make the best of it?

'I've been director of a company, in charge of purchasing,' John said. 'But the manufacturing base in this country has been undermined. I can't find work, not down here. And ageism? You can't ban it. As soon as people know you're sixty, they think twice. My partner's keeping me afloat.'

His wasn't a temporary blip like Jeremy's. There was real angst in John's disquiet, made no easier by the knowledge of how things had been.

'We're trying hard to be part of the culture, making friends and fitting in. But you can be strangers in your own road. Where I grew up, everyone was together.'

'Yes. And who do we find time to talk to today? The barber?' Whether I liked it or not, I was wandering down John's street. More so because there wasn't a hint of bitterness. 'You still have your idealism,' I hoped.

'Yes. I'm a 60s child,' was his answer.

So what did he wish for?

'To fulfil my destiny. I've a sense of it,' he said. 'Always follow your guardian angel. You have to believe in a spiritual world. That's what'll guide Little England back to where it belongs.'

It *was* affection. I'd never heard anyone talk of England in such terms, as though he had a personal stake in it and cared, much as one might for a dearly-loved acquaintance who'd lost his way. His aspiration reminded me so much of Jeremy's. Except that 'being happy' had turned into a deep-seated cry from the heart.

A touch after midday John and I parted company at a turn-off to Launceston. One lift had given me reason enough to be thankful for the burgerland escape. But as to whom or what I should thank, that was another question. Perhaps a Nissan Micra ought to be up there somewhere.

The Bridge

Had I spoken too soon? I was slap-bang on the hard shoulder of the A30, that juggernauting beast. And with no slip road in sight, I couldn't get off. The brio that went with Matthew's swagger was short-lived. Soon I found myself cursing; the verges, for example. Did no-one ever cut them? But uncut verges encourage wildlife, I reasoned. What? To get squished? That didn't get me far. And how far off was I anyway? I toyed with my target: about 800 miles to Dunnet I reckoned. How many miles a day could I cover? Surely 60 weren't out of the question. How long would that take? With a spot of short division, some carrying over and rounding up what was left of me, I made it a fortnight. That didn't help much. I was still where I was … stranded.

But I carried on contradicting. Tides turn. I'd never forget a time in my twenties when I hitchhiked through Sweden. With a non-stop procession of Volvos, Saabs and VWs, I plonked my rucksack down and waited. Then I saw a Morris Minor approaching. It had to stop. Lars and Barbro were going sailing and would I like to join them? You bet. We fished but caught seaweed. We sailed but the wind dropped. And, as the evening closed in to the smack of paddles and the sway of our makeshift songs, I'd never been happier. To cap it all, they lived in a turreted tower and I spent the night at the very top. The following morning, Lars ran me back to the road and, in one lift, I covered the 400 kilometres to Stockholm.

It's all about waiting for the right opportunity. Hardly had I thought it than I was joined by a quietly reassuring hiking partner – Patience Personified. The least I could do was entertain her with a little ditty:

> *Patience is a virtue*
> *She's a wonder to behold*

Endlessly repeated, it gave my steps the kind of yo-ho you'd expect from any shanty. Half an hour later, though, and still no suitable spot to hitch from, the relentless tramp, tramp, tramp was telling. Even pitching on the raised surface of the unbroken white line irritated me. I wanted a break and Patience paid the price. I tacked on a second couplet. It struck a more defiant note:

> *Patience is a virtue*
> *She's a wonder to behold*
> *But she's bloody hard to live with*
> *When lifts are going cold*

[DAY TWO]

Belting it out to drown the decibels helped me forget a pointless thumb. I had stopped signalling. Soon I had something else to think about – a bridge over the River Tamar and the county boundary. Cross it and I'd break through to Devon. But Patience was further tested. Major construction work meant the walkway had disappeared. Carry on and I'd be squished. A load of barriers criss-crossing the central reservation ruled that route out. Some heavy earthmoving equipment and a tower of scaffolding below made me wonder whether there might be a footbridge.

Having slithered down a rubble-ridden path beside the bridge, I found myself clumping across churned-up clods of clay which stuck layer upon layer to my boots. Though I was increasing in height with each step, I still couldn't spot a footbridge and any further progress towards the river was proving ... well, sticky. Workmen high above me on steelwork were oblivious to my predicament, so I shouted up to one of them, 'Any way across?'

'Swimming,' came the cheery riposte.

I clodhopped back up the same path with mud-spattered jeans and clay-caked boots. Next the assault course. I scuttled across to the central reservation, the only way on. Scaling barriers, shimmying beneath crossbars and squeezing between makeshift stanchions, I dashed to the safety of the verge beyond. Devon at last. A victory roll was called for but Patience wouldn't have it. Not on the uncut grass.

By the time I reached the next turn-off, it was two o'clock and I'd had a two hour slog along the A30. Patience merited a second verse. It went something like:

Patience is a virtue
She's a wonder to behold
But if she doesn't get a move on
I'll be far too frigging old

We parted company soon after, helped by the ominous hint of a blister.

The turning was signposted 'Lifton village' and, further on, a slip road rejoined the A30 in its unrelenting rampage to Okehampton. I gave the hitching one last shot but could almost hear the reproach of hitchhiking guru Matthew. 'You've got it all wrong, mate. Look as if you mean it.' It was a serious breach of a hitchhiking canon. My thumb had no conviction. I turned back and did a double take on the signpost. Right next to 'Lifton village' was another destination: 'Liftondown ½ mile'. Lift..on..down. Of course. Exactly what I wanted. The conviction was unshakeable. This was my direction. Dual carriageways could get stuffed.

The Farmhouse Restaurant

Sanity returned. I felt in tune with the fields, hedges, trees, folding hills and nestling cottages in a way I couldn't with the constant roar of traffic. Though cars were occasional, slower speeds held out the more favourable prospect of a lift. And I could pass the time of day on my way. At one house a smart looking chap was busy polishing a car. The car wasn't his. He ran a car valeting service. 'You should have seen it before,' he told me proudly. 'This'll sell it.'

'You don't do the same for boots I suppose?' I said, looking at the sorry state of mine. A flash of humour makes the best of friends and often earns good interest.

'Don't stop at the first B & B,' he advised. 'It's a bit pricey.'

This was the old road to Okehampton – about fifteen miles distant – now called The West Devon Drive. Gentry and gentility came to mind as I walked on in more leisurely vein. What a godsend these old main roads are, I thought. But better not spread the word in case the wrong sort gets to know. The road you travel tells you something about yourself. I liked what I was being told.

After my heathenish take on the A30, a well disposed feeling took its place. I needed no more encouragement to linger than a sighting of the Lifton Farm Shop … and a sign advertising The Farmhouse Restaurant. I sidled past an array of stonkingly healthy vegetables before being tempted by a fish pie in the restaurant which had been revamped only weeks before. Good taste was all around, from the stripped beams straddling the ceiling down to the chunky oak table I sat at, its top a full two inches thick.

While I waited, a man worked round the walls hanging pictures. He was meticulous, hanging them all at exactly the same height. That wasn't so notable. But checking with a spirit level that each one hung true was. I went over to compliment him. It was as if

I'd congratulated him on breathing. The prints were all of rural scenes. One was entitled *Chris feeding Suffolk Sheep*. I remembered my daughter bottle-feeding Snowy the lamb on one farmhouse holiday. Back again the following year, we didn't let on that he was mutton, ready for the chop. Another print showed a workshop with the paraphernalia of yesteryear's working farm. All I saw was a jumble.

A diner joined me. 'That's a Lister engine,' he pointed out, as if identifying an old friend in a faded photograph.

We progressed to a print of a Massey Ferguson. I reminisced about a Field Marshall tractor my son had pretended to drive on the same holiday.

'Cheapest you'd pay for one of those single cylinder jobs would be seven grand,' he said.

I was an outsider but those prints took me inside. My meal arrived. Fish pie isn't normally an epicurean delight but there's a way of dressing a plate that re-defines a dish. This one allowed each ingredient its place: two nicely rounded potatoes, some lush swede, carrots and curly kale sitting happily alongside a handsome helping of pie, with the fish well founded. And the plate, a large white oval platter, helped root the sense of occasion.

When the strains of Samuel Barber's *Adagio for Strings* wafted in my direction, I was on top deck and the sunset over the Aegean had no words to describe it. I want to live here I decided. As I ate, a girl wiped each table and then each and every table mat, used or unused. She wouldn't have been out of place in a hospital. I called her over. Too easily given to griping as we are, I like to play an even hand and while about it I commented on the meal.

'I was brought up on a farm,' she told me, 'and the food here tastes just like my mum's.' She knew about the *Romanesco* cauliflower. 'But have you heard of the graffiti cabbage?' she asked. 'We had it in the other day. It's bright purple.'

When I finished the meal, I was even more aware of the size of my platter but the picture hanger's precision had got to me. 'Can I borrow your tape a moment?' I asked. I wasn't imagining it; the plate was all but a foot long.

'Who's behind all this?' I asked the waitress collecting my plate.

'It's Jo,' she said.

I searched her out. A culture like this takes its cue from the top. She didn't witter on. 'Simple,' she told me. 'I come from a farming background myself. We know about good food, that's all. No additives. It's us versus the supermarkets. We have to do our own thing. Early days but I hope we can show the way.'

I'd been shown. I might think that a lift is the way forward. But what a lift I get from being where I am.

The Present

I could have carried on hitching. The fifteen miles to Okehampton weren't a big target. But The Farmhouse Restaurant made me feel I belonged, so I made for a B & B, the second one. The walk took me through Lifton to a hamlet beyond and Tinhay Mill Guest House. They only had doubles, John the proprietor said. But £57 was more than I'd bargained for. After a civilised British compromise of £40, John showed me to my room, apologising for the central heating or, rather, lack of it. 'I've not got around to adjusting the timer,' he explained. Of course. The clocks went back not long ago. 'But it'll be on soon.'

No tea in the room but there'd be a cuppa downstairs whenever I fancied it. So after I'd settled in, I wandered down a bewilderment of passageways to a seat by an open fireplace and the sound of chiming. I couldn't but be aware of time, not just because it was a quarter to four. There were clocks everywhere – grandfather, grandmother, long case, short case, every sort of case – an omnipresence only rivalled by the wincy, chintzy patterns swirling over floors and walls.

A makeover guru would have had a field day 'blanding' this place. But the black beams, brasses and chinaware displays would be estranged. So would Margaret, John's wife. Small in stature but big in presence, she soon sorted out my cuppa and her provenance. Starting off at a local hotel, she became second chef, then ran her own outside catering business before taking on this challenge. That included a dust recce as she spoke, to shelves she could hardly reach. 'It gets everywhere,' she complained. I was exhausted just watching.

She wouldn't have been impressed with the makeover I gave her room: the damp carcase of my tent spread out across the floor and assorted underwear that I'd washed dangling from the now functional radiator. Taking off my boots brought one pleasant surprise: the hint of a blister turned out to be some grit in one boot. After a long shower, shave and a nutty russet apple from the farm shop, I pulled out the one book that I'd brought with me. *The Power of Now* by Eckhart Tolle had been recommended by a friend.

It was heady stuff; about how we identify with our mind, how thinking with all its labels, words, judgements and definitions creates 'the illusion of separateness' and cuts us off from the present. 'Thinking has become a disease' Eckhart warned. 'Watching the thinker', he argued, is the way forward. The moment you start doing it 'a higher level of consciousness becomes activated' and you 'realize that all the things that truly matter – beauty, love, creativity, joy, inner peace – arise from beyond the mind. You begin to awaken'. I must have tapped into that inner peace. I fell asleep.

Day Three

Lifton to Crockernwell

'Now is all time and no time at all'

The Time Traveller

I woke at 4.36 or so my watch said. Something possessed me to set the Dream Machine Digital Clock Radio beside the bed. Hardly had I done so than it reset itself to 5.07. I gave up. My mind was working overtime. Had the A30 really been a metaphor for my hurry-scurry mind? What ought I to be doing? Watching what I was thinking, Eckhart told me. And what was that? Thinking up questions. Not good enough. I had to watch what questions I was thinking of. Now.

I needed to go beyond generalities. If someone said, 'My grandchildren give my life meaning' I'd ask, 'Tell me one thing they taught you.' I drew up a list of questions:

>   1. What led you to do what you like?
>   2. How easy or difficult was it to do?
>   3. What gives you most pleasure?
>   4. What dream remains unfulfilled?
>   5. What disturbs you about life today?
>   6. What one thing will you never forget?

Then I conked out and surfaced at 7.15 with another thought: could Margaret be a guinea pig? Having chosen Welsh Rarebit for breakfast, I embarked on my test run. 'What led you to be doing

[DAY THREE]

this?' I began in the kitchen.

'I've always loved cooking,' she said.

I probed.

'It comes from my granny I think, though I never knew her. It must be in the genes. I love dealing with people', she went on. 'It puts you in ... .' She broke off abruptly. 'You'll never believe this. I come down this morning and in my mind's eye see a fox in the corner of the garden. When I look it's not there. But there it is now, eating the seed dropped from the bird feeder.'

We watched it take a last snaffle. 'Have you seen it in the past?' I asked.

'Well, yes. In the early morning. But never this late.'

The precognition of the fox quite consumed her. For Margaret, now was then. What was this business with time? But I had to pull both of us back to the questions.

'How easy was it to do what you wanted?'

'Oh, it came natural. I fell into it.'

'And what gives you most pleasure now?' I might have anticipated the answer.

'Wildlife, without a doubt. We've been to Alaska and Canada and seen the bears.' Margaret couldn't contain her enthusiasm. 'I can't wait to go back. We saw them from the coach. So we walked eight miles into the wilderness. We didn't catch sight of the bears again, but the wildness, that was lovely.'

'Well, I think you've covered the other questions,' I said, 'oh, except what disturbs you about life today?'

'The way the world's going, the politics, the lies. It all feels out of control.'

I took a walk round while she conjured the Welsh Rarebit. A clock chimed. What *was* the time? I hadn't put my watch on. Spoilt for choice here, it didn't matter surely. Until I looked. The choice was spoilt. Each clock had its own idea. I took the collection: 5 to 7, 13 to 9, 28 to 9, 22 to 1, 20 past 12, 26 to 5, 10 to 12, oh and another 13 to 9. So was it 13 minutes to 9? Did one corroborate the other? Well, no. A minute on and one still showed 13 to 9. The synchronicity was coincidental. Timekeeping had become a pick'n mix irrelevance.

My Welsh Rarebit arrived. I ought to have known that mustard was an ingredient. I knew now. Mustard was all I tasted. I didn't blame Margaret. The fox did it. And the bears. The present had gone on safari. If there was one lesson I took away from Tinhay, it had to be that now is all time and no time at all.

The Wistful Sailor

On the road again and I'd acquired a devil-may-care attitude. The morning was bright and breezy. So was I. Through patches of blue sky, the sun flicked glances at the late autumn leaves, flashing the richness of their colours. If I'd had a hat, I'd have doffed it all round. How blessed to be walking along a pavement. But when that disappeared and I had to shrink into a hedge while the occasional car bowled past, my blessedness persisted.

I was in Devon, on home ground. Those rolling hills were mine, the winding lanes were mine and the air was definitely mine. I hoovered up lungfuls. As for hitching, I didn't mind if I didn't and I didn't mind if I did. My thumb was tempered with content. So when Clive stopped, our meeting was as casual as a tap on the shoulder.

His cloth cap topping a chisel-chinned face made me feel I'd joined the country set. 'I can take you a few miles,' he said. 'Used to hitch myself. I know what it's like.'

Introductions over, I launched into the questions.

His father and elder brother started him off. 'They loved sport, and sailing best of all. That's where I got my love of the sea from.' With the merchant fleet in decline twenty-five years ago, the Navy was his obvious career choice.

And what was it that grabbed him about that sort of life?

'The freedom,' he said with relish, 'and opportunities. Every day's never the same. That's what the sea does for you.'

Yes, how was it we got stuck in routines? Every day *is* different.

'Wish I was there now,' he volunteered.

'So your dream is ...?'

'... to spend more time at sea', he added wistfully, 'on a little yacht perhaps.'

And what gave him most pleasure now?

'My family, my wife and daughter. Sharing family life – that means most.'

What disturbed him was the lack of tolerance in the world. 'There's too much short-termism today. Overnight results rarely happen in history,' he said. 'You only have to look at Iraq and Afghanistan.'

What was the one thing he would never forget?

He hesitated. 'Our wedding. We married young. I was only eighteen ...' – he was talking slowly – '...when my father died, on the eve of our marriage.'

I didn't know what to say, helpless as one feels, close to someone's sadness.

'I can never sleep without remembering, never forget.'

'Was it that close?'

'The night before.'

I couldn't think of a crueller blow. I thanked him for the sharing. What consolation was there in words? A headmaster of mine trotted out 'Time is a great healer' on my mother's death. But how could time heal Clive's memory, that aching juxtaposition of happiness and grief? 'Every day's never the same,' he'd said. At sea. A strange form of words. Perhaps it picked out the difference. That day would always be the same, the one day that always is.

Our paths had to part. Clive turned to me and I noticed the red poppy pinned to a fold of his sweater. Of course, Remembrance Day tomorrow. Today. Every day.

'You might be interested to know,' he said, pointing to some buildings on the other side of the road, 'that's where Jethro lives.' I must have looked a bit quizzical. 'The comedian. Risqué jokes and all that.'

I'd heard the name but never seen him perform. 'Well,' I said, on the unthinking spur of the moment, 'perhaps I should drop in on him.'

The Blue Comedian

Yes. Why not? It wasn't yet ten o'clock. I had time on my side. But there was more to it than that. This journey was all about direction and how you find it. To follow any direction, you need a sign. The very fact that Clive dropped me off at this place now meant something. *The Power of Now* was called for; to wake up to what was happening. Signs change. So do directions.

A plaque announced 'Jethro's'. A signboard proclaimed a restaurant. What looked like a stable block on the far side of a yard had a lorry in front emblazoned with 'Jethro's Bloodstock Show Team'. A stable hand suggested, 'Try the bar. If he's around, that's where you'll find him.' The bar was deserted, and I might have aborted the whole idea had not the counter persuaded me to hang on. Lined up on it were a *Daily Mail* with a pair of specs on, a crumpled packet of Mini Cheddars and the morning's post, unread. He's bound to be back soon, I thought.

While I waited, my eyes strayed to a portrait of Winston Churchill over the fireplace, and some words to the side.

If for warmth you do desire
Poke your wife and not the fire.
If you live a single life
Go out and poke another's wife.
Poke another's or poke your own
But for Christ sake leave the fire alone.

With Winston Churchill presiding and what I'd seen outside, another picture emerged. Here was a man of many interests and eclectic tastes. I decided to tinker with my questions. 'What dream remains unfulfilled?' became 'What malarkey will you get up to next?' And 'What disturbs you?' turned into a salacious 'What gets up your fanny?' I was wrestling with more vulgarity when a door opened. I had no idea what Jethro looked like. If I imagined he'd have a stage presence, I was wrong. But his very ordinariness made me not assume. With generous beard, sideburns and loose sweater, he had the look of a benign gaffer. 'Jethro?'

'Yes?'

I explain what I'm about and how I happened to gatecrash his bar when he cuts in: 'We were doing a show at Bridlington. On the day of the show, mooching around town, we came across a bowling club. Me and my mate walked straight in and sat down, enjoying ourselves. "We'll be thrown out in a minute," I said. Then a big fat lady came over. I was never more taken aback when she said, "I've just made a pot of tea. Would you like a cuppa?" That's how I remember Bridlington.'

That's all right then. I settle myself on to the bar seat, while he's on the other side. How did he start? He came from a musical family. 'Burnt toast will make you sing' his mother used to say. He joined the operatic society in St.Just – perhaps that's why – and was given a comedy role. 'The lines were scripted but I sang them the way I felt. I went on to sing in a pub and tell a few stories. The stories got more and the songs less. Then I went out as a comic.'

This man hardly needs any questions. And certainly not my dodgy ones. His language is as clean as it comes. So what gets him going?

'Nothing much,' he says.

I'm not convinced. 'You wouldn't think it looking round.'

'No? I've achieved more than I ever thought. Been down most avenues, business-wise and entertainment-wise. But I'm running out of ideas. You don't get the buzz when you've done it all before.' He eyes my get-up. 'I walk thirty or forty miles though, every week. I enjoy walking. Keeps me trim.'

'You must take a lot in,' I suggest.

'I notice nothing.'

I give a sceptical look.

'No. Really. I'll drive the car and see ten times more. Unless there's a deer in front, it's tunnel vision. Five miles an hour is what I do. I used to time myself up to a gate. I've got to have a target – twelve or fifteen miles say. And all I can see is the finishing line. Sometimes the hardest part is putting the boots on and leaving home.'

'Don't you get blisters?' I ask.

'My boots fit perfectly,' he says. 'Know the secret? Run a bath nine inches deep, the hottest you can bear. Put your boots on and dangle 'em in the water for ten minutes. Wear 'em till dry and they'll fit like a glove.'

I take him back to the 'not noticing' and tell him about the fox at breakfast.

'You know, when I was a kid – seven or eight I'd be – I was petrified of foxes. Out one day, I ran down the lane and climbed on top of a hedge. I swore I'd seen a fox in the field. But I'm still not sure if I imagined it.' Jethro has some memory and an unconventional one at that. You'd have to, in his line.

The comic business then; what about it?

'I've been in it thirty-two years. People say, who's the best comic?

But there'll always be something about any of us that appeals to someone. You need to know how to play an audience. They're all different. Humour's a funny thing. Here,' he says. 'It was August bank holiday at Perranporth and this lion and Bengal tiger were walking across the beach – can you believe? – at three o'clock. So the lion turned to the tiger and said, "For an August bank holiday, not a lot of people around, are there?" '

I laugh as the light dawns.

'But some of the young chaps who come in 'ere, they've got their own ideas. I tell you what amuses them. It's stupid: what's red and invisible?'

'I haven't a clue.'

'No tomatoes. They laughed themselves silly.'

I chuckle politely, fearing I could let myself down badly in this masterclass.

'And then there's the political correctness these days. It gets tricky. Three babies got mixed up in a maternity ward recently.'

Was he being serious?

'The parents were West Indian, French and English. When I heard about the problem, I said to my daughter, "You'd think, with a bit of parental instinct, they'd know their own child." Anyway, the doctors called the parents of the English child in first and the father spoke up. "The black one's definitely mine," he said. "No mistake." "How d'you know?" they asked him. "Well, one of the others is French," he said, "and there's no bloody way I'm chancing that." '

I have to steady myself and the seat. What is it about the French that sets us off?

Jethro has a show coming up soon, in London. He can't remember the last one. 'I don't keep memorabilia,' he says. 'There's no future in the past.' It sounds like a mantra. 'And I never know what I'm going to say. I've done it so many times before.' He didn't even prepare for the Royal Variety Show. 'No nerves.' Then he confides, 'But reading a lesson at the Royal Jubilee frightened the life out of me.'

'How's that?'

'It's myself, isn't it? It's different when I'm Jeffrey Rowe. I can be embarrassed even presenting prizes, as I did at a Prince's Trust do.'

His honesty is disarming. How comforting it must be to slip from that vulnerable self into the confident cut of his on-stage persona. 'I'm almost a recluse,' he contends. But he does enjoy good company. The Bishop of Truro once told him "We're in the same business really. Of course, it's a different message. But unless we tell the stories right, people won't listen." '

A barwoman arrives and tidies up, ready for the day's business. 'Here, d'you fancy a cuppa?' he says, with a glance in her direction.

Jethro is in a more philosophical mood after the tea arrives. 'This is a concert,' he reflects, 'not a rehearsal. Man's been on earth a fleeting moment, two and a half seconds in the scheme of things. Our time is short. It's your way of life that counts. If you don't want to do something, don't, I say. Know your limitations. Do simple things well that you can cope with. Much better than doing clever things badly. But never knock how others get their enjoyment. They pay their taxes. So respect them. That's how I see it.'

Jethro has strong-minded views but there's a liberal vein running through. So what doesn't he like? 'What gets up your nose?' is the decorous way I put it.

'People who don't put something back into the country, but only take out.'

And what would he do about it?

'I'd say, "Go to that firm today. Help 'em out. Let the boss tell you what to do, not the state." They'll soon learn. It's old-fashioned discipline. But it works. You know I'm very much a countryman and traditionalist. Why change? Change isn't for the better. I haven't seen it.'

We're sipping the tea now and I'm astonished to still be here. He's given me far more time than I thought. And Jethro's straight talking is a tonic. You might not agree with everything he says but you can't help liking his forthrightness. I say something to that effect and he's at pains to discount any way with words.

'I'm no academic. Never read a book in my life,' he asserts. 'But I do love people with a command of the English language, those who condense a situation to a few words where others take fifteen paragraphs. The master's John Betjeman.' And rather contradicting himself on the book front, he quotes the phrase 'crunching over private gravel' as an example of the poet's economy with words. 'It says everything. You know someone's presence isn't welcome.'

It isn't a cue for me to leave but I don't want to overstay my welcome. I can't go, though, without asking Jethro what he'd never forget.

He doesn't hesitate. 'My first job.' It's as if all his answers are pre-programmed. Quick-wittedness must be second nature for a comic. But in this case, it goes deeper.

'I trained to be a carpenter, working for a Mr.Eddy. Lovely man and a real gentleman. Learned my trade there and served my time. Due to a brain tumour, he'd had part of his skull removed. They tried to graft on to what was left but it didn't work. After that he was shaky with his hands, so I worked with him. He'd be the brains behind the window we made and I'd be his hands. I'll never forget that.

'When he died, I heard about his funeral. But I was too busy to go. It didn't matter then but looking back it does. D'you know, that's the biggest regret of my life; that I didn't find time to go. Most days I think about it.'

A poignant note like that seemed a fitting point at which to end. But Jethro couldn't let me go without one last word. 'If there's one comic I'd like to meet on my birthday, it's Les Dawson.' He gave me a reprise of one Dawson gem.

'I'm awake. It's three a.m. and I can't sleep. But I'm thinking how incredibly wonderful is the endless space of eternity. I'm marvelling that out beyond the wisps of gossamer-like clouds shimmering in the moonlight stretch the realms of the infinite, with galaxies strung out like sparkling jewels on a crown and the firmament of stars like silver sequins sprinkled on black velvet, when one flash goes through my mind: what the devil's happened to the roof of my shit house?'

I had absolutely no idea how I was going to make sense of all that, when I bade Jethro goodbye. But I did know that I had to watch out for signs, wherever they came from. Or led.

The Lay-by

An hour or more with Jethro and there was only so much I could take in. I'd seen how a private face differed from the public image. I'd met the man. And I'd been caught off guard with my preconceptions and his punchlines. The English landscape was not what it seemed either. Beyond some trees I spotted a field … of ostriches. It's all change, I thought. Once this very road was a stony woodland track and the long lay-by ahead a grassy glade. There was still ample tree cover and a sign, Combe Row, evoked cosy memories: a Goblin Combe of my childhood; a Burrington Combe of happy caving days in the Mendip Hills.

I parked myself at the start of the lay-by. But after a few cars passed, I paced up and down impatiently, until something made me stoop. One of the cars must have struck a blue tit, lying motionless on the tarmac. I picked it up. It fitted snugly into my palm, eyes tight shut. But warmth was still filtering into my hand. I felt for breaks. The breast bone was projecting slightly perhaps, but I wasn't sure.

Shock can anaesthetise. I'd seen a pigeon hit a window and sit stunned on the ground for ages before flying off. Could I bring this little fellow round? I spoke to it. 'Come on now. You can do it.' Was a whiff of breath within? I whistled. If only I knew a blue tit's call. Then I stroked it lightly, the feather softness beneath my finger unruffled. Only then did I notice the thinnest streak of red lining its beak.

I'd never seen this commonest visitor to our garden in such close-up. Its colouring had a virtuosity that bordered on the exotic – a shame that a bird had to die for me to realise it. Its wings, a deep Prussian blue, were tipped with flashes of white and the softest olive green feathery down between. A rich midnight blue to the nape of its neck branched off to a black stripe crossing its eye. Gently I turned it. A chinstrap lined a stylish beard, sharply defined against high white cheeks. On its underside a yellow shone out, of a more vibrant shade than I'd credited, and all of this topped by the cap in a bright tint of blue.

This was a priceless miniature. Anyone wanting to lay down accomplished brushstrokes only had to consult this little chap. Interior designers ought to be inspired by his flair. He deserved commemoration: a blue tit room. Could I commit him to the tarmac again? No. I looked round. At the edge of the lay-by were sycamore saplings. I plucked a large crinkled leaf and selected a sapling with a suitable fork in the branches. I bedded the leaf into the crook and placed the blue tit, side on, in its cradle. I paused for a last look, then walked back slowly to the start of the lay-by. Hush. Could I really hear leaves falling in this woodland glade?

The Wildlife Rescuers

After the brashness of the A30, this was a place to savour, so I didn't will cars to stop. Though the day was young, I had already slowed down. I was in 'let it be' mode and, when you hold a maybe in your mind, perhaps the right answer comes along.

It was Joe and Jean who came, faces with like-minded smiles. Before I knew it, my rucksack was in the boot and I was on the back seat with Glen. We were heading for Okehampton and I was trying to cope with *the* most ferocious welcome. If gladness was a dog, Glen would be ecstasy. I thought if I thanked him with enough slaps, jiggles and pats, I might earn a respite. That was naïve. The best strategy proved to be the clamp of an outstretched hand over this rapturous, writhing reception committee. As fast as I'd been assailed, the frenzy was over. The Welcome Terrier curled up and fell asleep. He'd done me proud.

Neither Jean nor Joe seemed to notice the excitement. What they did pick up on were people and attitudes. Jean had a story to tell. 'I got knocked off a moped some time back. I couldn't move my legs but, when a car came along, the driver took one look, drove round me and went on.'

'You know what it is,' chipped in Joe. 'People are frightened in case it's a trap.' That was some comment. How deep mistrust can run. 'I get fed up with people who don't think,' he added. 'With my sticky legs I can't get out of the car without opening the door wide. You'd be amazed how close some park.'

They'd moved from Kent sixteen years ago and Joe had concerns. 'There are plenty of brownfield sites but more and more people are building in their gardens. We've lost so much green space.' Another thing was the cruelty to animals. 'We'll never forget coming across some pheasants in the road. I flashed drivers to slow down, even signalled by hand. When we went back they'd been mown down. Out of fourteen, only three survived.'

Crass ignorance I'd have called it but cruelty by default. It's what happens when a car distances you from life. I mentioned my blue tit find. My questions had gone by the board but I might have guessed what drove them on; they rescued animals.

'We've bought some woodland,' Joe told me. 'There are buzzards and sparrowhawks all round.' Then story after story. Two geese kept in an old cellar and only fed on grass were found wasting away. 'Now, given corn, they're back on form and conversing,' Joe said, as if that was the ultimate test of a healthy goose.

Jean mentioned the baby rabbit that one of their rescued cats brought in. 'We only found it hours later under a corner unit. All she wanted to do was love it.'

I knew. A cat of ours caught a baby rabbit but spent ages licking its fur as though it was a newborn kitten.

'Every one of our cats comes in at night,' Jean stressed. 'We don't believe in inflicting cats on other animals.' She's rehabilitated battery chickens. 'With up to ten in a cage they can't stand properly. I've spent two or three days showing them how to walk.' That meant physically walking them. But her dedication was rewarded. 'You can't beat that feeling; seeing a chicken walk again when it didn't know how.'

That had to be one thing you'd never forget, but it triggered a thought. 'Can you bring birds back to life?'

'Yes, of course. It's not easy but we've brought several birds round. Seeing animals survive is wonderful.'

'How? How do you do it?' I told them about my amateurish efforts.

'Rubbing their chest helps but mainly it's the kiss of life.'

If I'd thought of that, would I have tried mouth to beak? I doubt it and not after I'd seen that trace of blood. Meeting these wildlife rescuers straight after my blue tit encounter was extraordinary. And I had to remind myself: the day had started – a long time ago – with a fox.

We reached Okehampton at lunchtime. Joe and Jean put me on to a Victorian Pantry near the Museum. 'Hey, don't forget your rucksack,' Joe reminded me as I made to go. 'No,' I said and screwed my head back on, asking myself as I waved goodbye, why hadn't I noticed Jean's jacket before, in that very blue tit shade of blue?

The Rescued Couple

I like to follow up leads but the Pantry's tables were packed and I couldn't wait. I shopped for emergency rations in a mini-market: two Cox's apples, a packet of ginger nuts and a tuna and sweetcorn sandwich, specially created for me (so it said) by Brian Turner who smiled from the label. Thanks, Brian. You can have a conversation with packets these days. After some chocolate pyramid thingummies flashed their wrappers next to the counter, I succumbed to the offer of three for 99p. While about it, I asked the chap serving, 'How do I get on the old road to Exeter?' I was hooked on old roads now.

'Head up the hill to Sticklepath,' he said. 'That'll take you there.'

I pushed on out of town and up the hill. Except that part way up, I was nonplussed. Ten yards or so ahead a tall chap stood on the pavement looking straight at me. Apart from Matthew, I hadn't bumped into any other hitchhiker and I'm thinking ugly; he's in front and I'll have first thumbing. But he's not thumbing. Nor am I … yet. And he's not walking. But I am. Soon I'll be in front and when I start hitching, what then? He'll be first. Is that it? He's waiting for me to go past. Nothing of the sort. When I reached him, there was no confrontation. He floored me.

'You're heading for Sticklepath, aren't you?'

'Well, yes.' I must have looked as though I'd seen an alien. 'How do you know?'

It turned out that Marie, Robbo's partner – he nodded towards the parked car – overheard me asking for directions in the shop and said, 'Let's give him a lift,' when she recognised me. More touching – after I settled myself on the back seat – was their concern. They knew this road well; winding and narrow in places, too risky to walk and not conducive to hitching.

The lift was one of the shortest – they were only going to Sticklepath – but I hardly had time to introduce myself before Marie told me where her direction came from.

'I used to be stuck on drugs,' she said, 'heroin, the hard stuff.' That was in Cambridgeshire. 'For years and years I tried to fight it. My friends got so worried about the state I was in that they went into church and prayed for my salvation. Within a week I had a phone call to say there was a rehab place for me in Devon. It popped up from nowhere.' She put it all down to God's influence and the power of prayer. Now she was getting her life back together. She'd met Robbo in rehab and her youngest daughter had just moved to Devon. Her eldest wanted to come too.

If there was ever a case for ready access to drug rehabilitation, Marie's story made it. I'd heard about pre-conditions for admission to rehab programmes – odd when rehabilitation seemed the pre-condition for coming off drugs. And I couldn't overlook the influence of her religious convictions.

'The more positive thinking I put into Him,' she said, 'the more God works.'

There was nothing soft about it. Her grittiness struck me; the determination to live her belief. I couldn't ignore that. I wouldn't have been where I was – safely in Sticklepath – without her intervention. I hadn't even thumbed. But then, if I hadn't lingered over those chocolate thingummies, would she have overheard?

Robbo dropped me off in the village and I had to take a photograph. They stepped out of the car and posed; he bespectacled, in a black bomber jacket and a head taller than her; she a slight figure, with open-necked blue windcheater, in her late thirties perhaps and older than Robbo. But what had age to do with it? With her head nestling against his shoulder and arms round one another, they looked a couple so naturally at ease that I know what I felt like; a sentimental old softie.

The Lateral Thinker

Further on, successive bends made hitching impossible. Just as well: I needed time to adjust. There was something almost pre-ordained about the way events were clicking into place. I wanted that to go on but no use raking over the whys and wherefores. I had to watch the thinker, as Eckhart had said. The tiniest decision made a difference, like when I found the Pantry full. I didn't faff around. I moved on and that led to the chocaholic fix and the lift with no thumb. If things didn't work out, they came good when I went along with a change of course. That was as much watching of this thinker as I could do.

The road started to level off with open views and straight

stretches where I could hitch. My luck held. A Land Rover pulled into a farm gate entrance and I piled into the back. The couple in front were discussing some plans and, apart from saying where I was going, I could only talk after the driver, David, dropped off his wife.

Hardly had I begun than he stopped again, at Whiddon Down Services, and our exchange was confined to the few moments after he parked ... with the engine running. I had no choice but to make it a quick Q & A.

'Well, hitchhiking from Bristol to Florence was fun and I've sailed halfway round the world,' he said briskly. And jobs? 'I farmed for twenty years. Now I'm a businessman. But I'll tell you what started me off; doing art at school.'

It was the gift of an answer. 'How d'you mean?'

'It's given me everything I wanted. It's a way of looking. I think more laterally now. Mind you, we had a fantastic art teacher. She was Elgar's grand-daughter.'

And he had to go. No time to ask how she'd taught or what he'd done with his art. He was running out of diesel. But he wasn't short on positivity. 'Look, this next junction could put you on the road to Scotland. I know for a fact, some of the lorries go right there. You could do it in one.'

What? Here we go again, I almost groaned. Yet this was the very 'anything-is-possible' attitude that Elgar's grand-daughter induced. I lived on the edge of the Malvern Hills for three years. I breathed the air of Elgar country. One abiding memory is being given long-playing records of the *Enigma Variations* – a gesture by my form teacher that helped wean me off a teenage obsession with pop music.

What if Elgar's grand-daughter had taught me? No. I couldn't hark back to the past. There was another choice to make – a more immediate one – where was I going? There were three exits at the junction.

The Face Painter

No contest. One road led back to the A30 and Exeter. Thumbs down to that. Another sign flagged up the A38 with a lorry icon alongside. But the chance of a quick fix to Scotland was old hat and the lorry was the colour of dissuasion, coffin black. The only other sign read Hittisleigh and Crockernwell. The light in the sky hinted that I'd be heading due east, hopefully on an old road to Exeter. But the names were enough. Head for them and I'd be a fighter who, for all his punch-ups, crocked up rather well. So I padded along but, dazed from the last few rounds, found it hard to focus. Where the feet went, the mind didn't follow.

A gate was enough to pull us both through. Beyond it was a travellers' site; trailers and trucks that told of other ways of living. I thought of Muggy, Helen and Shy. This was their sort of life. How might it work out to live like that, not outside Gibraltar, but in the leafy lanes of Devon?

The site was one long straggle of homes in a sleepy mid-afternoon lull, but I was drawn towards one that oozed character. The back of this truck had been fitted with dark-stained French doors opening out to an improvised veranda. Beside the doors was a pine-clad panel on which two hatchets, a short-handled shovel and bow saw had been hung. Above these was a board with racing green background and gold letters advertising a 'Lounge Bar Restaurant'. On permanent loan I guessed. On offer were 'Real Ales, Bar Meals' and 'Open Log Fires' with a claim to be 'Open All Day, Every Day'. I opened up too.

'Hi,' I said to the cheerful young mother busying herself with a toddler. I was Laurence, she was Tash and he was Ziggy; she with a generous lick of brunette falling to one side of her face and ginger highlights flashing from the other, while he had a crown of auburn fringed with white. And I whitest grey, explaining my mission. We talked, surrounded by a survival kit of water carriers, petrol cans, gas cylinder and oval pail that suggested Victorian bath times by the fireside, while Ziggy ran in and out.

School had meant nothing to Tash but she'd got a degree in environmental science. 'We went round Europe after that,' she said, 'jumping trains. We got fined but never paid, not in those days. They couldn't track us down.' The travel bug bit her. It still did, judging from the pile of National Geographic Magazines on the veranda.

Now she did kid's parties. 'I do face painting and sell hair braiding.' What bothered her were 'kids starving abroad when there's loads of money about.'

'And in this country?'

'Grim council estates and modern day life.'

How did they manage here?

'The council let us stay if we keep quiet,' she said.

'There are no neighbours though.'

'You wouldn't think so, but people ten miles away complain about our parties.'

I wondered whether they got landed with Council Tax.

'We don't pay,' she insisted, 'or it would have to be an official site and the council don't want that. It's only as permanent as the site lasts.' The children did get free schooling and that was a blessing. One thing she'd never do was live in rented accommodation again. 'It's good living like this,' she said. 'We're just one big family.'

She didn't need to play it up – the freedom and warmth of a community. Not everyone might relish being so close to one's fellow humans but no-one could argue about the richness of lives and relationships lived out in the open. If things got hairy, there was always an escape route – her dream; to take the truck around the world.

'That will have to be a bit later,' she said, patting her tummy, 'after the next one: another boy.'

I hadn't asked about her partner but had to move on. I left her sitting on the veranda, one arm clasped round Ziggy's legs and smiles that didn't need to be painted.

The Magic Circle

I hit the road with high hopes. But if this was the old road to Exeter, people had deserted it. One car belted past with hoots and cheering laddish faces. What to stop someone ploughing into me and laughing all the way down to his forked tail? I needed to put that thinking to bed. Bed? With scarce signs of habitation, the chances of finding a B & B were as distant as the folds of hills rippling all round. A farmer I passed said there was a camping site about a quarter of a mile on. Part way there I came to a halt. On the roadside verge was a huge half-circle of plate-size toadstools, about twenty in all. The other half disappeared into thick undergrowth. At ten feet or so across, this wasn't so much a fairy ring as a hobgoblins' henge.

While I speculated, the same farmer pulled up. 'Sorry,' he said, 'but I've remembered; the camping site closed last week.'

'Dammit,' I muttered, but defiantly, 'I'll have to talk them into it.' I didn't have much choice. The light was fading fast. 'Oh and, how do you think *that* happened?'

'It's the spores,' he said. 'They're cast in a circle.'

I didn't buy that, nor would the hobgoblins. They'd look for meaning as they hobnail-booted round the henge. Greeting a new moon, they'd hawk out a gruff old chant, *we're going round in circles, in circles, in circles*. That's what *they'd* make of it.

A bar was clunked across the track leading to the Barley Meadow Camping and Caravan Park. But the absence of a 'closed' sign gave me tacit permission to duck under. There was no-one around. With earthmoving equipment on hand and churned-up ground, the site looked as though it was being revamped.

I picked a discreet spot under a young oak tree and swung off my rucksack. The 'lift-off' was instant and the escape from gravity exhilarating. I did my own dance to the toilet block with springs on. Spotting a swing, I tried to emulate the challenge of my youth, gearing up to near level with the crossbar. But after a sudden jolt when the chain went slack, I came back to earth rapidly. Did I really want to be air-borne? Besides, I kept noticing a posse of clouds scudding in from the west.

I pitched a quick tent and, lying inside after dark, savoured my well-timed dryness while the rain spattered and hefty squalls tugged at the fly sheet. But a flashing light, raking my tent soon exposed any smugness. A fair cop. This squatter deserved what he'd get. Eviction?

'You all right?' a voice queried.

'Uh ...yes,' I said tentatively, feeling sure I soon wouldn't be, and tried to explain away my slight oversight at the barred entrance.

'Well, sorry about the state of the site,' it volunteered. What!

'Oh no trouble,' I said and should have added, 'I've seen worse.' But, taken off guard by the apology, I grovelled, agreeing to settle up with the disembodied voice in the morning. At least I could sleep soundly ... after a parting smile from the tuna and sweetcorn sandwich.

Day Four

Crockernwell to Honiton

'I had to question the very idea of randomness'

The Family Business

The night threw up the unlikeliest dream: an eagle in a tree that turned into an American Indian woman – attractive despite the beaked nose – who had problems with her skin. I took her to the doctor's, piggybacking her part way, but when I got there, she'd gone. Flown off, I suppose.

What was that about? It's what happens when you start jigging about on swings, having disembodied conversations ... and hobnobbing with hobgoblins. Those toadstools kept breaking into my minimal breakfast of an apple, ginger nut biscuit and chocolate thingummy. Was I going round in circles too? Things were repeating: the blue tit find and straight after, the wildlife rescue people; Muggy, Helen and Shy morphing into Tash and Ziggy; the funeral Clive would have wished to miss and Jethro's regret for the one he *had* missed. And what about the Roman soldier? Where would this wheel of connections lead?

I de-camped, stopping to gaze at a scene in a field on my way to settle up: simply one bull, a cow and calves, but a sight as unfamiliar as any dream. How far from normality this world has strayed when a family in a field commands attention. On one farm holiday we were kept awake all night by a cow mooing. 'She's missing her calf,' the farmer had explained. 'We have to take it away after three days.'

Last night's voice belonged to a face about twenty years younger than I'd envisaged and I ended up a modest six quid lighter. 'Good chap, that farmer,' the younger man told me, nodding towards the field. 'He's gone organic. But it all goes to London. People won't pay the premium he needs down here.' Wouldn't you *want* to pay the extra, I wondered, if it put a family back together?

It was 'that'll do' to the weather; a hangover of mizzle in the air but peeps of blue between white-edged greys. And the wind had dropped. What hadn't changed were the wheels. There were even fewer this morning. The only distraction as I tramped through Cheriton Bishop was an overhanging tree. Just within reach an apple dangled, deliciously flecked with blood red darts as if branded with flashes of summer sun. I wanted that taste. But it was tart, a bittersweet declaration of the gap between what we like to imagine and reality.

When I passed Woodleigh Coach House and Café on the outskirts of Exeter, the gap in my stomach yawned. 'Backslider,' I berated myself, pushing at the door. I chatted away to the girl behind the counter after settling for cereal and toast. They'd only been going two months. She worked in childcare before. Her sister, Cherie, had finished uni with a degree in film and communications. That was her sitting down over there with Baz, her fiancé. 'He's a labourer,' she said, as if that mattered. They were all new to this and helping out best as they could, as was her brother.

'So who's in charge?' I asked.

'Oh, that's mum,' she said. 'Mum wanted to get out of London. We've all joined in and it's starting to happen. We're getting regulars now.'

While I waited for breakfast to surface, an older woman bustled in.

'Are you the one behind this?' I called out cheekily.

'Lot to learn,' she said quickly. 'We've all got to pull together.'

Before I knew it, she'd yanked out a chair to sit down and I was asking what brought her here.

'I've done loads before. I used to teach the piano. Had my own pine furniture business once, staining and polishing. Then I ran an off-licence grocery for a while.'

This was a one-woman employment agency. Dynamo came to mind.

'I've done hairdressing, painting and decorating too, but nursing mostly. Had my finger nearly chopped off once by a patient.' Little things didn't put her off. 'Safety's dull,' she pronounced. 'Gives you a false sense of security, that's what.' She didn't have that here. 'Finding out what they're best at; that's the problem. Anyone can do what they want. That's what I believe. They've got the potential. And they'll do it, as long as they really want to.' It was a personal credo delivered with passion. 'Whipping the family into shape is what I have to do.' And she would. 'We're all the sum of our experiences, aren't we? But I don't know how it'll work out.'

Her experiences had toughened her resolve but would her 'whipping' work? After all, they were still learning what parts to play. I told her about the Lifton Farmhouse Restaurant, though her challenge went further than choosing the right plates. 'Listen to your customers,' I counselled. 'They'll soon tell you if you're doing the right thing.' That's what my years in sales came down to.

My breakfast arrived. So had more customers. The mum, Michelle, made off and so did Cherie, leaving Baz sitting by himself a couple of tables away. With dark hair swept back and slicked close to his face, black T-shirt and black leather slip over the shoulders, he looked smart enough.

'Mind if I join you,' I said, curious to hear his side of the story. How had he become involved? The stud in his bottom lip, bobbing up and down, lent his words an engrossing authority; that and a quiet, confiding voice.

'I grew up in Manchester but moved to Cambridge. That's where I met Cherie,' he said, 'She was me landlord. But, when she sold up, we went to live with Michelle in London till she had this idea of buying the café. Trouble is,' he said pointedly, 'people don't agree on the way to go. I'm always patching things up.'

'Sounds as though you're a mediator,' I said.

He told me about his time in Manchester. 'There used to be forty or more of us kids hanging around a street corner. The old lady who lived there kicked up a fuss at the noise. But I was one of the leaders and once, after we'd had a snowfall, I was waiting for the rest to show up when she came outside and said, "Can you do me a favour luv – build a snowman for when the grandchildren come round?" So that's what we did and after that she wasn't too

[DAY FOUR]

bothered. She put up with us.'

The thought of those kids building Mr.Snowman was engaging. The satisfaction showed in his face.

'Anyway, we got talking and I told her we 'ad nothing to do. "I've got a friend on the Council who might help," she said. They found us one of those metal shipping containers and put it in a field nearby. We got furniture in and decorated the walls. Magic it was; our own den. It got us out of the rain and the flats. Worked so well, they put up another four or five.'

The more Baz talked, the more I was impressed. Unassuming he might be, but his ready response to the needs of those around him showed real mettle. Then he told me about the other end of the street.

'There was a load of druggies always making trouble. They lived above the shops. Great help that was, 'cause they kept breaking into 'em to fund the habit. Several of me friends got beat up and had mobile phones nicked. So me and this lady got a petition up to get 'em moved out and it worked. Another time, a friend of mine had his bike nicked. But I knew who done it. I walked straight into his house, nabbed the bike and took it out.'

Baz told his story as if he was reliving it. 'Me and two others tried to keep the group together doing summat useful. I got it so we went to the swimming baths every fortnight. Me mam used to pay half. She liked the idea of me keeping 'em off the streets. But I got a job at sixteen and made new friends.'

'And how did they fare,' I asked 'after you moved on?'

'Fell apart,' he said. 'Two got arrested for mugging some old lady and another got caught stealing cars.'

Understandable without Baz's leadership. One conclusion was clear: if Michelle wanted someone to build a team spirit, she need look no further. If this soft-voiced labourer coped with those kids, he could certainly teach them how to get along. I wished I'd seen Michelle before I left. 'Give him his wings,' I'd have said, 'and the business will really go places. He'll get things done. You won't need to do any whipping.' It could be a business with real heart. I found that prospect strangely moving. And then I thought … the world needs Baz.

The Best Friend

I wasn't looking forward to the trek through Exeter. Luckily, just before a roundabout, Roger stopped; in his late twenties, I guessed, same as Baz. Heading up his deep green T-shirt was a face so flushed with life you could almost see the blood corpuscles partying. But soon after I mentioned my mission, he said, 'Sorry if I have to break off,' and with an intent look, 'I'm expecting an important call.' That call hung like a spider from the ceiling over our conversation.

He'd reached a crossroads a couple of years ago. After working in catering, he'd driven fork lifts on construction sites. 'But after five years of that I'd had enough and packed it in. Trouble was I got depressed between jobs, not knowing what I wanted to do.' Then he heard about The Prince's Trust.

It was my turn to look intent. When planning this trip I had decided to donate five pounds for each lift, split between two charities. One obvious choice was The Prince's Trust with the vital work it does in helping young people gain a sense of direction.

'Enough people want to do it for them to have to select but, if you miss out on one team, you'll be picked for the next. The leaders try to get a good mix of people to bounce off each other, even if that means conflict. I was lucky. I got recruited first time for a small team.' That experience gave him such a boost in confidence that he was chosen to run his own team. He must have shown leadership qualities. 'Since I was one of the older members, a lot of the messed-up ones looked to me,' was how he put it. He worked for a friend's building company for two years and, having just completed an HND in Business Management, project-managed the business.

'The turn-round in your attitude must be huge,' I suggested.

'You don't know if you don't try is what I say.' But he was quick to put his achievements in perspective. 'For someone else to think, "I can now go to a shop for a pint of milk without my friends", that's success too.'

'When you don't have to think twice about something,' I said, 'you never realise what a milestone that might be for someone else.'

If only Baz's group had followed in Roger's footsteps, what a difference that might have made. Having a role model was one thing, but a framework for encouraging young people's initiatives was crucial. A relative of mine working with the unemployed arranged for a group to barter talents, such as doing garden work in return for some typing. That really fostered a spirit of enterprise.

We'd reached the far side of Exeter and Roger had to drop me off but, as he was pulling up, his mobile rang. 'It's that call,' he said quickly. I could have gestured a goodbye but not after the first few words. Roger's short interjections were loaded with concern.

'How serious? ... He's in hospital? ... Yes? ... They don't know? ... Oh Wonford ... Can we? ... No? ... Not yet?' When the call finished, he said, 'You'll understand if I'm a bit down. It was about Luke, a friend of mine. He's tried to kill himself.'

Luke's girlfriend, Amy, was only eighteen, ten years younger. 'He wanted to settle down but she wanted her freedom. When it came to a split, Luke couldn't take it.' He'd gone round to her place and stabbed himself in front of her.

I was staggered that a setback like that could provoke such an extreme response.

Roger wasn't sure what damage he'd done. He'd known him from primary school days. Luke was an only child and his father's death two years before hit him badly. His mother found it hard to cope in her seventies. Roger encouraged him to embark on a Prince's Trust programme but, after his father died, he'd become more reclusive.

This news came as a real shock. To what depths of despair had Luke sunk that he could knife himself in front of his girlfriend? Roger had seen the warning signs but looked to himself for reasons. 'You know, me and my girlfriend have been together a good while. I think he might be jealous of our relationship and that's kind of rubbed it in. Luke's always compared himself with me.'

'I'm sure there's much more to it than that,' I said, trying to reassure him. 'Well, I really hope he pulls round.' I shook Roger by the hand, opened the car door and reproached myself: so close to someone else's tragedy yet in a few short steps so distant.

The Wacky Dresser

One reason for this journey was to put myself in touch with today's world. When someone wanted nothing more to do with it, I could hardly shrug that off. I'd seen what family meant and how devastating a break-up could be, dire enough for Luke to try and end his own life. It was as if by stabbing himself in front of Amy he'd said, 'This is what *you've* done.'

How did she feel, seeing him do it? Crushed for sure. She'd need help, poor girl. How many times would she ask herself, 'What else *could* I have said? I *am* only eighteen. I don't want to get tied down.' Nothing wrong with that.

But reasoning didn't come into it, not for him. That break-up was a knife to the heart, plunged in with all the other hurts; the loss of his dad, the helplessness of his mum. And what else? The hurts we feel, the hurts we inflict on ourselves and others; they go on, repeating and repeated until something breaks through; a coming to terms, a glimmer of light, a hope. Would it break through for Luke? His trial was a solitary affair by the sound of it. Even his close friend, Roger, hadn't been able to help. What *would* it take for Luke to let go and move forward?

Those were the jumble of thoughts that littered my path as I stumped through the outskirts of Exeter looking for a way on and anything but the A30. A side road looked promising. A last row of houses led on to open countryside. I had to ask, to talk to someone. I don't know how I knew but one house seemed to have life in it. A youngish mother, Emma, answered the door. Yes, this was the old road. It would take me through Ottery St.Mary and beyond to Honiton.

'Great,' I said and told her of my plans. Despite the competing attentions of children, Emma listened patiently. I talked about my last lift and how difficult it was for kids to get a sense of direction.

'I know exactly what you mean,' she said. 'This girl came into my shop some time ago. She'd been going from shop to shop asking if there was a chance of a job.'

'Good of her to try like that,' I said.

'But they all took one look at her and said no. Then she came to me. You know, it was that something different about her that I liked – the wacky way she dressed for one thing – and I took her on. She's only twenty but that girl has so much experience with the things she's done that she acts like thirty.'

'She's still with you?'

'I'll say. Wouldn't be without her. She shows so much patience and interest. She'll spend half an hour with customers just to make sure they're happy with a purchase. They love her for it.'

She painted such a glowing picture of this girl. Only after we parted did I realise that Emma had helped me too. I needed to be consoled and she'd done it; showing me, as if I hadn't already known, that the answer comes if only you reach out. You can find the way on. All you do is knock. And give time. I walked. I wanted time too … to myself and the walking worked. A mile or so on, a sign greeted me: 'Welcome to Clyst Honiton on the Trafalgar Way.' Winning words, I hoped.

The Nine-out-of-Ten Sculptor

A long lay-by in the middle of the village left ample space for cars to pull in. One or two did, but only for parking purposes. While waiting, I sampled the distant views of the Devon countryside, unbroken by rolling hills. When another car stopped, I held back … until the driver opened the passenger door. I was there in a bound.

'I passed you earlier,' he said, 'going the other way.' Simon, a young guy, thirtyish I'd say, looked laid back but a round face was underpinned by one of those chins that says quietly determined. The inside of the car had that lived-in feeling, an easy indulgence with the marginalia of life that usually comes from a preoccupation with more important matters. And so it proved. Simon was lucky to be a sculptor, though he didn't make a living from it.

'I'd be surprised if you did,' I said. 'We don't value the arts in this country.'

Simon got by, working as a technician in a College of Art, but sculpture was his passion. 'I've been working on the same sculpture for two years now,' he said. 'It'll take at least another two years before I finish. I've got a photograph somewhere.' He grubbed about in the dashboard compartment, but to no avail. 'Tell you what; I'll take you round to my studio if you like.' I jumped at the chance.

On the way he told me where the idea came from. 'They say ten per cent of people have ninety per cent of the world's wealth. That means nine out of ten – those who live in poverty – don't. I started thinking how best I could show that.' There were going to be nine heads. 'I see them in water and drowning – like in a big fountain – and all different. They'll be cries for help. One will be a mother holding a baby.' He wanted to build in hope somewhere but hadn't worked out how. And money was tight. Having the steel galvanised was costly.

When we reached Simon's studio, a garage at his parents' house down a long country lane, I was impressed with his meticulous research. A book lay open with picture after picture of different expressions. It looked as though he'd photographed a chap in a bath. The water was lapping over his wide open mouth, hair clinging to scalp and eyes staring, riveted, transfixed. Simon hadn't underplayed the horror. On the floor was his interpretation in metal; a head part-finished, four or five feet long down to the top lip, with shiny steel strips welded across the cheek. What struck me most were the pupils exactly centred in the whites of the deeply recessed eyes. The effect was one of intense focus but at the same time of total absence, as though the being behind the eyes had flown, leaving only fear.

Simon led me outside, then left me to view more of his work.

Propped against a raised border was a finished head with bare scalp that made the gender ambivalent. This head was riven with an anguish laced with anger. Both sets of teeth were bared, with the mouth a dark, empty abyss. The facial features were sharply defined with angled facets to the cheeks tightly stretched down the length of the face. This was metal welded to raw emotion, the feeling stripped to the tensile, muscular bone.

Simon reappeared holding the photograph he'd hoped to find in the car: a head, with arms raised, in a landscape setting. 'They'll be fifteen to twenty feet tall', he said. The impact would be staggering; the monumental equivalent of Edvard Munch's *The Scream*.

'Do you see them in a sculpture park,' I asked as we headed back.

'No, more of a public place,' he said. Simon had other work exhibited at an arts centre and sculpture garden but this project needed to be in the public eye: an open space bordering a city thoroughfare, or maybe even a lake. But his immediate concern was funding the next head. An idea like Simon's doesn't just happen. You'd need a deep-seated conscience to be that touched by the plight of the world's poor and strong reserves of skill, energy and motivation to carry it through.

Where did that come from?

'Well, my grandmother was a painter and grandfather a potter cum sculptor. I used to spend lots of time with them as a kid. We were surrounded by grandad's figures and pots at home.'

'I taught ceramics once,' I said. 'What was his name, out of interest?'

'Same as mine: Ruscoe.'

'What?! I used a book by someone called Ruscoe for reference. I still have it at home: *Sculpture for the Potter*.'

'Yes, that's him – William Ruscoe.'

Unbelievable. I was talking to the grandson of a man whose advice I had drawn on years ago. Rubbing shoulders with him, so to speak, after an apparently random lift, I had to question the very idea of randomness. The odds might not be that great. But what did odds count for against the reality of this whole encounter?

It wasn't easy to say goodbye. Contact with creative people always pulls on my heart strings. As I stepped out of the car, I noticed Simon's leather jacket had two parallel white stripes running down from the collar and sleeve pointing straight to his hands. From head to hands; a direct route. It couldn't have been more appropriate for a sculptor.

The Caterpillar Tracks

Strange but, fresh from the Gulliver-scale heads, a Lilliputian caught my eye; a black haired caterpillar on a perilous journey across the road. Wasn't November an odd time for it to be here? Climate change? Or yet another example of my ignorance about the natural world? Yes, I decided; caterpillars must pupate over the winter and some later than others. Perhaps some did and some, who left it too late, didn't.

Caterpillars are such a paradigm for change. Did it but know, this multi-legged, perambulating tube was destined for a bendy straitjacket; a small sacrifice for the spell-binding transformation to come. The wonder was that wings could be fashioned within, with such tapestries of colour and pattern. I can't see any caterpillar without remembering an analogy related by Bill Arkle, a poet and painter whose mystical philosophy had a great influence on me in my twenties.

'Imagine a caterpillar on the edge of the table,' he said. 'That is the end of its two-dimensional world. But, looking on from another dimension, you know there is more to its existence. One day it will fly. Then imagine you are the caterpillar. Are you ready for take-off?'

Out I came with the same answer I always did: 'No, Bill. I'm as earthbound as ever; still looking over the edge, worried how far I might fall.' My encounters had taken more out of me than I'd realised. Clinging to hedges with no chance of a lift on this narrowest of B-roads, I took a wrong turning towards Exeter until a chap in a front garden put me right. 'You want Ottery St.Mary,' he said.

I demolished the almond and apricot crumble that I'd bought at the café and my last russet apple. Then I trudged towards the centre of town, passing the leviathan hulk of a switchgear factory, a washed-up redbrick relic of the one-time great manufacturing base in this country that gave so many hands and eyes a purpose.

Ivy tendrils and vandals were performing the last rites.

For all the mindless drudgery of production line work there can be a comforting camaraderie. Working long shifts in a bakery once, I enjoyed the good-natured badinage and occasional George Formby turns with a brush for ukulele. There were other consolations. Flicking cuts in the bloomers with rat-a-tat flashes of the knife was one. Another was diving into the dough with pinched fingers, to fix the top bun on a cottage loaf. Perhaps that's why, later, clay grabbed me.

Groups of people were going in my direction. Outside a church, a cameraman waited. A few policemen took up positions. People were gathering in a side road, some lining the street as if to witness a carnival procession. How could I have forgotten? Remembrance Sunday, of course.

'They're eight minutes late,' I heard one person say. Lucky: I might have missed the chance to pay my respects for the sacrifice so many had made. More than that though; I'd include all the wishes and regrets of my fellow travellers. They'd be there. And so would the memory of all those who'd brought me to this point, stretching way, way back; a small town's tribute and a lone hitchhiker's thanks, hand in hand.

The veterans were getting ready to march in rows further up the road. The strident skirl of the Scottish piper at the head of the procession resounded. At its cue, the thinning ranks of elderly servicemen, bereted and be-medalled, broke into step followed by other local worthies, the scouts and guides, presences signalled by standards borne aloft, some held reverentially in white-gloved hands. What a welter of private thoughts marched with them. How upright-and-eyes-forward were those with a cause to believe in. All too soon, the marchers were gone and so were my reflections, hived off by the comment of a middle-aged woman at my side. 'And what they want, they get today,' she said, with a touch of bitterness. 'It's a throwaway society we live in.'

I nodded blankly. But I played with her thoughts as I walked on. They seemed at odds; get but don't keep. What can we hold on to? What do we really want? That was a question I returned to time and again.

The Lookalike Bookkeeper

Waiting for a lift always gave me a buzz. True, the buzz palled the longer I waited but I had to go through the waiting for the right person to turn up. Standing by the gate to a field just out of town, I reckoned that a lift couldn't be long coming. There had to be charitably-minded people around on Remembrance Sunday.

When Hugh pulled up in his silver car, it wasn't his stopping that struck me or his charity. Hugh's face was the unmistakable image of my caterpillar sage, Bill Arkle. If I mentally removed the woolly hat, he had the same long, slender face, the same pronounced cheek bones and strong jaw line. The likeness was striking. But his eyes were the most telling. Their reflectiveness identified a similarly deep thinker.

Hugh used to work for the Forestry Commission and was now a self-employed bookkeeper. 'I feel that I'm helping people by keeping their books in order,' he said.

'Doesn't sound as though that's what you live for,' I said.

It wasn't. Hugh worked with another kind of balance sheet. 'From the age of twelve,' he said, 'I was aware of the difference between right and wrong. Conscience, I suppose you'd call it.' As an adolescent, he'd asked: 'What is life about?' At university, he joined the Christian Union. 'I've been following Christ ever since I was nineteen. And now I'm fifty-five.' It had given direction and meaning to his life.

Perverse perhaps, but a commitment like that arouses in me an uneasy admiration: fortunate to be anchored to a faith, yes; but a certainty I'd forego, like a lift that gets me there in one. So when Hugh said, 'Jesus was either a liar or you believe what he said,' I was tempted to put some greys in. Could we trust reports of what Jesus said? It was easy enough to darken white with hints of black but it felt gratuitous tendering scepticism when Hugh's very convictions probably earned me this lift.

Instead I murmured, 'It's what people do with the truth that bothers me.'

'*The heart is deceitful above all things and desperately corrupt: Ezekiel*,' Hugh proferred.

The biblical quotation backed up what I'd said but it was a blanket statement I'd want to qualify. Surely the heart knows best *sometimes.* He must have sensed the uncertainty in my 'yes'.

'It's about sin,' he said, definitively. 'Humanists say men are good but I say not all.'

I had to agree with 'not all' but I felt sure that humanists held human beings responsible for their actions – good or evil. 'Look what man's done to man; those we're remembering today; those who died and still are dying. And what for?' I protested. 'Do we learn from the past? Is there hope?'

'Well, the past tells us how we got here but not where we're going. That's the point.'

'Isn't it all pointless though when man keeps on repeating the same old mistakes?'

'I don't think so. If life doesn't have a meaning, it's a sick joke.'

I could hardly deny it. Every time I looked at Hugh I was reminded of Bill. Could that and all other connections on this trip be purely random? Might an analogy help? 'A casual look at the night sky and you'd think the stars are scattered any old how. But pattern and order's there. You'd have to see meaning in that, wouldn't you?'

'Exactly,' replied Hugh.

But it was my own reasoning I doubted. Did pattern and order equate with meaning? And what meaning was there for lives caught up in the chaos of war? I was getting tangled in philosophical knots. We were nearing Honiton now, dusk was upon us and I had to confront a more pressing issue; where to shack up for the night?

'Might be able to put you in touch with someone,' Hugh said. 'Rod lives in Honiton. Used to be a teacher. He's a brother in God. Let's see if he's in.'

The Repointing Teacher

When we arrived, Rod wasn't exactly in. He was up, repointing ridge tiles on the roof. Did Christian fellowship extend to bringing him down from his perch? It did, but after Rod came to earth the serious expression crossing his craggy features made me sense a problem. His wife was away and he wasn't sure which rooms had been slept in by the last visitors. It came down to whether the sheets had been changed.

'How about using the inner sheet from my sleeping bag?' I suggested.

That sorted, we said our goodbyes to Hugh and repaired to the house, passing on the way to my room the hallway radiator which sported the motif, 'The joy of the Lord is our strength.' Warmth too! While Rod carried on pointing, I introduced myself to the fluffiest, haughtiest feline I have ever met, with eyes so all-seeing that only total transparency of feelings would do. I obliged. Lucinda Nora, or 'Lady' for short, was an American Maine Coon, a pedigree she didn't have to assert.

Over a chicken tikka masala that Rod kindly offered to share he talked about his journey. As a young lad, he'd felt supported by older Christians. 'That loving cradle' he called it. But 'I was also aware of the demonic,' he said pointedly.

I raised my eyebrows.

'Demons are angels gone wrong,' he added. One of his grandmothers was a fortune teller – 'tarot and tea leaves sort of thing' – only because she needed the money. 'But I've had to disown all of that,' he said. He studied chemistry at Birmingham University. 'I played at making fireworks,' he explained, 'and always liked making explosions. But then,' with a wry grin, 'that got moderated by my beliefs too.'

He'd suffered from bad back problems – vertebrae compressing the spinal cord – having to work bent over to ease the pain. Part way through a PhD, he took up teaching but became concerned about an irascible Buddhist Head of R.E. Then not doffing your cap could earn you the cane. But one kid riled the Buddhist so much that he gave him an uppercut, knocking him down some stairs. I laughed at the thought of a boxing Buddhist but this wasn't a punchline. There was a more profound message.

'After that, God spoke to me,' Rod said. 'He wanted the Buddhist back. I was to approach him but not in the Common Room. We were to meet in a connecting passage with the kitchen at eleven a.m. I was told.'

How specific was that!

'OK, God,' Rod had said. 'I agree.' With that, a hot pain shot down his back. 'From that day on, my back trouble went,' he said. 'That's my testimony.' And what *could* be more convincing than lasting relief from chronic pain? His wife bore witness to the power of faith too. Her arthritis and a benign lump disappeared after a faith healer's intervention.

'So faith is rewarded,' I said.

We were enjoying a delicious tiramisu when the phone rang. It was his wife. Rod's voice carried. I couldn't miss one snatch: 'I haven't fallen off the roof today, dear. Or, if I did, I'm all right.'

'Nice to know you're being thought of,' I commented after. 'But then, it is Remembrance Sunday.'

Rod sat down, looking if anything more earnest. 'There's something we've just found out: where my other grandmother's grave is. We're sorting out a memorial. D'you ever hear of the Brighton trunk murders? She was a Mafia Moll – Violet Kaye, a famous dancer – one of the victims.'

I'd read about it sometime in the past.

'Back in the thirties, it was,' he said. 'The body – hacked up – was hidden in a trunk in the left luggage department on Brighton railway station. They reckon she died of shock following a depressed fracture of the skull. Terrible business. I've lived with this since I was fifty.'

I couldn't imagine how one adjusted to such horrendous news.

'My father only found out when a foster-uncle of mine had his tongue loosened by drink. The awful thing is that the chap who murdered her got away with it. Norman Birkett – defence counsel – acquitted him in 1934. Later he said it was his worst day's work. The murderer confessed in 1976 but died shortly after.'

I understood now how important it was to respect their grandmother's memory and why family meant so much to Rod. We talked about drugs. A relative of Rod's had written of his own dependency on heroin. He'd likened it to a girlfriend you couldn't split up from. Thankfully, Rod's relative had come through the experience. But what did heroin do for you that you couldn't find elsewhere? Was it a substitute for the meaning one didn't find in relationships or life?

Rod spoke of his step-grandfather. 'He was an old sea salt – sailed round Cape Horn several times – in the days when men were men,' he said. Where was the challenge today? Was that what was missing? Rod had some work to do after our meal, so I took the opportunity to retire to my room.

The Dancing Shadow

I had much to mull over. If talk of funerals, an attempted suicide
and a notorious murder wasn't enough to get me thinking, what
would? It brought me back to the question I'd posed after the
procession: what can we hold on to? One answer stared me in
the face. Hugh and Rod shone a light on it, as Marie and Robbo
had before them: religion. I could see what strength it gave. It was
written on Rod's radiator! But this was the very thing I baulked
at.

It wasn't that I decried religion. No, I'd defend to the hilt people's
right to hold their beliefs as long as they respected others' right to
hold different ones. But if doctrines and dogma bred intolerance,
I had qualms. That shining light of certainty could be treacherous.
How certain could anyone be that their beliefs were right and
others' wrong? There are many spiritual paths.

But Hugh and Rod's convictions floodlit my uncertainties.
What *did* I believe in? How *should* I travel? Matthew's hitchhiking
code of practice had served me well. What I needed now was a
philosophical sort of Highway Code: not something airy-fairy,
but wrought from experience. All very well my asking everyone
else but this journey, this life on the road, was teaching me *my*
direction. And how would I describe my belief system? 'Keep it
simple, stupid' – or 'K.I.S.S.' – I was told during my selling days,
so let's call it 'The Hitchhiker's Way'. And **Tenet One** should stop
me being dogmatic: *There are many routes to a destination.*

It wasn't an earth-shattering revelation but enough to make me
feel I'd earned a good night's sleep. I slipped into the inner sheet
of my sleeping bag, turned out the light but didn't turn over. The
wind was riffling through trees outside and, by some unfortunate
alignment of a streetlight, one tree, and my bedroom window,
I was disturbed by the dancing shadow of a branch on the wall
opposite my bed. Soon every twig, every leaf bud and node
was as personally known to me as if we'd been in a permanent
handshake.

The initial irritation had me wielding secateur-ridden threats
but I rediscovered a philosophical turn of mind, conjuring up an
image from Plato's *Republic* that had always fascinated me. The
story – allegory really – goes something like this. Prisoners were

shackled deep in a cave, where a fire cast shadows of objects carried along a causeway in the cave on to the far wall. Because the prisoners knew no other existence, they took the shadows for the real things and, when one escapee tried to put them wise, they killed him. They wanted to hang on to the world they knew.

Why was I grabbed by this image? I saw a link with my query about pattern, order and meaning. Suppose I was a prisoner in this room and privy only to this dancing shadow of a branch, my understanding would be limited to what I could deduce from the pattern of twigs. But, if I went to the window, I'd start making connections – to the tree, the wind, the streetlight – that explained what I was seeing. I could attribute more meaning to the shadow from the extended pattern of connections. But it didn't stop there. Where did the light come from that cast the shadow in the first place? Track back from that and I'd have to conclude that the further I looked, the greater the depth of meaning I could attach.

So did pattern and order equate with meaning? There was only one conclusion: yes, but it's all relative. So much pattern; so much meaning. That sounded like **Tenet Two**. How would it go? *The more connections, the greater the meaning.* Yes, that would help a hitchhiker make sense. Not a bad night's work either.

Day Five

Honiton to Bath

'How tempting it was to explain away the unlikely'

The Confirmed Dealer

Before breakfast I caught a piece on the telly in my room about people who don't get enough sleep. A rarely diagnosed disorder – obstructive sleep apnoea – stopped enough air getting to the lungs. That made me sit up. My brother-in-law suffers from such a condition. He was lucky not to be killed when he fell asleep driving across a bridge in Sweden and collided head on with another car. Now he has to use an air pressure mask at night to keep his airways open.

I couldn't help thinking about Luke. A suicide bid took more than an air mask to deal with. But a fat lot of good it was standing on the touchline of tragedy. Then I remembered Marie – prayer had worked for her – and Rod's hotline to God. Why not plug in? I'd ask Rod about this talking-to-God business over breakfast. Come to that, what happened to the Buddhist boxer?

Rod was up and about. I could hear him talking downstairs ... to Lucinda. 'Salmon steak or roast pheasant this morning, My Lady?' I imagined. When I did descend, it was to the strains of a guitar and a rousing Christian song from Rod. My appetite sharpened by the musical hors d'oeuvres, I stepped up to the breakfast table, with a view of the garden and Lady Lucinda pussyfooting some sadly wet grass.

'That Buddhist,' I began over the cornflakes, 'you never said what happened.'

'Oh, I carried it through. I found myself on the way to the kitchen at eleven and, believe me, that was the first and last time we met there. And I delivered my message, like I'd been told.'

'And ...?'

'I don't think he took any notice,' Rod said lightly. 'He'd become anti-Christian. He just looked at me, almost embarrassed. But he did smile.'

There hadn't been a Damascene conversion, but Rod had kept his side of the bargain and the brisk westerly still brushing the trees helped keep me focussed. 'How does that talking to God work?' I asked.

'When you give your life to Jesus, you get pointers, you know, and God *can* speak to you. Not always, if I'm honest.'

So the line broke up on occasions. I liked that. It made the whole thing more plausible. But how did Jesus fit in?

Rod believed that Jesus was man and God, unlike the Jehovah's Witnesses, who maintained he was a god. 'They reckon he was the archangel Michael,' Rod said matter-of-factly.

I'd never heard *that* before. There was a lot I didn't know about beliefs, but I ruled nothing out or in, even archangels. My ecumenism included regular doorstep meetings with Witnesses. I'd quiz them about Michael next time we met. In the meantime, I trotted out one of my father's mantras: 'How can there be *any* God, when animals have to kill to survive?'

'Well atheism is a real faith,' he reassured. Dad might have had his doubts about that. 'But there's no evidence for there *not* being a God. If you chuck a load of soil in the air, what's the chance of a typewriter coming down?'

I laughed. 'That's a tricky one.'

'The order's got to come from somewhere; someone or something. Science helps. One law of thermodynamics deals with entropy. Without energy in a system, it tends to become disordered. So the universe shouldn't exist.'

I was cracking open an egg, peeling off the broken bits. 'The need for order's inbuilt, isn't it?' I asked, 'but I've always liked *some* chaos to get to work on.' I told him about the teaching job I took on in a rundown pottery. The kids had run riot and left clay prints all over the ceiling. 'I don't think they believed in God.'

'God's a potter,' Rod said. 'See *Isaiah 29:16*. King James Version, that is. "Can the pot speak against the potter?" *That's* the question.'

Rod's ability to quote chapter and verse put me to shame. My father had treasured *The Rubaiyat of Omar Khayyam*. But I could recite only the briefest phrase: 'Who is the potter and who the pot?' How much more telling was what eluded me! It was a good point to bring in Luke. Rod was only too pleased to put together some sort of prayer.

He looked up and down, rearranged the cutlery and the words materialised from somewhere. 'Dear Lord, if it be your will, we pray that Luke may survive, that he will forgive himself for what he has done, find whatever meaning this experience has for him and look for the light that comes out of the darkness. Through Jesus Christ our Lord and Saviour, Amen.'

It was a simple enough prayer. We fell silent for a while and the sense of completion was greater than at the end of any meal. Then he had some news. As a stamp dealer now, he'd been planning to purchase some stamps in Taunton. If it was any help, he could give me a lift there. If!

We shared the honours at the sink while Rod regaled me with choice idioms. 'You're all behind like a cow's tail,' he said as I dallied with the drying. I'd come to appreciate his frankness, laced with darts of humour and generosity. Rod only wanted sixteen pounds for the B & B. I had to persuade him of the merits of twenty. I would have taken my leave of Her Royal Highness, except she'd curled up in a cardboard box, playing the most sumptuous, deep downy cushion that any prince might wish to lay his head on.

I packed my rucksack and tried to revamp my questions for the day's lifts but gave up when I remembered where pre-planning had got me. I'd let directions emerge from the talk. Plain enough where Rod's direction came from: on the way to Taunton, he told me that he asked God whether he should still sell stamps. And why not? I could relate to God the Father, not so sure about God the Son, but definitely God the Careers Adviser.

But God the Son had a message for me, so Rod led me to think. 'He gave up everything – paid the price on the cross – so we could benefit.'

'How?' I asked, feeling slightly mercenary.

'If you're born again, giving your life to Jesus, you become part of a royal priesthood, exalted in high places.'

'Gosh, I'm not sure I'm ready for that, Rod.'

'That's how the Book of Hebrews and St.Peter put it. But you have to commit to Christ before you die. There are rewards in heaven.' Reassuringly he added, 'All men are precious in God's eyes, whatever they've achieved or aspired to.'

I have to say I abetted Rod's talk of heaven. Ever since reading Dante's *Inferno* I'd wondered how life might shape up on the other side. Rod painted a glowing picture. There were mansions, banquets, a lot of singing and mingling with angels. 'Party time,' he said.

'But I wouldn't want it too good,' I argued. I couldn't hack an overdose of angelic singing and celestial eating.

'People who believe in heaven talk about the amazing colours you'd see and how they link with music,' Rod encouraged.

Extraordinary that he should come out with that. In my twenties, Bill Arkle, the caterpillar analogy man, introduced me to the music of Delius. One day I put on a record of *Song of the High Hills* and dozed off to the ethereal sounds. When I opened my eyes, I was staggered to see what was coming out of the speakers. Wafting gently upwards were filmy, undulating slips of colour, changing shape subtly in harmony with the music, each a distinct tone of purple or blue. So pleasurable was the phenomenon that I wanted it to continue. I tried to maintain the same dreamy state, but the colours soon faded, then disappeared.

I've experienced nothing like it since. Colour and sound synaesthesia I have read about but only in the sense that hearing a sound will evoke in the mind a particular colour, not produce a free floating image. Such a link made heaven worth a pilgrimage. But I'd want to come back! Rod indulged my lyrical account of the experience as if it were a description of a Shangri-la that he too had visited. If so, he didn't let on. Perhaps he wanted me to feel that I'd found an undiscovered land.

We were nearing Taunton and more immediate concerns. 'I'll drop you at the Monkton Elms Garden Centre,' he said. 'It's a good place to hitch from.'

My stay with Rod had been particularly warm and revealing, and I don't think either of us was ready to part. 'What about a coffee in the Garden Centre?' I asked. Over a cappuccino and a generous slice of carrot cake, we nattered like lifelong buddies and Rod told me about best friends of his who dug holes for the water board. Back to earth.

The Resolute Drifter

I'd shaken off the spectre of the A30, and the A361 here was a much more approachable beast. At half past twelve, I started hitching and my thumb couldn't believe its pulling power when an old white van drew up twenty minutes later. Straggling brownish hair trailing to the shoulders convinced me there was a woman driver, until a bristly faced Mick turned round. I'd hardly said, 'Thanks, anywhere north' before we were rumbling towards Glastonbury and Mick was rattling off too … on his own track.

'I was going to Canada. Had a few drinks before with some mates – party it was – an' left a bit late for the airport. But there's no one at the checkout. This Sheila turns up an' says, "*Is your name Michael? Know how much it costs to keep a plane waiting?*" "My mate phoned up," I said. "*Good job he did, or you wouldn't be on it,*" she says. So I 'ave a G & T, can o' beer, smoke a joint, gets out the other end and there we go. What 'ad I done? Left me fuckin' money at me mate's place, 'adn't I. Couldn't even read the map but I'd worked out where I was, roughly. Collapsed at a roundabout I did. There's twenty-five fuckin' people hitchhiking, so I wraps the bag round me fuckin' feet an' sits on the stanchion.'

'Stanch-i-on,' he says. But what *is* he talking about?

'So this hitchhiker writes me a sign: Manchester.'

'What?' I say. 'I thought you were in Canada.'

'No mate. No money. Listen. I'm coming back now… '

'Right.'

' …an' a fuckin' black man drives up in a Merc. "*What the fuck have you been up to?*" he says. "I've been on 'oliday," I says. "It was a mistake: a fuckin' waste of time." Then he's stopped doing a ton, up the motorway. Jaysus. I nods off an' I wakes up. "*How old are you,*" he says. "Twenty-four," I says. (He's got to be thirty plus now, unless his face is telling porkies) An' he gives me a talking to. "*Give up the drink 'n drugs, man,*" he says. It's this black man telling me! Get that?'

[DAY FIVE]

'Yes.' He makes sure I pay attention, then he's off again.

'Listen. We're off on 'oliday, this girl and me, to this commune in Wales, both skint. "*I'll get the bus,*" she says. "I'll hitchhike," I says. So I 'eads out of Wales on a slip road.'

Whoa. Weren't they just going? And now he's coming back?!

'But the fucker was cordoned off. Seven-mile walk it was, an' three hours later I'm well behind the fuckin' schedule to Manchester when I get picked up by this dude. I'm dead to the wind at fuckin' ten at night and I've got 36p. *36p.*'

He says it so loud you'd think he's just found the hole in his pocket.

' "How fuckin' far can I get with 36p?" I says, 'an' 'e drives me to this station. Cost £4.40 to Wythenshawe. "*You'll have to walk mate,*" the geezer says at the barrier, so I jumps it, straight on to the train. If I 'adn't, I'd 'ave 'ad to walk fifteen fuckin' miles to me ma's and never met up with Julie.'

'Well, at least you'd both got together.'

'Yeah. "*Did you 'ave a nice trip?*" she says, when I get there. "Oh yeah," I says, "an' where's the fuckin' cider?" '

Fat chance they're still together. Better not ask. I blurt out, 'Done a fair bit of hitching then?' Mick doesn't need cues.

'I was hitchin' in the fuckin' winter once, just outside Birmingham. An' there was all this writing on the crash barrier. *I've been here four hours,* one said. There was more on a fuckin' post: *Well done, you've just discovered the art of invisibility,* and this other: *God is everywhere but he ain't here.* People don't know 'alf what life's like. Walk into a bus station at night an' it's like *Blade Runner*; everything's smashed up an' I'm scared shitless, dodging the blacks. One time this old woman comes up and says, "*I'll wait with you.*" An *old* woman.'

He softens his voice at the memory of it. Touching. But who was helping who?

'Friend of mine said, "*Never look at people. Too much ugliness'll do yer 'ead in.*" This lorry pulls up ...' (so we're talking hitchhiking again) 'an' this fuckin' dude opens the door. First thing I notice: his wrists. *This* big' (he puts a hand round his leg) 'an' brute of a face. Boxer type I'd say. "*I don't like fuckin' beggars,*" he says. Put me on edge that did. "*I was in the army but I 'ad an accident, see; fell on me face.*" I didn't laugh. Just as well. Turns out we're the same age an' it was no joke. When he 'ad the accident, no-one came to see 'im. I felt sorry in the end.'

Trying to keep track of Mick's stories, I've lost my thread altogether. As for the landscape we're travelling through, only Glastonbury Tor registers, but its myths and legends hardly rival the world of monsters and mystery I'm engulfed in. And there's plenty of plot left in Mick's tales. The slightest conversational touch on the tiller – like me picking up on the begging – and we're off on another tack.

'Yea, I've tried begging. No luck though. One girl came up – in Stockport, where I'm from – and said, "*You're fat enough already. Go and get a job. Act like a man.*" '

So many people tell him what to do, I figure. But he's not telling himself. Or is he?

'So many ways to go in life,' he says. 'For all me drifting, maybe I should've got married, 'ad a couple of kids an' the rest of it. But what would I 'ave missed?'

I recognise that thinking!

'If I end up with a mortgage, me whole life's mapped out. Whip all the energy out of me, it would. As it is, if I run out of social, I'll ditch the van an' hitch to London. But you can end up not taking orders from people. That's the trouble.'

'What jobs have you had?' I venture.

'Bricklayin'. Electronics. Didn't last. Tell you the best time: near Minehead I met a girl on a bus, years back. Turned out she lived in a bender, next to a waterfall. So I got one for meself, six by six, dark green camouflage, an' so well hidden you wouldn't know it's there. I lived in it two years off an' on. It's got a wood burner an' a gas ring. An' I rigged up a flexible steel flue that loops over an' up outside.'

The way he's talking, with hand gestures to match, this tent must be the closest to what he'd call home.

'I 'ad to leave the flap open for oxygen. Best in winter it was; less of a challenge an' no mosquitoes. You just 'ave to keep warm but the novelty's gone off now.'

I'm sorry. The tent was there waiting. Mick isn't.

''Ad a puppy once. Fred I called it. Spent all me money on 'im. We was hitchin' to Taunton in the rain when this woman stopped; for the dog not me. Poor perisher was shivering. "*I lost my husband*

four months ago," she said. "D'you miss him?" I said. "*No. I fuckin'
hated him,*" she came back. "Did you have the insurance then?"
"*Oh yes,*" she said. "So you got the house paid for an' 'e got the
answer to the big question," I said. "Was 'e mushroom soup?"
"*No,*" she said. "*He died of natural causes.*" '

Mick's natural born humour spills over. But he doesn't find
himself amusing and I hardly have time to laugh. He has to turn
off a short way ahead. 'I'll drop you at a lay-by with a bus shelter.
You can go in there if it fuckin' rains,' he says.

Now there's someone who knows about life on the road.

'I don't know wha's the matter with me mates. Some 'ave
gone religious. Must be scared of Sooty or something. And wha's
worse, some of 'em 'ave become nondescript adults.' That was his
parting shot.

'So what now, Mick?' I say.

'Go to the pub, get drunk and get some sleep,' he says.

We shake on it. I watch him drive off in his old white van. An
hour's gone and half of me is still ticking away, living his anything
but nondescript life.

The Tipping Chips

I tried hitching from the bus stop lay-by but not for long. Straight
ahead were some traffic lights. When they were red, cars would
only stop once. Green and they'd race past to beat them. Though
the next lift should have been the main attraction, right opposite
was a warm-up act: a small transport café, The Green Ore.

The fug was not for the faint-hearted. I wasn't sure whether the
walls were yellow out of choice or chip fat charmed by fingers of
smoke into co-habiting. I perched on a metal-framed red chair that
looked at me angrily. The PVC seat was split wide open, foaming
at the mouth. Other mouths were puffing. A copy of *The Sun* set
the tone with a headline: 'What a repulsive creature' and a picture
of a snake round someone's neck. I couldn't be bothered to find
out whose repulsive neck it was or why this warranted half a front
page. Much more disturbing was that an item headed 'Four British
troops killed' merited only one sixteenth of the same page.

Having been badmouthed by the seat, I consulted the menu on
the wall for better news, though the clock alongside offered only

one choice; a quarter to ten. I made it five past two. From the nosh on offer, beans on toast with chips and a cuppa seemed the least unhealthy option. The waitress took my order with breathless brevity.

'Thanks,' I said, thinking this is going to be a great meal, and continued to breathe while I consulted the map. A little further on, the road met the A37 to Bristol and rejoined the A39 soon after, heading towards Bath. Bristol was a more direct route to the north but I might get bogged down in the suburbs. That decided it: I'd take the Bath option.

Then my mind went back to Mick. What a jolt. But what a revelation. I couldn't get over his rough and ready rootlessness. His lifestyle might be subsidised by the state, but wasn't society richer with a healthy degree of nonconformism? One business guru maintains that, if firms are to innovate, they need anarchists to disrupt conventional thinking. Look beyond Mick's language, drink and drugs – if you could – and you'd find someone resourceful and open-ended in his thinking: so open-ended that he was always in transit! Drifting was one way to characterise it. Divergent might be another. Was that the thinking I needed for my Hitchhiker's Way? It sounded as though he'd written **Tenet Three**: *Direction can come from avoiding destinations*. Where would *that* take me? Well, away from Bristol, perhaps. *And fixed ideas*. I liked that. I'd tack it on to the Tenet.

The baked beans arrived riding *two* slices of toast, bumper to bumper. The chips, which I feared might be limp and greasy, were as crisp and golden as the promise of an advertising slogan. Having cast aspersions before, I had to compliment the waitress. 'What's the secret of your chips?' I asked.

She thought for a moment. 'Clean oil,' she said, 'and chilled chips. We *never* use frozen.'

I was shamed. Never jump to conclusions, I told myself. The chips tipped me off. And Mick.

The Otherworldly Herbalist

If Rod was a bedrock of belief, Mick was like that load of soil Rod wanted to chuck in the air. And how would Mick land? As an actor? Storyteller? Extreme events organiser? He'd be well qualified to be a drink and drugs counsellor. Not a cardboard box resident in a boarded-up doorway, I hoped.

My course was hardly decisive, winding up, down and round with no sign of a stopping place until I topped the brow of a hill to earn the reward for a two or three-mile hike. A thick-piled carpet rolled out before me, with the intricate traceries of birch, oak and a few poplars patterning the landscape, a clearing sky and a swish of feather dusters sweeping the horizon. The driveway to some cottages provided a pull-in. Perfect. I stationed myself there, happy with the view … except that a lanky buddleia growing out of a wall obscured it.

What caught my eye often proved significant. I couldn't ignore **Tenet Four**: *Watch out for signs and learn how to read them.* What might a buddleia tell me? Here was a plant that fetched up in the most unlikely places – a barrier-jumper like Mick. But the scent of this opportunist's flower attracted those most flitting of insects; butterflies.

The irony appealed to me: the wanderer finds a home, only to discover that it's a magnet for other itinerants, and certainly not nondescript. Well, I wouldn't budge from this place till my lift arrived. That was decisive. But what exotic traveller might be winging his or her way to me now? It seemed like no time before Matthew H. arrived, though with my musings and the view to occupy me, twenty minutes might have passed.

'Hi,' I said. 'Thanks.'

He smiled and, glory be, he was heading for Bath. I could have described him as in his thirties, clean-shaven with close-cropped black hair, receding slightly and looking smartly casual in a loosely-zipped jacket. But overriding all that was his expression: as if he knew what I was going to say.

At fourteen, he was into CND marches and annoyed at 'the system'. After college, he lived in Israel. From the way he talked, I wasn't sure how far he identified with the Jewish faith. 'Some Jewish people are quite extreme in their thinking,' he said. For a while he did gardening at a Mushav (where you get paid), before moving on to a kibbutz (where you don't) at Elat. It was there he fell in love with Ginnie, a nurse, before she went off to Thailand. Short of money, he couldn't join her but kept in touch. He fell out with the farmer at another Mushav. 'He'd been a general in the

Israeli army and barked out, *"No time for joking, only working"* when I tried to crack jokes.'

Someone said he might find work in Jerusalem. He stayed at a Palestinian guest house for several days but found nothing. 'I was getting desperate; down to my last twenty quid, plus a few shekels.' The owner made Matthew an offer: "Find other people to book rooms here and you can stay free." It didn't work.

At a really low ebb, he said to himself: I have to get a job. I've got so little money. Four or five shekels would be something. And I could do with calling my dad. Three or four phone tokens would be enough. And I need some chewing gum. 'My breath', he explained, 'and the smoking. I didn't want to put people off when I spoke.'

He set off to look for a job in hotels. At the first hotel they kept him waiting, only to trot out 'No work'. The same went for the next two. His spirits sank. But he gave it one more go. When the manageress, an Israeli, told him, 'No work', Matthew said, 'No problem' … like you do when you've given up thinking. 'But then she said, "Wait a moment." I thought, what's she gonna come back with? Some food? Or does she know of another job?' She didn't, but returned saying she had some things for him. Matthew held out a hand and she dropped into it, one after the other: five shekels, four phone tokens and three chewing gum strips.

'I closed my hand round them,' he said. 'I'd taken it in subconsciously but it hadn't quite registered. "Good luck," she said. My heart starts pounding. I need to look at what's in my hand but I can't believe what's there.' He was overcome with emotion: 'An overpowering feeling of joy, love and compassion flooded from the pit of my stomach and all over. I started to cry. Tears were running down my T-shirt. My hands were covered in tears. I washed my face with them.'

The emotion was still there. Matthew had to let it out. I'd hardly spoken. And what could I say? It's easy to let scepticism infiltrate open-mindedness. But I *wanted* to empathise and recalled an experience that chimed with Matthew's.

'I was at an all-time low in one job, dealing with rounds of complaints and swore at some workmates who were trying to help. Shortly after, a customer walked into the office carrying a box. "What've you got there?" I said, suspiciously. *"It's for you,"* he

[DAY FIVE]

said. Inside was the most beautifully iced cake with – would you believe? – three angels on it. "We haven't started your conservatory yet," I said, overwhelmed with his generosity. *"No, but we're so happy with the design,"* he said. That one gesture changed my whole outlook.'

'It must have.' Matthew nodded, looking out of the window. Low stone walls lining the road afforded wide open views of the countryside. 'I was between jobs when Ginnie and I got back together. She was living at the Lizard.'

'The Lizard?' I had to tell Matthew how fated Ingrid and Snowy were to buy the Most Southerly House. My digression must have seemed long-winded.

'Ginnie was still working as a nurse and staying in two converted railway carriages. We lived there eight or nine months; a beautiful area on the edge of a valley with a stream running down. Only ten minutes from the beach. You could hear the sea.'

My turn to nod. 'Wonderful.'

'We grew most of our own stuff: tomatoes, potatoes, Jerusalem artichokes and so on. We even had a polytunnel; vegetarians' dream.' He smiled. 'That time, that place: it was special. We really enjoyed the good life; a healthy environment and eating well. And then, there was one day ...' He broke off. 'You know I don't normally tell people these things, but I think I can. We went for a walk down by the sea. It must have been a late summer afternoon; beautiful day, not hot or cold. There were two ways to go; straight up back home or along the bottom of the valley, cutting across the stream. That's where we went. We found a spot by the stream for a rest and sat a foot or so apart on the same side.'

Why so specific? It keyed me up to expect something.

'We chatted about life in general, not *that* deeply. We must have sat for nine or ten minutes, with the stream only ... what, fifteen feet away ... and we've gone quiet; so absorbed in the present moment, looking at the view, that we stop talking, when all of a sudden my eyes are drawn to a stone about four or five feet away, maybe three feet across the base. A couple of ferns were growing there. The stone was a sort of conical pyramid, with moss on top. And I'm just looking when I notice it's starting to shimmer and almost changing. I blink my eyes. It seemed to be changing shape and ... yes, it was ... starting to form a human face.'

I am so stunned by what I'm hearing that I can only think of, 'No!'

'I said to myself at that point: it can't look more real. And then the skin of the rock ... face ... starts moving. The cheeks become animated as I look. It's the face of a guy in his mid-forties with long, wavy, straggly hair. Definitely the look of a Cornish pirate, but from two hundred or more years ago. I was amazed ... transfixed.'

'I'm not surprised.' I was anticipating like mad what might come next.

'So I said to Ginnie, "Can you see that?" She said, "*Yes, I can.*" "What?"

"*You won't believe it: a woman with long wavy hair, looking like a pirate.*"

"A woman?" I said. "*Yes, with a wizened face ... thin, weather-worn features.*"

'The two of us had seen it and that was the only thing we disagreed about. I said a man. She said a woman.'

'I suppose you might expect that, with the straggly hair.' I was thinking of Mick. 'But what did you make of it?'

'It wasn't something I tried to explain. Some things are just what they are,' he said. 'I accepted it for what it was. I have a great belief in the spiritual side of things.' He'd looked into Buddhism, Islam and Christianity, and used the *I Ching* (a Chinese system of divination), as I had on occasions. He found that it worked best with a clear state of mind, specific questions and no thought of personal gain.

I was still hyped up about the pirate but didn't feel disposed to probe in the face of his acceptance. Instead I asked, 'What about Ginnie?'

'We gradually grew apart, but parted on good terms – that was about eight years ago. I've lost touch now.'

'Aaah.' I couldn't disguise my disappointment.

'Yes, but you learn from good experiences to explore your thoughts and revisit situations. I get some comfort and joy from that.'

'And what now?'

He was setting up an internet business with medicinal herbs and superfoods. He planned to use a numerology symbol as the logo with interlocking numbers that formed two hearts. I couldn't have warmed more to Matthew. We were in Bath now and he invited me round to his flat for a coffee. I should have accepted but, with the light fading, felt I had to push on. He was good enough to run me to the outskirts.

As I made to go, he said, 'I've got something for you' and handed me a packet of incense sticks. 'To cleanse and purify,' he said. After he dropped me off I read the label: *This Jasmene Incense is prepared according to unique Technique of Traditional Tibetan Art. This incense can be best used for offering, purification, an air-freshener and for fragrance of Jasmene.*

A sweet scent and such shared confidences: I couldn't have wished for better gifts if he'd been my brother.

The Monkey Puzzle

Ironic that the two Matthews I'd met were at opposite ends of the spectrum; the down-to-earth Matthew whose advice I kept putting into practice and the otherworldly Matthew who took me to regions beyond the reach of any thumb. Just as well that I'd shut up hitchhiking shop. All I had to do was keep my eyes open for a B & B while I trudged up this hill section of the A46, wrestling with the esoteric.

It sounded far-fetched: those gifts from that hotel owner matching his wish list. Pity I hadn't told him about the day I had a whole sequence of wishes granted: a second-hand CD I was looking for handed in while I was in the shop; a book that was too expensive suddenly reduced to half price; an insurance claim met in full. It went on; small tokens individually but, one after the other, astounding.

Matthew's experience, coming all at once, was bound to affect him even more deeply. Synchronicity like that took some explaining. Some might put extra-sensory perception, or a spiritual agency, into the equation; others the law of averages or just good luck.

But where did the pirate come from? Was he a product of their daydreaming imaginations or a play of the shimmering sun? Perhaps the moss on the stone suggested a pirate's headband. How tempting to explain away the unlikely. But if I embraced it,

I'd be as out on a limb as I was looking for this B & B – no sign of a sign. I liked to think that my mind was open to all possibilities, but was it? The plausible would always put up a more convincing case than the improbable.

So what if a pirate, or rather his spirit, did inhabit that stone? If poltergeists can pass through walls, why couldn't another 'geist' inhabit a stone? A big 'if', I know. In the 80s we used to sit down with our kids totally engrossed in *Monkey Magic* (a TV series based on a 16th century Chinese epic) and one episode showed scores of spirits trapped in a rock. Was one apparition in a stone so outlandish a possibility? And what about slips of colour synthesising with music; how way out was that?!

These encounters begged many questions but if we didn't entertain the unfamiliar, how could we progress? No hitchhiker would get far unless he kept thinking that he'd be picked up, again and again. Or in my case, find somewhere to shack up for the night. Soon. At the risk of devaluing the tenet currency, there had to be another one, **Tenet Five**: *Follow the unfamiliar if you want to go further.*

Right now, I needed belief. I'd swapped the idea of a B & B for somewhere to camp when I saw a sign pointing down a lane to Upper Swainswick. That rang distant bells. Thirty or so years before, we'd attended a garden party to celebrate the opening of a home for severely disabled people. Friends of mine with a disabled daughter were the prime movers in setting it up, with the help of an unexpected legacy. I'd lost touch with them but thought that the place was round about here.

I knocked on one homeowner's door up the lane. Did she know of anywhere to camp? She didn't. Nor did she think it likely, with the steep slopes round here. Blast. I tried my second tack: was there a home for disabled people nearby?

'Fountain House?'

'Yes, that's it.' It was further up the lane. Perhaps I could camp in the grounds.

It took a while before one of the staff came to the door, but no chance to camp, so I mentioned my friends. Were they still around? They were. Great! And what's more, they lived in an annexe next door but she had no idea whether they were in. I crossed a small courtyard, knocked and held my breath.

The Venerable Architect

A short wait and the door opens. 'Helen, lovely to see you,' I gush, instantly reminded of the distinguished North American Indian lady that I always saw in her, perhaps because of a colourful hair ribbon she used to wear. And what does she make of me? Noticing a slight look of puzzlement, I add, 'Remember me? Laurence.'

'Of course,' she says. We hug. 'Do come in. Ronald's upstairs.'

How timeless time can be. Before I know it, I'm sitting upstairs – theirs is an upside-down house – with a cup of tea. The annexe is rather grand: open plan, with a vaulted ceiling and the evidence of Ronald's loving craftsmanship all round. Bowled over by our meeting, I'm not sure whether I've made it clear why I'm here. It hardly matters, because the very idea of my camping is pooh-poohed. Helen insists on my taking the guest room, and would I like to join them for dinner?

The years are letting some things slip. 'Ronald's eighty now. He had a stroke two years ago,' Helen tells me.

The elder statesman may have lost some of his vigour but he still has the mischievous light in his eyes. I well remember him performing Stanley Holloway's monologue, *The Lion and Albert*, to much applause. The authority in his voice always commanded an audience. But we're talking about today. Ronald's saying what an impoverished society we live in and that 'competitiveness is one of the curses.' He bemoans the attitude; 'I come first and everyone is there for my convenience.' But he's quick to add, 'There are a lot of good people.' They subscribe to a magazine called *Positive News*. Ronald was always full of that. He ran his own architectural practice and helped those new to the profession find their feet and set up on their own.

One commission he's particularly proud of is a Catholic Church. He presented his model to the whole congregation. The plan centred round the seven sacraments: baptism, confirmation, mass, absolution, marriage, ordination of priests and anointing the sick. Each sacrament had its appropriate location; the arrangements for baptism, for example, being at the entrance. It worked so well that they were convinced he was a Catholic. Ronald wasn't. His background is Church of England.

Meeting Ronald and Helen again is like retracing my footsteps to a time when I was finding my own way. My background had been C of E too, but in my twenties I dipped into a smorgasbord of philosophies, 'isms and 'ologies, amongst them Scientology, Theosophy, the Kabbalah, Buddhism, the Bahai faith and Sufism. The *Bhagavad Gita* rubbed shoulders on my bookshelf with the *I Ching*. But when friends of mine donned the Bhagwan's orange robes, I stuck with my Harris Tweed.

One movement which did attract me was Subud, at the heart of which is an exercise called the latihan. It was brought to the west from Indonesia by Muhammad Subuh, known to followers as Bapak. The exercise is one in which members submit to promptings from within, expressed in a whole variety of forms: chanting, laughing, crying, singing, walking, stretching, running, dancing, and more; allowing whatever feeling to surface without the habitual monitoring of the mind. The direct simplicity of it and the liberating effect of 'letting go' appealed to me, as did the freedom from dogma or proselytising.

Ronald was instrumental in bringing me into Subud and I have practised the latihan on and off ever since. The benefits can be many: a release from old habits and hang-ups, a new look at oneself and fresh thoughts about one's direction in life. As to the source of such benefits, that's open to conjecture. Some believe, as I tend to, that it's a reconnection with a life force all too easily masked by the demands and habits of everyday life. Belief in God or spiritual influences is not obligatory, though some followers maintain that it helps and that the exercise is a form of worship. There are times when it seems to go beyond previous experience.

One consequence of looking at oneself in a new light can be to feel the need for a change of name. I changed mine. The procedure is to send off to Indonesia – to Bapak when he was alive – for an initial letter. You then remit your own choice of five names beginning with that letter. The envelope-opening tension, wondering which name has been selected, more than matches 'A' level results. I was relieved when 'Laurence' emerged from the process and 'Christopher' quietly went to earth. It's a gamble. I might have been Llewellyn, Lucian, Liam or Leigh. Heaven forbid! Such changes can be contentious, especially for the parents who named you, and for relatives, friends and even workmates. But if you're scratching your head trying to remember someone's name,

[DAY FIVE]

it can be the perfect excuse: 'Let me see. Who are you now? Still Henry is it? Oh, fine.'

My change of name had been relatively painless. But it hadn't been easy for others to accept Ronald's new name, nor for him. James, as he was before, hadn't taken to 'Ronald' at all ... until, that is, he started looking at the origins of names and 'then the penny dropped.' He found that 'James was a supplanter, stealing his brother's inheritance,' whereas 'Ronald' carried the meaning of 'being on a ship on a journey.' Though most of his ancestors were crofters or farmers, they were seafarers too; not surprising since his family background was Orcadian.

That takes me aback. An intention I hadn't shared with anyone was to spend some time in Orkney on the northernmost island – North Ronaldsay. There *were* other reasons why I'd chosen that island but, if this was a sign, I knew how to read it. If, as I believe, coincidences confirm you're on the right track, it simply had to be 'Ronaldsay'. 'I'll send you a card when I get there,' I tell them.

I'm synchronising again: the timing of my arrival turns out to be impeccable. Ronald tells me that tonight is a latihan night (there are normally two a week) and, since he's the only one going, would I like to join him? He also wants to show me round the meeting place, the New Oriel Community Hall, as the architect responsible for its refurbishment.

We have our meal together and, afterwards, Helen busies herself in the kitchen. Ronald and I are relaxing over a drink when he gives me one of those 'knowing' looks. 'With you and your hitchhiking,' he says, 'I don't suppose you've heard about the woman picked up by a lorry driver who put his hand on her knee.'

'No?' I reply, innocently.

'She told him she was a witch.'

'Yes?'

'But he said, "No, you're not," and suddenly turned into a lay-by.'

It's a joke worthy of Jethro, though his spell wouldn't have stopped at the knee or lay-by! I'm still smiling to myself when there's a sound from behind. A connecting door to the main house opens and Rosie, their daughter, is wheeled in by an assistant. Without fuss, Helen and Ronald prepare for her mealtime. It's not easy being a bystander. I have no conception how they cope with

Rosie's situation day after day or what life is like for someone so severely handicapped. Specialist care and facilities are as indispensable as love and attention. I feel privileged to witness their kisses and infinite patience in feeding her.

'It's a shame Rosie isn't mobile any more,' Helen says. She'd been virtually bedridden since she had a stroke about three and a half years ago and then another one later. 'She has spasms though,' Helen adds, 'which are good in a way because they exercise muscles.'

I wonder how much Rosie can communicate.

'Well, we can't know what's happening inside,' she says. 'But she'll turn her head away if we haven't been around for a day or two. And she's tough,' Helen affirms. 'We thought she'd be on her way after the strokes, but she's forty-two now.'

I can see why belief is so vital. 'We can't know what's happening inside' holds a hope open; that Rosie might be far more aware than one thinks, and making progress in ways one can only guess at. It would be arrogant to dismiss that possibility when we spend a third of our lives in a subconscious state and benefit from it.

For an analogy, I can't do better than resort to my friends, the Lepidoptera. We see the roving caterpillar. We hardly ever see the chrysalis and never the transformation in that power house, from which the butterfly launches on its mercurial flight. Helen feels that Rosie is moving fast, 'with a whoosh.' How often does a revelation follow from a time of stillness and rest, indeed from our very dream time. I know a tenet when I see one, **Tenet Six**: *Out of stillness come new insights and directions.*

It's time to be leaving for the latihan. The assistant collects Rosie and Helen drives us to the hall. The women exercise separately from the men. After greeting the other ladies, Ronald and I retire to an upstairs room with chairs round the perimeter and another vaulted ceiling.

To begin with, we observe a period of silence: about fifteen minutes. The idea is not to just stop talking, but to quieten one's thinking, since the mind tends to block the spontaneity of any receiving. Eckhart Tolle thought that thinking had become a disease, and certainly it can cut across more intuitive responses. Try to 'not think' if you want to test its tenacity. If there is a key to dealing with this intruder, it's to leave the back door open so that he can let himself out. Thinking soon gets bored if you keep letting him go. That's what I think!

Once the latihan starts, the first intimations are often akin to the sounds and signs of waking, followed by whatever action or vocalization one feels moved to express. From the moment I open my mouth, the sound carries. The vaulted ceiling is such an asset. The uplifting acoustics encourage me to circulate round the room, allowing the sounds full rein.

Speaking – anything from intelligible words to apparent gobbledygook – soon gives way to singing, and Ronald's receiving seems to chime in with mine. Harmony isn't necessarily the result or the point of the exercise. Dissonance may be as much in evidence. And a group latihan can take on the character of a tropical rainforest, with swings of sound and the percussion of movement!

There are moments here when the sounds acquire harmonics of their own, winging way beyond this room into some universal space. It's a strange tribute to an architect to say that the roof has 'lift-off'. But Ronald's achieved it.

He's keen to show me round after the latihan – which only lasts thirty minutes – and I can see what an immense benefit to the community this hall is, with a stage and suites of rooms for a whole range of activities. I am particularly struck with a set of sparkling, spherical lamps which Ronald designed and made for the main hall. A string of bead-like lights spirals round the outside of each sphere; floating auras over the room to distinguish any occasion.

There's no doubt about the therapeutic powers of singing. I certainly feel in tune as we travel back on this starlit night. Sipping coffee upstairs, Ronald and I roam far and wide. His thoughts span the whole history of the Reformation: from Jan Huss, who defended John Wycliffe, through Martin Luther to the Moravians and John Wesley. It all leads up to, 'You don't need priests between you and God.' But the fate which befell early challengers of the church is terrifying. Huss, who was burned at the stake, first had the skin removed from his hands. It's a salutary reminder of the debt due to those who paid, and still do pay, a fearsome price for freedom of expression.

My thoughts turn to Rod and my speculation about how order

– the pattern of stars, for example – equates with meaning. Ronald recounts a time, a Bastille Day celebration, when Bapak was talking freely. 'But he fell silent for a while, gazed at the sky and asked an onlooker what he saw.'

"Space," he said.

"It might not be space as you think of it," Bapak said.'

Ronald told me of Bapak's explanation: that the universe was one single intricate machine; not like a typewriter ... (that's news for Rod then!) ... or car, but more like an electronic grid or field of force. He'd said that it moves out from its origin in a circular direction, condensing into lumps as it does so – the planets and stars – becoming refined and eventually returning to its origin.

When Bapak was asked, "Where is the origin?", Ronald said he replied with another question; "How can there be an origin of a circle?" That debate could go round and round! But if there has to be a resolution, it can only be that the origin is ... everywhere.

Ronald is happy to talk on but I can see he's getting tired and I want to be up early in the morning, so I bid them both goodnight with a parting bear hug for Ronald. He won't be up before I leave. I'll see Helen though. She's an early riser. It's only a few hours since I arrived, but I feel as though I've been back to my beginnings.

Footnote: I have to report with great sadness that Ronald died on 12th February 2010. His son, Brindley, wrote eloquently (next page) of Ronald's many talents. The consummate skills of an artist-craftsman and an all-embracing humanity were the inspiring hallmarks of this revered man.

[DAY FIVE]

Day Six
Bath to Derby

'Perhaps one needed to be waylaid by twists of fortune'

The Grand Parents

I switched on my mobile last evening at the usual quarter to six, so that my position could be relayed by GPS to the family. But not till three a.m. did the great memo pad in the sky prompt me to put it back on charge. When I re-emerged from the sheets, a short walk to the bathroom was all it took to reinforce the importance of family and, most of all, parents. On the wall were framed verses that one of his sons had written. The first celebrated one of Ronald's birthdays. I jotted down some of the words:

> *Ronald's the patriarch*
> *Accomplished, creative, the architect fine,*
> *The craftsman, the artist, the sculptor divine!*
> *A Dad full of fun, a designer of note*
> *And on this special day,*
> *Ronald White gets our vote.*

What an example! And here's a flavour of some touching verses about Helen, entitled Mum's Song. It talks about how she …

> *Brung us up with love and care,*
> *Made us lovely dinners.*
> *All us kids got big and strong*

Whilst dear old Mum got thinner.
We were young and wild and free,
Loads of aggravation.

Every morning she'd come down,
Bum against the Aga,
Light a fag and have a drag;
Stopped her going ga-ga.

Yes, kids can drive you mad. But the warmth of affection and sense of direction from parents – if kids are lucky enough – work wonders.

What about my own parents? My father was orphaned at the age of three and treated callously at a Birmingham orphanage. 'We had cold baths and toenails were cut till they bled,' he told us. But somehow he learned to play the trombone. That was his salvation. His musical gifts earned him a place in an RAF band and he was eternally proud of having played for Lawrence of Arabia on board ship. That brutal childhood, though, was damaging. He found it hard to trust anyone. It wasn't surprising that he joined the police force. He always regretted that he'd never been able to fulfil his talent. Losing his teeth cut short his musical career.

My mother's experience was one of ambition unfulfilled too. Before she met my father, she'd attended Art College, showing a real talent for clay modelling and sculpture. Where Dad could only draw a cup and saucer or steam engine, Mum drew anything, but especially people. She had a wonderful speaking voice. The confidence she gained as a tobacco factory guide encouraged her to broadcast her own account of a ramble in the Forest of Dean. She loved travelling. Dad didn't; not abroad anyway. When a wartime bomb went off while he was keeping the crowd back, he was blown in the air. He blamed that for his subsequent tummy troubles and migraines plagued him. 'All that greasy food' abroad was out of bounds ever after.

My mother's vivacity was hard to dampen. She'd make friends with anyone, from the Tizer drinks delivery driver to the workman who found an early Victorian florin in the drain outside our house. Typical of Mum that she persuaded him to hand it over. I still have that token of her outgoing nature. And did she glory in roses!

Fragrant Cloud was her all-time favourite. Even in the final throes of cancer, she wrote: 'You only appreciate the beauty of morning because of the darkness of night'.

When my mother died at forty-three, with me just fourteen and my sister nine, Dad did everything to compensate. If love could be served, he ladled it, laying on roast dinner every Sunday with the full works: Yorkshire pudding bubbling with gravy (no lumps), always followed by home-made apple pie and oodles of custard.

So what was their legacy? From my father, I gained a conviction that you couldn't shake off a wretched childhood. But though I might have been infected by his deep-seated distrust, I didn't take it on board. Perhaps my mother's optimism overcame it. And even Dad would tell and re-tell a story of how his innocence paid off. On the day he left the orphanage at fourteen, he asked the first person he met in a Birmingham street, 'Do you know where my brother Douglas lives?' That person did.

In the background, there was always the hope of redemption for hardship; that good might come of it; that the weak sapling would be all the stronger for surviving a harsh winter. But from both parents I learned one abiding lesson: do what you love doing. It's taken me long enough to get around to it!

Over breakfast I remarked on the poems and how heart-warming it was to see the parents appreciated in that way. Helen told me they had eight grandchildren and two great-grandchildren – some legacy. We talked about past times, but my time wouldn't keep quiet. Before breakfast I had taken out a folded map of Great Britain and one sketchy look told me I'd only covered one and a half sections of an eight-section map – less than one fifth. At this rate, I'd be on the road for another twenty days. And that was without North Ronaldsay. It was nearly eight o'clock when I stood at the front door, not knowing how to take my leave. I murmured something about Rosie.

'I love her enormously,' Helen said. 'D'you know, I think Rosie's only staying around to keep Fountain House going.'

I liked that way of putting it. 'That's good,' I said, 'and thanks for everything.'

We kissed goodbye, and I set off up the lane to the main road, under a quiet, grey, light-fringed sky. But slowly. Hundreds of leaves had fallen from a maple tree and been pressed flat by passing traffic, laminating the dull tarmac with the rich and dappled shades of late autumn. I couldn't rush this picture book. When I reached the end, I'd be starting all over again.

The Uphill Struggle

I might have a destination in mind. But my experience had been perverse. Every time I went forward, something brought me back. I was walking over pressed leaves to get there. Dipping into Ronald and Helen's life, I felt as if I'd dropped back home. It was a place I'd returned to and set out from again; a warmth I was loath to leave, a sense of belonging I was hesitant to surrender.

There was something else: I knew Bath. I loved Bath. I'd loved to have lived in Bath. How *could* I forget it? I'd fallen *in* the Roman Baths for God's sake in my teens and bussed back to Bristol in sopping wet trousers. In my twenties, I'd run a bread round there. I was 'Witts the Wonderloaf' man, plying my loaves up and down the seven hills of Bath. How could I have forgotten *them*?!

If I needed convincing that I was starting from scratch again, my absence of mind did it. I might not be snarled up in the Bristol suburbs but ahead of me lay the longest of long drags up the A46; a single carriageway with no stopping places, the steepest of hills and the heaviest of traffic making for the M4. No doubt about it: I was in for a slog. Lights flashed: 'Hardship ahead'. With hardly any verge in places, I had to walk in the road. Lorries cut in close to the continuous white line, threatening to tip me off balance. There's little scope for fine thoughts when you're feet away from a walk-on, carried-off part in *Casualty*.

I distracted myself, as I'd done before, matching word sounds to the traffic, except that they were ear-splittingly different. 'Phwoah, phoosh, whoomb, wharm, phwam' were my best onomatopoeic shots. The occasional 'bob, bob' when a car hit a drain cover came as some relief, but percussion was too close to concussion for me to enjoy the syncopation, and dins can do you in … if the monoxide doesn't get you first.

Sometimes I'd have to wait for a break in the traffic and duck under some overhanging branches, or play dodgems with brambles to reach a refuge. It was a battleground. Part way up the hill I sat out the next skirmish on a roadside barrier, gnawing listlessly at a Cox's apple that Helen had pressed into my hand. A little leitmotif passed: a van sported my old initials – *CPS, French Car Specialists*. 'Yes', I shouted. 'That's me: Christopher Paul Shelley.' Was my past overtaking me?

I endured over an hour of this war of attrition when a 'Welcome to South Gloucestershire' sign greeted me. What I wanted was a 'get-me-out-of-here' card. Soon after I picked up on a village sign, Nimlet. Into my well-worn, word association mind dropped another word: Kismet. Fate or destiny, wasn't it? A little further on, a redundant church came into view. I must have passed it many times on my bread round. What was it now? Artist's studio? Yoga centre? Dosser's den? On a spit of land in front was a caravan. The door was open.

The Professional Player

Like a feral cat, I peered through some bushes. A man who'd been busying himself round the back slipped inside. How would I accost him? Bowl of milk please? Drop of the hard stuff, more like. I was fagged out, but if idle curiosity could bend the truth to earn me a momentary respite, so much the better. I walked over. The leather jacket I'd glimpsed suggested a macho image and a blunt reception.

'Sorry to bother you.' I launched the words into the inner sanctum with all the tentativeness of an out-of-luck Kleeneze salesman.

The man shuffled to the door. 'Yes?'

'I've driven past so many times and always wondered about the church.' With a white horseshoe of a beard framing cheerful ruddy cheeks, silvery grey hair flip-flopping at the sides and a couple of zipped jumpers under his jacket, the chap looked a lot more benign. And he was keen to chat.

'Oh, this is an old Congregational Church. Hasn't been used since the forties.' It looked handsome from this angle, with a massive circular stained glass window and a castellated turret to one side.

'Do you own it?'

'Yes. I was passing by about thirty years ago, saw it was empty and bought it. Twelve hundred quid, that was all. D'you want to look inside?'

I could hardly believe my luck.

'Scottie,' he said. We shook hands and walked across the gravelly ground of what looked like a goods yard, with assorted cars, van, discarded hub caps, metal storage container, corrugated iron shed, tarpaulins, and all signs of work long in progress. We accessed by a side door, then along a corridor, to the main hall. A dining table of boardroom proportions took up much of the floor area but lining the walls were cupboards, dressers, ottomans, tallboys, bookcases and china ware – all the accoutrements of an antique dealer's emporium. Scottie was in the business, in Bath, and this his warehouse. But he was selling up.

'The congestion's terrible. Wherever you go, you can't escape bridges. And the parking's awful.' He planned to live here but had a lot to dispose of. One item stood out. Next to a lofty grandfather clock and a Dyson vacuum cleaner was the hugely mellow presence of a double bass.

Scottie's eyes lit up the moment I remarked on it.

'Made by Roff,' he said, 'a German instrument maker; from the 1830s.' And it wasn't for sale. He played in a band. 'We do a lot of weddings; 30,40,50s stuff and some modern. Seeing little kids – this high – dancing, it's great.' Scottie was away. 'That's now, but I remember the war – I was born in '37 – when the Americans came over with a different kind of music. Glenn Miller and the top bands took me on a different road.'

So what started him off?

'When I got a guitar. We 'ad pocket money for cleaning the stables and I was only a nipper – must 'ave been about seven – when I bought it. Had to 'ave one. Then I went on to sing in a choir. Music lessons 'n all that. Here, d'you want to see upstairs?'

I wound up the rickety staircase after him, only to be astonished by the surreal scene. A Dali or Duchamp would have revelled in these flights of piggyback chairs. The intertwined legs were like acrobatic body parts towering up to the rafters but these were columns of chairs with the teetering jimjams. If this is what Scottie had brought me to see, it was some feat; the gravity-defying pinnacle of antique dealing success. Funnily enough he made no reference to the chairs. He was going to turn all this into living accommodation now that the roof was sound.

'Bit of stuff to shift first,' I observed.

'Aw, no problem. I'll get another six or seven containers for that,' he said lightly.

And the rest!

'My great-grandfather was Scottish,' he said, as we clopped downstairs, 'from a little village outside Edinburgh. Before that, we were Irish. Cork – that way. I get a lot of Irish dealers.'

With a lot of chairs. I took the liberty of sitting down by the boardroom table while Scottie positioned himself at the business end, next to the double bass.

'It's a funny place to be; the world of music,' he said. 'Bit sinister, the modern idiom. I like some of it. But what can you believe in now?'

It sounded like a test of faith. He'd played trad jazz in Ronnie Scott's club as a session man and still did professional work, playing in Bristol, Cheltenham and London. There was pride in that. 'Tell you what – there's one tune I just can't forget; *Harlem Nocturne*. D'you know it?'

I didn't.

'Haunting. Makes my skin creep. I write my own stuff too. The chord structure's the foundation. Play a weird chord with a diminished note, for example, and it'll connect with another. Before you know, you get a phrase, then a tune. I'll show you.'

I was all ears. I wanted to be moved.

'Listen to this. It's an intro. You'll recognise the tune when I get to it.'

Scottie pulled the double bass close and started plucking his way through the introductory phrases. When he broke into the melody, he soon had my head nodding and toes tapping. In a moment all the antiques that lined the walls and floors melted away. There was only me, Scottie … and *Sweet Georgia Brown*.

'You make it look easy,' I said.

'Playing with decent musicians helps. You pick up from them. Rubs off, it does. It's a lifetime of learning; years and years of what you love doing.'

Never mind a mountain of chairs, life doesn't get much more surreal than this; having sweated up the hill, jarred and jangled by the cacophony of traffic, to be sitting at a boardroom table in this grand old church while Scottie treated me to a swinging jam session. He'd taken *me* away. I'd been transported. I thanked Scottie – hardly enough – and wished him well with his building plans. He couldn't have known how much he'd helped, how a little strumming had whisked away the hardship. There had to be another tenet here, **Tenet Seven**: *Doing what you love doing transports others*. If only my parents had had more of a chance.

The Accident-Prone Driver

Sweet Georgia Brown kept me company as I hummed my way towards the M4 junction. What a tune will do! The traffic thundered past on this level stretch of road, but my steps carried a rhythm and my mind a crusading optimism. It only took a 'Police Slow' sign lying flat on the verge – a relic of some past accident – for me to issue my own edict. I propped it up and lay in wait with my thumb. What would drivers gain by slowing down? Me! It made not one brake light difference. I ploughed on, and when *Mission Impossible*, a courier van, did a U-turn right in front of me, I wondered what sort of omen was that.

Soon I reached the M4 junction and a car park snack bar. A cuppa would go down a treat. Proximity to a motorway must breed a particularly bolshy attitude. My tea was served with a sideswipe, as the balding entrepreneur chatted to a lorry driver, puffing away at the counter. 'I used to run gangs for Manpower Services but, know what, I'd give piss all for most of 'em.' He shook his head contemptuously.

'Yeah, I'd shoot the criminals,' said the smoking gun.

Had I missed something? Rough justice rules by the M4. What struck me was the sheer number of cars parked but few signs of drivers. Not shot, I hoped.

'Never see 'em,' Mr. Manpower said. 'Car park's full when I get 'ere at six-thirty.' He reckoned they worked in London and that this was a car share pick-up point. Why not have car share points at other motorway junctions? City congestion solved: simple. We all agreed. Society's problems are soon sorted over a snack bar counter.

Hitting the road again, I was about to cross a junction on the other side of the M4 when a car pulled up.

'I hadn't even thumbed,' I said.

'You looked as though you would,' John claimed.

It was all very impulsive. He didn't even know where I was heading, not that it mattered because he was only going two or three miles up the road. Still, the boost to morale more than made up for the shortness of the lift. I'd hardly time to introduce myself before he was off ... on a potted history of his driving. His talking flashed past as fast as the countryside. I had a job keeping up. What I did notice was black: the car, hair, eyebrows, jacket, shoes.

'I'm a Class 1 lorry driver really,' he said, as though apologising for the car. It was clear why. 'Courtesy car this is,' he gestured with a dismissive flick at the dashboard and launched into a pacy account of how he came by it. 'Up from Bath I was ... dual carriageway ... going downhill ... pulled into a lay-by on opposite side ... bloody well did a U-turn.'

He was losing me already. Who pulled into the lay-by? And was he in a lorry or car? But nothing stopped him.

' ... Crossed double lines ... couldn't miss ... straight into the side of 'im. Mine was a write-off. All he 'ad was a dent. Bloody hell,' he broke off abruptly. 'Hey up.'

Rounding a corner, he slammed on his brakes and shuddered to a halt, narrowly missing the bollards and bars of a road block, and nosing out towards a car coming head on, straight for us.

'Whooo.'

'Sorry about that, mate. It's the talking.'

The driving, I'd have said.

'Yeah, mine was a write-off. All he 'ad was a dent.'

So it must have been a car. But he carried on as though nothing had happened, as if he brushed with near misses like toothpaste.

I laughed myself silly, like after a death sentence is commuted, thinking how close we were to a smash when he's talking about one. While he wittered on about his tradeplating days, a great truck stop somewhere and how I ought to go to Glasgow, I reflected how talking about trouble can land you in it, how it helps to be dressed for the part, and how the Chinese believe there's no such thing as an accident. When he pulled into a Gulf garage to fill up, I *was* miles away.

'Good place to hitch from,' he said, 'and this'll help.' He handed me a tachodisc, the circular card that registers all lorry movements.

'Just hold that up, mate, and you'll get a lift in minutes.' Standing still would do me for a while.

The Broken Pattern

The day had changed and I hadn't noticed. A mist was airbrushing out the distance. I sidled up to the garage and indulged in a comforting Peppermint Aero. The proprietor was planning a sex establishment next door. I couldn't see it – the good burghers of Bath going for something on the side, way out here. It might give a new meaning to 'filling up' but I'd had enough excitement. I walked on a little in the misty drizzle – soft, they call this sort of weather in Ireland – but, softly saturated, I sheltered absurdly under a leafless tree. Where was I? Diffusing like the mist. This search for direction was taking me backwards and forwards, and sometimes both at the same time.

I'd felt as though I was starting all over again when I left Ronald and Helen behind.

Ironic that my departure heralded hardship. It was hardship that my Dad had to live through before, first the trombone, and then my mother brought light into his life. She had her own cross to bear with cancer, a fact he kept secret for the eighteen months or so that it ravaged her body. I could see patterns repeating, repeating. My long slog seemed to mirror those periods in life when, no matter what one does, nothing works out. Yet I had my musical interlude that put the world to rights, like it must have done for Dad. Perhaps one needed to be waylaid every so often by twists of fortune. But what tricks those twists could play: they might open up a new path but just as well deal out a sudden accident or unexpected illness.

What did it all mean? Buddhists believe that life is an endless round of pain and suffering. Identifying with favourable or adverse events, we are hooked by the roller-coaster feelings attached to them. But what was it that Kipling said – in the 'If' poem that my father took such pleasure in memorising – about treating those two impostors, triumph and disaster, just the same? In his laughable way, John had shown me how. He took the prospect of an accident in his stride. **Tenet Eight** stared me in the face: *Letting come, letting go makes it so much easier to move on.*

That's why this hitching business gripped me. I had to accept whatever turned up and wherever it took me. It was so different from life's well-worn ruts. If I could live like this, I would. What was I thinking? This *was* a new beginning. But in what way? Too much thinking, I thought. Let the next lift sort it out.

The Rehabilitating Tutor

The road was level and the traffic lighter. But the leafless tree wasn't an umbrella. When I heard a car coming I'd slip my hood off, eyeball the driver and hope for a halt. John's idea of the tachodisc had one flaw: apart from a solitary Tesco lorry (fat chance of any little help) there were no others. They'd all headed for the M4. Holding the disc out to car drivers had about as much impact as … my 'Police Slow' sign. But a get-lift-quick attitude wouldn't get me anywhere fast.

Less than a mile on, I stationed myself before a turn-off to Old Sodbury and refused to consult my watch. It worked. I had no idea how long I waited before Nick drove up. He was pretty oblivious too: not at all bothered by my wet clobber. But he did have the look of someone for whom morning came too soon, with his hair still in mid-yawn and a face that looked as though it could do with a good combing.

After I delivered my mission statement, Nick told me about his hitchhiking days. The best lift he'd had was Bristol to Glasgow from a rock group with airline-type seats in their bus. And the worst? When he'd had to hike twenty miles between lifts. He was off to work now at a rehab centre near Stroud. He'd drop me there. 'I'm helping people who need rehab; anyone from seventeen-year old crackheads to seventy-year old alcoholics,' Nick said. 'I show them how to repair bikes; old wrecks mostly.' His 'clients' came on a six-week course initially, working a three-hour session each week. 'We advertise for old bikes and put them back in first class order. You should see the pride in a bike they've done up. And riding it.'

I'd seen that same look in the faces of pupils when they made a pot. A tangible achievement meant so much more than any paperwork grade, especially for the less academic ones.

'I've been doing it for a year, long enough to build up friendships,'

Nick said. 'Two guys got so much out of it, they asked to stay on as helpers.' But the rehab path is a slippery one. His voice dropped as he told me about one client who had had some major trauma in his life. 'He turned up the worse for wear after a few drinks and got kicked out. Great shame. He'd done so well up to then.'

Did anyone care what happened to him after? Nick did. I wondered whether his background helped him empathise.

'I'm no good at relaxing, what with work and the kids. I've got two sons, eleven and fifteen. They live with me seven days, and seven with their mum. It's not easy, coping. I get depressed a lot and drinking's no good. I've given up a few times and felt less rocky. But that doesn't stop you slipping back. Thank the Lord I haven't lost my licence. It's a real downer when you get into the criminal justice system. You don't want to go there.'

Being close to the demons his clients faced must have helped him come to terms with his own. And those who've had to live through heartaches are uniquely qualified to understand the challenges of others. There's something complete about a circle of shared feelings.

Nick felt things deeply. He'd never forget the birth of his youngest son. 'We'd planned a home birth and been to a few birthing sessions. In the end it wasn't possible at home but we were lucky to have an enlightened midwife. She watched while I delivered him myself. I did the whole thing.'

With a little help from his wife, of course. Astonishing that a midwife could exercise such discretion. How did he feel about the whole process?

'It's a mixture of emotions: the anxiety driving to hospital, the screaming with the labour pains and wanting all the bleeping machines out of the way. It's scary and fascinating. I was crying and smiling with joy all at the same time.'

Nick must relive those feelings when playing with his youngest son. But tangled up, there had to be regrets about the split-up. He harked back to another break in relationships. 'I was living in Bristol at the time and my mum was in Cornwall, not well. When I called her, she said, "Don't worry about me, son. I'm all right." So I didn't go. Then a phone call came to say she'd died. Not being with her when she died: that still hurts.'

I understood. When my father was seriously ill, I had just

started my first permanent teaching job and wasn't there when he passed away. I should have been. No job is that important. Nick was nearing his workplace. Our conversation had touched some raw nerves. Close as we'd been, I wanted to take a photograph of him.

'No photo please,' Nick said. 'I'm a photographer and I always look scraggy.' But life can *be* like that, I thought, after we parted.

The Source of Light

I walked the short distance to Stroud, valuing the chance to be alone with my thoughts. I couldn't get over how Nick had confided his feelings. If anything guided his passage through life, it was those. And what a mishmash of contradictions they were: the satisfaction of his job but concern for his clients; the joy of delivering one son and seeing them both grow up, but only every other week; and the loss of his mother compounding the split with his wife.

Even before Nick picked me up, I'd questioned how detached we could be about feelings. Emotions like jealousy, envy, regret, anger or fear can take hold and advertisers play on them. I'd learnt that as a fledgling copywriter. A.I.D.A. isn't an opera by Verdi. It's the acronym for Attention, Interest, Desire, Action. That's how we plotted the path to sales. But emotions like love, compassion or generosity, can suggest new directions. Another acronym sprang to mind: A.R.C. It stood for Affinity, Reality, Communication; the prerequisites for understanding. If you like a subject enough, you find out more about it. That makes it more real so that you like it even more, and latch on to deeper levels of understanding. The A.R.C. triangle was one 'tool' from my Scientology days that served me well.

So often 'I like it' is derided as a comment on, say, a painting. We demand intellectual rigour, a considered critique. But that misses the point. 'Liking' persuades us to delve deeper. The implication is clear. *Let what you feel passionate about lead you on*. It sounded like **Tenet Nine**.

English Literature meant most at school because it was taught by a teacher I liked who had a passion for the subject. Hardly surprising that I wanted to be a writer when I left school. And what about other decisions? We might rationalise about buying a house, but so often gut feelings – 'it feels right' – are what clinch a purchase. Ours persuaded us to buy a house in Poole, Dorset, and the owners liked us enough to say, 'We can see you living here.' We did ... for twenty-three happy years.

As I tramped into Stroud, I was taken by a poster advertising a programme of music by Purcell and Handel. It was headed 'Eternal Source of Light'. Enlightenment! What power music had to lighten a mood, to stir emotions, to *move*. That's what my new start was about: getting a move on, with feelings to light the way.

The Hurdy-Gurdy Girl

Stroud had happy memories for me. As a newly promoted accounts executive in an advertising agency, I was sent out prospecting for business. It was probably an act of desperation: advertising budgets had shrunk in the 60s under the Labour government. But in and around Stroud, small enterprises beavered away, and that was where I started cold calling. My first success was an order for a modest campaign, promoting what I branded 'The Dipple Dorstor', a storage rack hung on a larder door. We didn't grow fat on it.

Decision time: I wanted to head up the A46, then turn off towards Gloucester and the A38. I stationed myself on a wide, tree-lined stretch of road leading into town. There'd be a lot of in-town traffic, but a good few drivers going further. Fixing my eyes on faces, I couldn't have been more delighted when the unlikeliest face stopped; that of a lone, youngish woman driver; Clare.

I knew she was 'Clare' because, when I wrote down her name without an 'i', she leaned over, and said, 'Yes, you've got it right there.'

Every 'Clare' I've ever met has been a particular sort of person. A 'Clare', with or without an 'i', is clear about what she wants and very clear about getting it. Hard as I tried to steer clear of preconceptions, this was one that Clare did her best to confirm.

'I'm making for the M5,' she said. 'That OK?'

'Uh, well. Yes, all right.' I ditched the A38 with hardly a thought, even though I'd forsworn any motorway travel before I started this trip. The fact that my thoughts had to compete with a continuous skirl of music from the tape player helped. It sounded Scottish

– sort of bagpipey – and one question I didn't dare ask kept time: could she be heading for Scotland?

Clare looked a little defensive after I'd explained my mission but had every right to be circumspect about confiding in the bearded weirdo who'd just hopped on board. Handing out my card helped establish my bona fides and she was happy enough to tell me that she had graduated from Lancaster with a degree in ecology.

How had her ambitions played out?

'I'd thought of being a landscape architect. But you can have too much studying.'

'Funny, that's what I fancied doing and I couldn't take another seven years either. But what *did* you do then?'

'I got a job in advertising; an agency in Preston.'

'My first job!'

She'd finished up as an account director but hadn't found it that fulfilling. 'A lot of fun, but shallow' was how she put it.

My feelings too. I'd learnt to take coincidences in my stride on this trip. But then she told me how she chose her career.

'I went into a nick-nack shop one day and happened to see a scroll with all the birth signs on. It showed which jobs suited which star signs. For a Taurean like me, it was landscape architecture or advertising, so I plumped for that.'

She'd ratcheted up the coincidence stakes. Not only was I a Taurean but I'd also consulted the stars over my career choice. An astrologer once told me that I'd make a good teacher (which I was at the time, I hope) but that I'd do well in work which involved buildings or sales – one reason why I started selling conservatories. I hedged my bets: combining the two.

I wondered how her career track developed. With the common ground we'd established, she seemed more comfortable about opening up.

She worked in London for seven or eight years, before moving to Cornwall. 'For the sailing', she said. She was married by then and they'd bought an office equipment company, with the goodwill and stock. But the previous owner did the dirty on them: he owned only half the stock and goodwill was non-existent. Within eighteen months, they were declared bankrupt.

'Yes,' Clare trumpeted over the bagpipey blare and punched a hand in the air, throwing me into startled confusion. 'See that?'

'What?'

'A 2CV just *overtook* us.'

'Really?' To think you'd celebrate being overtaken.

'Yes, I used to have one of those.' Her car was a Corsa now, but the Citroen had been the love affair. And still was.

My only contribution to the ensuing eulogy was to recall the car's idiosyncratic windows flapping non-stop on some dim, distant journey. But what happened after the bankruptcy?

Clare told me that they set up again, renting premises, and built up a successful business over seven years. But, as can happen when a couple live and work together, there were strains in their relationship. They divorced.

I left it at that, not wanting to probe, but Clare didn't sound regretful. Her resilience was up-front. So was the music. I had to ask her about it.

'A hurdy-gurdy,' she said, with relish.

'You must love it.' She didn't pick up on the not-to-my-taste sub-text.

'Love it? I play it.'

She'd gone out of her way to buy two instruments: an eleven-hour journey to the South of France. She played in a duo; her and a piper, with weekend gigs all over the UK. And no, it wasn't Scottish music. They played French-style dance tunes mostly, and what she called Borders' music. And Scotland wasn't in her sights. She'd drop me off at the Strensham Services, this side of Worcester. Ah well: another dilemma I wouldn't have to face.

'Worcester: I did my teacher training there,' I said and, with the Malvern Hills rearing up on the horizon, I pointed. 'That's where I used to live.' As a mature student , I rented a wooden chalet, Bamboo Cottage, for £2.50 a week in the grounds of an estate. With a Victorian plant collector's garden, two swimming pools, an orchard with every variety of apple free for the picking, and stunning walks over the Hills in the footsteps of Elgar, I was in clover. Enjoying weekend visits from my wife-to-be, I led a charmed life in that love nest, though our romantic trysts were besmirched by nightly visits from less lovable mice.

My abiding memory was of the day everyone gathered on the Hills before dawn to celebrate the summer solstice with an early morning breakfast, courtesy of Charlie who ran a small café at the

[DAY SIX]

top. I knew him intimately from his sideline; striking statuesque poses as our life drawing model at college. The sunrise was more veiled. We saw the merest glimmer through a blanket of fog, but the eerie Gothic images of figures drifting in and out of the mist have stayed with me ever since.

Clare added her own treasured memory. 'I'll never forget an experience in Cornwall. We lived on the edge of the Lizard, near Helston.'

Matthew H's apparition leapt to mind. Not *another* pirate surely!

'I'd taken the dog for a walk and it was getting dark. We were walking over a field – it was convex, first up, then down – when I saw a light coming over the top of the field. I couldn't believe it: the full moon rising, and so suddenly. It had a huge impact on me; it was something I'd never seen before, or since.'

I'd never thought of a moonrise, let alone seen one, but I had witnessed the ghostly glow of moonlight in a woodland glade. Perhaps there is a touch of the supernatural about light streaming across a landscape, before the moon slips into sight. But we were approaching Strensham Services and I didn't know what Clare did now.

'Oh, I work for the NHS in admin,' she said dismissively.

'And you live in Stroud?'

'Yes, but I'd like to change my neighbours. They've painted their house blue and both are mad.' She sounded indignant. 'He's in his seventies and talks at you. I hate that. I'll have to move; a bigger house would be nice; somewhere, anywhere.'

If anyone could show you how to move on, Clare would. Her sparkiness was infectious. Clare couldn't have been far short of forty, but she spoke and acted like someone much younger. She might be hung up on 2CVs, hurdy-gurdies and blue houses, but she certainly followed her feelings and welcomed fresh starts. I liked to think that was something else we had in common.

The Numerate Trucker

It was half past three, close to my shut-down time but Premier Travel Inn's best bed price here was £50, so I stayed open. I owed it to Clare to think afresh and thumbed from a verge near the exit point. Car after car went past. But lorries parked further down hadn't registered. When one pulled away, then stopped, that didn't register either. The driver had to sound his horn before I spotted him thumbing *me*. As I ran towards the lorry – a massive tractor and trailer unit – doubts rushed in. A mighty machine conjured up macho man. Would I be mash to his muscles?

Clambering up into the cab was enough. Having jumped onto a narrow foothold, I had to rivet myself to the door handle while opening the door. Leaning out, with the rucksack threatening to up-end me, I swung round to the other side to gain entry. It was hardly the North Face of the Eiger but I had enough presence of mind left to resist a wimpish, 'Bit of a climb' when I sank into the passenger seat.

'Thanks a lot,' I said. 'I'm Laurence.' That was as much as I could manage, till I got my breath back.

'Malc,' he said, nodding but straight-faced. 'I'll be hitting the M1. Any good?'

I hadn't a chance to look at the map but 'no' wouldn't be on it.

'Junction 25'll be best,' Malc said. 'You're not far from Derby there.'

'That's fine,' I said, in a state of mild euphoria at the thought of the immense distance I'd be covering, seated, and free of decision-making.

Malc wasn't the pumped-up, muscle-flexing type, but a straight-shooting kind of guy with built-in sights. The black dots in his bluey-green eyes zeroed in like an integral part of a laser-directed missile system.

After I asked about the size of the lorry, back came the answer, bang on target. 'The trailer's 45 feet and the tractor unit 17, but the net length's 56 feet.' I guessed that's when they were coupled up.

And what was he carrying?

'Flat-pack deliveries for Argos, MFI and Homebase. And it's me, 99 per cent, that does the loading and off-loading.'

It sounded a hard life. He worked up to fifteen hours a day – nine driving – and spent five or six nights a week away from home. He'd got used to it. The bed-sit arrangements at the back of the cab even took in a telly. But he didn't like what was going on in the haulage business. 'There's plenty of hauliers,' he said, 'but not enough drivers. We could do with a third more.' The gap was

[DAY SIX]

being filled by foreigners. Why? While he might get £450 a week, Polish truckers would be happy with £250, doing the British out of jobs. 'What's more, their driving standards are questionable,' he complained, 'and so's the condition of their trucks.'

The light was fading fast and the traffic was heavy, especially when we reached the M42. Malc's driving standards were impeccable. His eyes flashed to and from the mirrors all the time, not just when he overtook. An attitude like that starts somewhere. Where?

'I joined the army at seventeen after I left school. My father was ex-military, so it was natural for me to follow and that's where I got my HGV licence.'

And what did life in the army do for him? I'd hardly put the question before Malc was off. But his eyes, darting to and fro told as much, with 'stupid bugger' hurled there and fond flashback lobbed in my direction.

'Well, when you join, you don't have to think. You're told to sit down, shut up and do as you're told. There's even procedures for tying up shoelaces. But then you get tested.' They had to travel 50 miles with a telegraph pole overcoming obstacles. 'It's to build stamina and see what initiative you show in a team.' They'd have route marches, scaled up from 5 miles to 7, then 15, 25 and 40. And carry backpacks weighing 75 lbs. But, battle-ready with ammunition and weaponry, those could weigh up to 130 lbs.

'That's over nine stone!'

He didn't sound as though he'd been fazed at all. It put my burden in perspective. My rucksack weighed a tiny fraction of that.

'When you work your way up,' Malc told me, 'there's a lot more decisions to take – like where to pitch camp or set up guard posts. Depends on your rank and the chain of command. If you're a lance-corporal, you're responsible for three or four people; for a corporal it's eight or nine; and a sergeant thirty-six.'

He did six years' service and it was eighteen years since he'd left, but you'd hardly know it. With Malc's reminiscences, our time passed all too quickly. We were now well up the M1 and he had to drop me off on the slip road.

'I'm waiting to sell up,' he said, 'to move to Cornwall. Ilkeston to Hayle, that's my idea. I love Cornwall and the Cornish. And the fish, specially mackerel.' Then he turned nostalgic. 'I used to keep chickens, you know – ten of 'em – and a cockerel. We used to get up to thirty-six eggs a day, except the fox cleaned 'em out.'

He'd report on any skirmish in the same tone of voice. What discipline and order can do. Numbers mattered to Malc. His answers were calibrated. And the precision was even-handed. He might count the cost but he also weighed the gain. I resolved to remember that as I set off towards Derby in the pouring rain.

The Dean

The auguries weren't good. I had to pull on my hood to ward off the watery salvoes. The A52 was a surrogate motorway, teeming with traffic. Who would shudder to a halt for a hoodie in the dark? With wipers whipping from side to side and the glare of headlights, would anyone even see this spook? Wading through clumps of wet grass and gangly weeds, I reconciled myself to a sodden slog. It wasn't defeatism but realism, I argued, until I realised that was how my father had justified his pessimism.

Quantify the reality: that's what I had to do. Malc would have done. He'd said it was about five miles to Derby. Not much pain. Pain?! What was I thinking? Getting this far had been a giant leap. I was seven league boot strides from Bath and five miles were a pinprick; the smallest on Malc's route march scale. What about the gain? I had to measure that too. At three miles per hour, I'd reach Derby by half past six. That would earn me one and a half hours' more thinking time.

The day had begun with an uphill struggle. But if *Sweet Georgia Brown* and the best day yet for lifts were payoffs, I could live with that. Would this little test turn up trumps? I picked up one lesson quickly; you get a pocketful of rain if you keep your hands in your pockets. That was a payoff too! Small reverses and big challenges were all the same: you learn something. There, I had it – another gain – **Tenet Ten**: *Difficulties are the route march to discoveries.*

Could I lump all difficulties together though? Malc's route marches were neatly graded, with self-belief in step with stamina. But you might have to walk away from the difficulties Nick or Clare met in their relationships. Nothing in life is clear-cut. I thought my boots were waterproof until my socks told me otherwise. When I reached a place called Borrowash, I sensed the promise of a shower and respite from my soggy state at a B & B advertised by the roadside. But it had closed down. And positive thinking deserted me when Spondon loomed up out of the darkness. 'Despondent' leapt into my mind ... with good reason.

I was trapped by a lofty roadside barrier, with a foot-wide ledge between me and the thundering traffic. Unless I backtracked to the Borrowash slip road – and I couldn't face that – there was no escape. I could only cling to the wire grill of the metal barrier and edge along sideways, hoping drivers wouldn't snick the overhanging rucksack for six, and me with it. At such times I like to think that the universe operates an arcane emergency response plan. And I know what it's called: 'Dean'. 'Dean' isn't an acronym. He's an alert young chap in a white van who's driving along the residential road on the other side of the barrier when he spots me hand-hopping along the wires of this cage.

He jumps out of the van in black overalls and shouts, 'You can get arrested for that.'

'I'm more worried about being splatted,' I blast back.

'Can't you climb over?'

I'm taking a serious Jonny Wilkinson look. The barrier rises about eight feet above a two-feet-high concrete wall. With the wire grills running between metal box sections, I'm thinking of monkeys at the zoo. 'I'll have a go.'

I stand on the concrete wall and hump the rucksack over the top for Dean to catch, before clambering on to a horizontal box section and toe-capping up the wire grill. He climbs part way up on his side and helps me straddle over the top. Then it's a bit of a jump down to a bent-legs landing and 'Thank God. You're a saviour.'

Dean is as pleased as I am at my arrival – perhaps for keeping the crime figures down – but his is a quite extraordinary, extraterrestrial intervention. It puts me in mind of the many unprompted gestures that do so much, in the cliché, to restore one's faith in humanity. How priceless are the words: 'you can pay me, love, next time you come,' after you run short of cash in a shop. They help put the lie to the cheerless headlines that dog us day after day.

Dean's good-heartedness didn't stop. He offered to drop me off at a local hostelry, The Moon Hotel. As we parted – with a totally inadequate handshake – I snatched a glance at the van. The signage said something to do with aggregates. I was delighted to be added to the collection of someone I could only call 'The Dean'.

The Blackness

The Moon Hotel had changed hands only two weeks before and, despite my volunteering to occupy any remotely vacant space, they couldn't or wouldn't put me up. I consoled myself with a long lager before guessing why. Black smears and streaks made me look as though I'd come straight from a coalface.

Wet and weary, I plodded on with mud-spattered trousers slapping my legs. Derby seemed distant as dreamland when I was hailed by a smart-suited gent standing at a bus stop. 'Is there a bus?' he asked. 'I've been waiting half an hour.'

'No idea,' I shrugged.

'How about going halves on a taxi?' he suggested.

'Fine,' I said, before I could think.

He was tapping out a number on his mobile when, wonder of wonders, a single-decker hove into view. He signalled vigorously. So did I. Arriving at a bus stop as a bus draws up is as good an indication you should jump on board as I know of. Besides, 'The Dean' was obviously still at work and I'd be well advised to play along. His agent didn't know Derby well enough to recommend a B & B but, after disembarking at the City Centre, I fell in step with a young couple – she a lot older than him – and such was their cheery chirpiness that it was easy to muscle in. Hardly had I opened my mouth than she was saying, 'I'd have offered you a room at my place,' – perhaps she hadn't seen my black side – 'but I'm not going home tonight.' I left my thoughts alone and took up her suggestion of The George Hotel. 'Only £25,' she said, 'and it's good.'

The George was under new management and the rate had gone up to £28 by the time I arrived. 'You'll pay sixty-five if you go up the road,' the preoccupied landlord said, and no, he didn't do breakfast but, 'You'll get a good'un for three pounds at Gee's.' That'll be *down* the road then, I thought. He wanted payment before showing me to the room. 'There you are' were the words.

If refurbishment was in the air, it hadn't reached room eight.

I did have a tea-making facility, but there were holes round the socket. Old metal pipes trailed across the ceiling down to a light over the washbasin. Everything was on show. Loose change was lying about, loose: 7p on the mantel shelf and 1p on the floor. That didn't bother me, but concerns about when the room had last been cleaned did. The dirty blue colour of the carpet didn't help and a stain on the towel positively hindered. The tone of the room was set by the door, painted matt black. If I'd had a stick of chalk I'd have scribbled 'Today's Lesson' on it. Opposite the door, black curtains continued the theme, and a duvet shading to black over the sarcophagus of a bed completed the funeral parlour ensemble.

It was then that it hit me: I was black too. I matched. The implication was self-evident: not that I'd passed through the pearly gates but that, as I was, so was my environment. It was a chameleon-in-reverse paradigm: as I changed, so did my surroundings. **Tenet Eleven** took a bow: *Change yourself if you want to change where you are.*

Exhilarated by this discovery, I had to laugh at the state of the room. How fitting it was to be here. And how vital to prepare myself not to be … by changing. First, the hunger: I snapped up a Szechuan duck with fried rice from The Emerald over the road. Then the disrepair: I draped my wet vest, shirt and socks in front of an electric heater and started drying out my trousers and jacket ready to brush off the splodges and streaks. Finally the unsavouriness: a shower down the corridor helped me change … position, alternating from 'ooh' cool to 'jump away' hot and back again. Drying took a little longer with only my face towel to fall back on. Soon the transformation was complete and now I'd proved I was alive, it was safe to sleep. Almost. I padded across to the bed wearing spare socks to avoid skin contact with the carpet before sliding into … my sleeping bag sheet liner.

Day Seven
Derby to Chesterfield

'Sometimes things have to get a lot more turbulent'

The Little Lifts

I surfaced at a quarter to eight. The blackout helped. It was still dark. But the night had been dark too. I dreamt I'd moved into a shed with stuff piled up to the roof. A friend said, 'it's riddled with vermin', so we cleared everything out but no mouse was to be seen. Had I been too hasty in my judgements about the room?

I pulled back the curtains. What a change: a bright blue sky. Perhaps my change had done the trick. I tried washing. The tap gulped, then gushed, and continued with its dribbles and spurts while I stuttered through my ablutions. No wonder my shower had been such a tepid and torrid affair. I put the kettle on to think through the day's plans with a cuppa. Nothing. Perhaps the kettle was kaput. But the heater which I'd left on low to dry my kit was dead too. I plugged the kettle into a corridor socket. Still nothing. I gave up. Either there'd been a power cut or the nightshift heater had sent a shockwave through the new management's balance sheet.

Today was enough of a challenge without troubleshooting this mess of pottage. Time to get out but, with no sign of the landlord, I dropped the keys on a desk. It was odd departing without a goodbye. A lot more was left undone behind. A week after leaving the Lizard, I should have been reflecting on what I'd learned. More pressing was a strategy to get through the city to the A6, without a bus. I decided to look for a petrol station and start hitching just beyond, before drivers picked up speed. A mug of tea and a tuna baguette at Gee's were *my* fuel.

First impressions count, but I didn't want my opinion of Derby to be coloured by one experience. At half past nine I was crossing a bridge when I heard the most exquisite of chimes, so sweet against the roar and rumble of traffic. 'Like a child's musical box', I remarked to a young businessman.

'That's St.Mary's,' he said, 'but you should hear the Cathedral's intricate chimes.'

Friendly and well-informed: that was my impression of Derby people. Rounding a corner, I passed a postman being checked by another chap. 'Is he finding the letterboxes all right?' I observed cheekily.

'He is,' said his supervisor, 'but it takes years of training.'

A good sense of humour – thanks, Derby – to add to my tally. Then a poster had me reeling. It was for tic-tacs, those little minty pellets as close to a pick-me-up placebo as you can get. The slogan screamed at me, 'Full of refreshing little lifts.' I couldn't have made it up. Exactly how I felt: uplifted. A few light-hearted remarks and I was in a positive frame of mind again, yet one small lapse, like the loose change left in my room, had led me to fear the worst. My glass was definitely half full now. But then I had changed. Black had been given the brush-off ... well, most of it.

When I came across a cluster of businesses around Duffield Road, King Street and Lodge Lane, I had to make a note of them. Octopus Tattoos, Linda's Lunch Basket, May May House (English & Chinese Meals), Pretty Petals (Florists), Five Lamps Bathrooms, Top Chef Fast Food, Tan Shack and Creative Interiors all brought their own distinctive touches to this part of Derby. I love to see small businesses thrive. Entrepreneurs who invest in their own talents are often the backbone of a community. Their success is crucial, not only to the livelihoods of their employees, but to all fugitives from clone cities.

I always feel like celebrating individuality. It's all too easy though to 'brand' people who work for retail chains or global corporations. But they're individuals too, with their own agendas. Instead of drawing the money out at the cashpoint I chose to go into the bank. 'How are you?' I asked cheerily, as Raj Chahal handed over the £40.

She grimaced. 'It's 25 per cent off at Debenhams today, but no way I can get there.'

'Aah. Sorry about that.' A boss might dismiss her regret but I could sympathise. In her thwarted wish, she represented all those for whom work patterns involved unhappy compromises. With time on my hands, I could forge my own direction. I'd better not forget it.

The Habitual Victim

After an hour's trudge through Derby, eureka! The promise of deliverance at the end of a road – a Murco sign and petrol station forecourt. I strolled over to a chap who'd just pulled up at the pumps in a van. 'Excuse me,' I said, 'am I OK for the A6?'

'It's quite a walk; about two miles,' he said in a deep-throated voice.

I reckoned on hitching from the exit but, as I sidled over, the gravelly voice stopped me short. 'I'll drop you there if you like.'

'Very kind,' I said. Some understatement. And, while he re-fuelled his pick-up – in mint condition – I sat in the passenger seat relishing my good fortune.

'Iain,' he announced once he'd paid, 'the Scottish Ian.' But he hardly sounded Scottish. The shiny black leather jacket with reddish trims to the collar and gold watch band gave him something of a young rocker look, at odds with the greyish hair bordering a bald crown.

Iain was a trade-plate man and he'd hitched at times. 'Not many people stop these days,' he said. Often he'd pick up a car after he dropped one off, as on a Swansea to Ludlow run recently. It saved him having to hitch.

With clear blue eyes peering over the top of his glasses, he had an impish look. But when I asked about his life's direction, that vanished. He couldn't begin to describe what had happened to him years before: the feeling of being plunged into darkness, of being choked and suffocated, like a zombie in a nether world. Iain had been caught up in the Channel Tunnel fire of 1996. The fire started on an HGV when the train was well into the tunnel on the French side. Along with 30 or so other passengers, he was trapped for about twenty minutes, having to lie on the floor to get enough air, before they were evacuated.

'If it had taken another ten seconds to get out, we'd have all been dead, I'm sure. A girl who was eight months' pregnant lost it,' he said. I guessed he meant self-control. No-one died, but he'd needed two and a half years of counselling to come to terms with the experience. Within ten seconds of death: could anything affect one more?

Iain gave a wry grin. 'But I haven't learned. About a year ago, I was in Bulgaria when an artic shoved me off the road at eighty miles an hour. Luckily I ended up on the verge. Too many nutters driving around, that's the trouble. My mate was asleep in the back at the time.'

'Not for much longer then,' I said. I didn't mean to be flippant, but the way Iain recounted the experience invited an almost casual response. There was more.

'Eight months ago, I had transmission failure on a truck and the brakes locked. A rag from the road wrapped itself round the prop shaft. When that seized up, the truck somersaulted. Terrific bash it was. They sent for the air ambulance. Didn't think I survived. I'd only cut my arm but the shock was bad enough. The doc said, "You'd better come off the lorries". So I did.' His voice had the whiff of victory as much as relief; that he'd diced with death again and won.

'You're not heading for the cats' record then,' I said.

'Hope not,' he rasped. 'Three's enough.'

'Bet you say your prayers?'

'Sometimes.'

Iain sounded matter-of-fact about his brushes with death. Perhaps that was how he'd learned to live with them. We'd reached the A6 by now and no time to find out how all this had affected his outlook on life. Our brief chat made me realise how heavily our minds are hard-wired into threats. Easy for me to shrug off a distasteful experience with a few light-hearted remarks, but the trials that Iain had endured were etched into a mindset.

I thanked him for telling me his story and set off, strangely heartened. Then it dawned on me: another refreshing little lift – that's what it *had* been; from the way it began to the openness with which Iain spoke about his ill luck. I couldn't help laughing. It wasn't to be taken lightly, but his ironic account hadn't been without its black humour.

The Wizard Systems Fixer

The A6 was a good choice. I enjoyed the human scale of the workmanlike stone cottages lining village streets, and when the Allestree Methodist Church noticeboard declared that 'Love is Sharing', I assumed that passing drivers would stretch the sentiment to a passenger seat. When, at half past eleven, a sign welcomed me to 'Amber Valley, the Heart of Derbyshire', I was ready for the green light.

This dialogue with signs was becoming an integral part of my journey. I read them as messages for me, as if the very fact of my noticing personalised them. A far-fetched thought maybe, but if these signals held up a mirror to myself, I'd better pay attention. **Tenet Twelve** stared back: *Signals from one's surroundings help one make sense of situations.*

As I was speculating Pete drew up. A dark-suited man with a stud in the dimple of his chin and one ear-ring, he reminded me of an old boss who wore an ear-ring and waved to people he didn't know as he drove. It was a nodding concession to the nonconformist streak of his younger days. And people waved back. Music was thumping away as I clambered in. Pete stubbed out a cigarette and after the usual exchanges – he'd drop me off at Belper – I broached the direction question.

'I've headed in so many directions,' he said, 'but I've been forced down this road.' He fixed business systems for companies and was on his way to a job. 'I've got to make a living somehow – I'm thirty-six, married, and a father. That means sticking to what I know.'

How many chaps like Pete are forced down a road, with the responsibilities of fatherhood and a mortgage? The demands of a job often mean that the very rationale for it – sustaining family life – is undermined. After I went into selling, I worked most weekends at a garden centre and had precious little quality time with my kids. What had Pete done before?

His eyes lit up. 'Had a great time living out of a canal boat, and a bender and caravans. Then I became a hippie – dreadlocks and all that – shacking up with friends in squats. Dirty, but all part of the creation of character,' he added wryly.

'Misspent youth some would say.'

'Yeah, but I went to uni after that. Took a four-year sandwich course in computer science and got very bored. And look at me now - a fish out of water.'

'Still swimming though.'

'Suppose so. I'm living within,' he said.

'That's sad,' I said. 'Not enough, is it? How do you see life working out?'

He fixed me with a look. 'I'll grow a beard. Become a crazy old wizard guy, an unkempt Druid.'

'And what will your kids make of you?'

'They won't care by then.'

Was he right? Maybe in time his kids would recognise that their dad's locked-in life had to be let out. They'd be old enough to sympathise, wouldn't they? Pete didn't seem so sure. And wasn't it too long to wait?

We reached Belper and I'd only glimpsed his frustrations. 'When my son walked for the first time, I wasn't even there,' I said. But had I missed the point? It wasn't so much the job taking him away from his family; it was the sacrifice he was making. He wanted to break out of his unsuited suit and the techie role. Fixing other people's systems, he wasn't free to see to his own or chart the other life he might live.

The music was still drumming in my ears when we pulled to a stop. It occurred to me to ask what one song he'd pick out from his music collection. He thought hard, fingering his stud. 'It's punky hardcore stuff,' he said. 'The group's American, called *No Means No*, and the piece, *The day everything became nothing*.'

'Which means most?' I asked. 'The music or the lyrics?'

'Both,' he said, emphatically.

But it was angst I read into his choice. While 'no' kept meaning 'yes', that day might be closing in. 'I must get the CD,' I said. It was one way I could keep in touch with Pete's feelings, and remember … what? My own dilemmas?

I took a photo of him before I left but not before he began smoothing his hair. Why? It wasn't straggly; not even long. 'Don't bother,' I said. 'Just as you are, that's fine.'

The Spinning Leaves

Walking through Belper, I found myself following in the footsteps of John Wesley. A notice at the Central Methodist Church announced that he preached near this place in 1786 and that 'the Good News of Jesus Christ is still preached here today'. Would that help Pete rediscover a life worth living? I'd want to hear why Nick, the Rehab Centre tutor, had to live through his heartaches or how Iain, the trade-plate man, might break free from his accident chains. They were like miscast actors still looking for the right roles, but what haunted me was the most poignant symbol of that mismatch: the stud in Pete's chin. It was a question mark stubbed in my face, not his.

Life must have been much easier when you looked to a Wesley for answers. But my needs were met when I was trapped on the A52. I had to remind myself of that. 'The Dean' had come from nowhere. I remembered another time I'd felt trapped; by that garden centre job. Working all the hours God gave, I'd reached an all-time low when a woman came into the sales office. She said, point-blank, 'Why are you here?' before walking out. I ran after her. 'I can't believe you said that,' I blurted out.

'Oh, I always have to say what comes into my head,' she said disarmingly.

'Well, please keep doing it,' I said. 'That's exactly what I needed to hear.' Those words prompted me to leave and set up my own business, working from home.

The intervals between lifts were often occupied with inconsequential observations. At twenty past twelve, I sat on a roadside wall and cut open the wrapper of an almond and cherry flapjack on the jagged edge of a rock. While I chewed away, the smell and sounds of a crackling garden bonfire put me in touch with everyday lives, as did a ram in a meadow trying to hump an unwilling ewe. Life went on, but not always in the way one might hope.

Seeing clusters of autumn leaves along the foot of the wall, I wondered what vagaries of wind brushed them here or there. Their locations might appear random but didn't they result from a combination of forces and circumstances? The mathematical equation would have to account for the direction and strength of wind, the mass and aerodynamics of leaves, along with the configuration of the wall, but I soon deduced that I (innumeracy) x T (time) = D (dead loss).

As I was about to set off, my eyes strayed to the river which had been an on-and-off companion. Leaves were drifting freely in the fast flowing waters. Others lay stranded in clumps of water weed but those that spun endlessly in whirlpool eddies absorbed me. What forces would it take to release them from their entrapment? I watched mesmerised, as if their plight was mine, until I saw a branch disrupt the swirling pattern and sweep leaves back into the full flow. The conclusion was clear; for a pattern to be broken, there had to be an intervention. In life, that might be an unexpected event, an upset or any experience that changes perceptions.

Sometimes things have to get a lot more turbulent before one is goaded to act. I left an advertising agency job after a stormy exchange with the boss who constantly interrupted my telephone calls. I know of other histrionic departures. A Head of Home Economics, totally frustrated by the demands of her job, threw down her books in the corridor one day and ran out of the school where we both taught. I saw her a few months later. 'It was the best thing I did,' she said. 'I've taken up piano playing. At last, I feel human again.' If difficulties are the route march to discoveries, *challenges to a routine are the springboards for change.* Welcome aboard, **Tenet Thirteen.** Perhaps we get the challenges we need.

The Emphatic Emigrant

Passing The Hurt Arms shortly after one-thirty, I thought The Tired Thumb might be more appropriate. Legs might be hanging half off though and shoulders slumped to your chest, but the sound of screeching brakes perks up the slouchiest hitchhiker. And if the hulking brute of a lorry draws up, with armour-plated ribs round a bison-like body, the least you can do is feign resilience.

The skill of a broncobuster doesn't go amiss either, so I was quite pleased when I mounted the beast with a degree of aplomb. This time I got things right: open the door first, step up a couple of footholds, flop in and close the door. Simple as that. And when I did, a yellow and white fluorescent-jacketed Dave faced me, with bare arms, black-rimmed specs and blunt moustache. Not an ounce of spare flesh on him, and even the balding forehead had a punch about it. Dave wasn't just high visibility, he was high octane.

I'd hardly introduced myself and mentioned the word 'direction' before he launched into something of a tirade.

'I hate this country,' he said. 'I'm emigrating.'

I gave a quizzical look.

'This country's all soft when it should be hard, that's why.'

I nodded. So where was he off to?

'Canada, on a dual passport. Spent years in the army there. I like the philosophy. Give you an example. It'll surprise you. We went to the shopping mall in Edmonton. I had Union Jack shorts on, with a skull and crossbones T-shirt. Know what? I was arrested for insulting the queen! In Canada! And hands pinned behind my back.'

He insisted that he'd signed an attestation to the queen. That made no difference. They still held him for three hours. He didn't sound displeased. Dave liked to know where he stood. If you didn't put down markers, he would. He was moving to Alberta and had been offered two jobs: one with the Canadian Post Office; another from a farmer. 'You've got to keep your speed up,' he said. 'There it's 75-80 mph. Here it's 56 max.'

Dave wanted to shift. No messing.

'Not just you is it?'

'No, I've a wife – married twenty years – and kids: three of them. One's eighteen – he finishes school in April – a fourteen-year-old, and another six months. That was a surprise.'

'A nice surprise?'

'Sure. But I won't have my kids going the way I did. I spent twelve years in the army. Everyone in my family were soldiers. But it stops with my generation.'

Dave spoke with real passion. I soon knew why.

'My best mate Stuart was killed four months ago. Five kids and no father. We were in the army together. Close, real close. In the Gulf War and Bosnia. I was a REME recovery mechanic there and shot at. Don't mind telling you; I shit myself. Your mates are everything out there. When I heard he'd been killed, know my reaction? I didn't tell the wife this, but I asked for the volunteer reel. That's how you sign up again. I wanted another three years to get my own back.'

I guessed it hadn't gone through.

'So far, 103 UK soldiers killed in Iraq. This might sound strange but if I was in Iraq, I'd be doing exactly the same as the Iraqis. It's all about oil, and Americans are the biggest terrorists in the world. I don't like 'em. They try to belittle you. That's my experience. It might be different if I went to the US, I don't know.'

We'd reached Matlock Bath. 'You should see this in May,' Dave said. 'It's biker heaven.' He'd had his fun. 'Lots of lorry drivers are bikers,' he said. 'You need good road sense for that.' That triggered off another thought as we headed up the A632 to Chesterfield. Dave told me that kids had dropped a whole paving slab through the windscreen of a mate's lorry. It broke his arm and collar bone, and the mate was lucky to survive when the lorry jackknifed. 'Lorry driving's the third most dangerous occupation,' he asserted. 'More dangerous than being a soldier.'

What was it that made kids commit such mindless acts? I wondered.

Dave drummed his fingers on the steering wheel and looked reflective. His voice dropped. 'When I was a nipper – only nine years old – my dad said, "I know something's wrong. You're being bullied, aren't you." I broke down. It all came out after an hour and a half's talking and sobbing. But he told me, "The only thing you've got to fear in life is fear itself. Control your own fears and you'll be stronger for it." '

'So when I went back to school, I started jumping on this bully, Darren. Really tore into him – he was bigger than me. When I'd finished he only had one kidney left and fifty per cent liver function. He spent weeks in hospital. I had youth custody for three months and under curfew till I was fifteen. Funny thing is, Darren was bullied when he was fifteen. "Now I know what I put you through," he said. So I told his bully, "You deal with the two of us." I speak to Darren most days and we meet at least twice a year. We're great pals. No-one stands up against bullying more than him.'

For a man who'd spoken about the traumas of war, talk of Darren brought him as close to a show of emotion as any tough army type could get. It took guts to divulge such a painful episode.

I wondered whether any of his children had to cope with bullying.

'Not really,' he said. 'My eldest has dyslexia, but he deals with his problems. One thing I can tell you: my kids have never been smacked.'

He was pulling into a quarry now – Goddards Quarry, a sign read – when his mobile rang. The cab juddered while the engine

[DAY SEVEN]

was idling. 'Ah, that's good news,' he said. 'The gaffer called and I've finished for the day.' He carried washed fines and powdered limestone but wouldn't have to pick up another load till tomorrow.

'You must be looking forward to Canada,' I said.

'I've had such good times there; rock climbing and white water rafting, all laid on by the army,' he said. 'It's sad I have to emigrate. But it's the way this country's going. Give an example: my mother-in-law – she's sixty-seven – brought up six kids and always had jobs. Now the kids have grown up she wants to exchange her three-bed house for a one-bed flat. Know what? All seventy-five flats where she lives, in Sheffield, have been allocated to immigrants. I'm not racist, at least I don't think so.'

'No,' I said. 'I can understand how she must feel, and you.'

'But sometimes they're too bloody hard. A mate of mine who's in Doncaster prison phoned me the other day. He's only doing time because his house got burgled. He tracked down the chap who done it and did him over. I'm not making excuses but they've banged him up for ten years. What he wants me to do is take his kids over to see him. He says I'm the only person he can trust.'

His mates would always look to Dave for support. He said what he meant and did what he said he'd do. You had to respect his views. They carried the conviction of experience. Dave went out of his way to drop me off on the outskirts of Chesterfield before heading off home. I really appreciated his grit and practical humanity. I'd miss that. So would Britain.

The Spare Room

It was nearly three o'clock; a little early to be shutting up shop. But I'd come to the end of a chapter. There might be a hint of hope out of the sadness but I wasn't ready to read on. I needed a B & B. 'The Dean' experience taught me that help might be close at hand so, when I crossed paths with the first woman in Chesterfield, I said, 'You're the very person to know where there's a B & B.' And she did, directing me to Brampton Guest House. They were full, but the owner suggested The Red Lion Hotel.

Following up leads was ingrained in me after years of selling. Looking for accommodation soon after we married, I knocked on six or seven doors before being told to try Mrs Elgar down the road. The name was auspicious. As she trotted out the same 'no room at the inn' story, a voice interrupted from inside. Mrs Elgar reappeared with a new story: a tenant had overheard and decided to vacate her room on the spot. We spent the first six months or so of married life there. Ever since, I've had that 'spare room' mentality, believing that you need to *knock on enough doors to open up opportunity*. That had to be **Tenet Fourteen**.

A few words with the bargirl at The Red Lion and I knew I'd arrived at the right place. Like a pet dog offered a treat, I followed her upstairs to an en-suite double with tea-making facility and telly. Pillows were plumped up and the duvet cover matched the curtains, in burgundy, not 'George Hotel' black. I snapped it up. For a double, £30 seemed cheap and I'd manage without loose change … on the floor.

I had an evening in, polishing off a prawn and pasta salad I'd bought in Amber Valley. I wrote cards to send home, one with a picture of a fox to accompany my story of Margaret's precognition way back at Lifton. That seemed like an age ago.

Too often one can be bedevilled by past misfortune, as Iain had, but good experiences can be trail-blazers. Margaret was drawn to Canada again for the wildlife and Dave for contradictory reasons. His Canada was a flag-waving antidote to the malaise he felt about this country and, like my spare room, a metaphor for the hope of a happy outcome.

Day Eight

Chesterfield to Newcastle-upon-Tyne

'Chance often mocks our efforts to organise and explain life'

The Crooked Spire

I slept well. Breakfast was minimalist: one pear, an apple and oat slice, and a cuppa dunked with a solitary digestive biscuit. A quick dip into breakfast telly revealed the day's preoccupation; sedentary lifestyles. That was my cue. I made the earliest departure yet, at twenty past seven, rewarded with a cooling breeze and a blue sky lightly shadowed by cloud.

On my way I bought some more postcards, one of which showed Chesterfield's famous crooked spire. I couldn't miss this architectural divertissement; a spire with a diverting direction all of its own. The Leaning Tower of Pisa has competition. This spire doesn't just lean – 9'5" from its true centre – it twists.

> *'Whichever way you turn your eye*
> *It always seems to be awry'*

… went a pithy couplet and eight cavorting faces catch that eye. Astonishingly the wooden spire isn't fixed to the tower but simply sits on top. Held in place by 150 tons of its own weight and 30 tons of lead, it has weathered storms for over 600 years. It's an animated presence on the Chesterfield skyline, a finger-wigging reproof that our gaze is not directed more to the heavens.

I speculated on its eccentric appearance. Was it the result of a geometric miscalculation or an underestimate of the long-term stresses and strains on wood? Or simply the legacy of carpenters who really enjoyed their work … and the occasional tipple? My postcard purveyor had her own explanation. 'Midges,' she said, 'and weather' as an afterthought; bizarre hypotheses in keeping with the spire's erratic behaviour. Whatever accounted for it, this key visitor attraction had clearly benefited the traders of Chesterfield.

The shop assistant's advice about my route – to make for Junction 29 on the M1 – matched her previous inventiveness. One glance at the map and I saw I'd be heading south. The A61, north to Sheffield, looked a much better bet. Slow moving traffic and a smattering of lay-bys were good news. So was the existence of a snack bar; an apple tree that overhung the verge, studded with crimson red-skinned apples. I reached up and collared one, only to find the skin scarred and blemished with black pockmarks. Tentatively I bit into the flesh. Free fruit is always more pleasurable, but the sweet juiciness of that first taste was all-surpassing. Near the core the flesh was translucent – something I'd never seen in an apple – and at its most luscious. I pocketed a clutch of them, all similarly blighted, and entertained myself with the thought that imperfections may turn out to have the most delicious twist, something that those wayside apples and the wayward spire certainly had in common.

The Campervan Man

Between hitches I often found myself more preoccupied with roadside rubbish than the landscape beyond. In bygone times, the playground game used to be to flick a cigarette card on top of someone else's to 'bag' it. The new game is tossing packets out of windows, but that doesn't hide the warnings. I started collecting them: *Smoking clogs the arteries and causes heart attacks and strokes; Smoking kills* (couldn't they have added 'slowly'?) and *Smokers die younger*. But for those living on, it wasn't just their future at stake: *Smoking may reduce blood flow and cause impotence.*

The message that would really have alarmed me – and I used to smoke – was *Smoke contains benzene, nitrosamines, formaldehyde and hydrogen cyanide*, without any explanation of the effects. Damien

Hirst used formaldehyde to pickle his cows and sharks. I could only imagine what that did to one's insides. But the most powerful dissuader I've seen was a blackened lung at an exhibition of 'plasticized' human remains. That image should be on the back of every packet.

So when a big white van pulled up at a lay-by, it was a surprise to be greeted by Ron, puffing away. If he let himself go in that direction, his hair was going that way too. Long white strands fell loosely round his head, each with a mind of its own.

He wasn't going far … he wouldn't at that rate, I thought … turning off a little way on but I was welcome. I climbed in and muttered about my mission. Ron cackled, as we drove off. 'I got divorced two years back,' he said, 'and I'm still celebrating.'

I wondered whether his ex-wife might feel the same, but laughed as heartily as he did. Crooked spire, delicious blemishes and now divorce revelling: these twist endings were really getting to me.

'Yeah, and that was the second time round,' he sniffed. 'I wouldn't get married again. Never.' That had decibels attached.

Ron had seen the light. A Stannah Chair Lift Lorry passed us. 'You're not ready for that then?' I nodded as it flew up the tarmacked staircase.

'God, no. I've just started living. A mate of mine who got banned had to get rid of his campervan quick. Wanted three hundred quid. I bit his hand off. You can't beat it. Most weekends I'm off somewhere.'

Ron so enthused about his new life that I was sorry not to share it longer … the enthusiasm, if not the smoke. It was packaging in the back, he told me, as we parted, crammed to the ceiling no doubt with empty cigarette packets. And 'campervans make a new man of you' scrawled all over them.

The Ex-Nightclub Manager

Traffic sped past my next lay-by station. Reality can slip through your fingers when your thumb loses its pulling power and you only have zoom, zoom, zoom for company. After my useless digit was passed by a car with the registration BU51MEN, I was incensed that someone could even think of flaunting their busyness. Short of throwing myself into the road, what would it take to stop all these busy people in their tracks?

It triggered off Harry Potter syndrome. With a flashing jiggle of fingers and thumb, and a spell-binding 'izzywizzy, get unbusy', I imagined them all shuddering to a halt. Then I released drivers from the fluence long enough to challenge them. 'What's all the urgency?' I'm sure I heard them say with one voice, 'Everyone else was rushing, so I thought I'd better rush too.'

Fantasy apart, there was more to my frustration. Close as these people passed, those 'little boxes' cut us off. Whatever the reasons – privacy, security, convenience, time pressures – that was sad. The intimacies of hitchhiking encounters made me aware how little we were in touch with the rest of humanity. What might the next lift bring? Looking drivers straight in the face, I hoped that thumb and eyes would do the trick. That tactic worked before, but I'd become so hypnotized by cars not stopping that I didn't spot Graham when he pulled up at the far end of the lay-by.

I apologised for keeping him waiting. 'Miles away,' I said. 'Thanks.'

'No trouble. I can take you to Dronfield.'

Never having heard of the place, I said, 'Fine.' Anywhere was better than nowhere. Graham had a friendly but shell-shocked face, a bit like a battered boxer, ears bent forward as if to catch any elusive remark and hair with curling tendencies. But what struck me most was his sombre suit. When he turned to me, I noticed the black tie.

He explained. 'I'm off to a funeral. A friend's wife. Only thirty-seven.' She'd gone out shopping one day and came back with a headache. The next thing her husband, Billy, knew was that she'd died; a massive brain haemorrhage. 'Billy was really cut up, as you'd expect,' he said. 'I've been ringing him every night.'

'Makes you realise what a fragile hold we have on life,' I said and told him about a friend of mine who returned from a walk rather tired and sat down on the sofa while his wife prepared dinner. 'When she went to fetch him, he'd died. Not a sound. What upset her most was the smile on his face.'

Graham was too wrapped up in his thoughts to respond. 'Anything can happen,' he said. 'Six years ago, I was a nightclub manager when there was an armed robbery. They shot their way in to scare us. But the laugh was on them. They only got away with three hundred and we had nine thousand quid on us that night.'

'And you weren't hurt?'

'Possibly,' he said. 'I reckon my arms had been weakened. Six weeks later I was pushing a caravan when my arm slipped. My hand went through the back window. Cut it clean off. You probably haven't seen.'

Graham hadn't told me half of what he'd been through. Had he wrestled with the gunmen? I looked down and saw the prosthesis for his left hand, darker than the other, resting on the gear lever.

'They tried to sew the old hand back on. Had eight operations altogether before they gave up.'

'What? Eight operations!' This poor chap's been crucified, I thought.

He managed all right now but had to grapple with a long-term problem. 'I'm left with this phantom limb pain. It's as if I'm going through the accident again and again. The pain's unreal. I've had every drug in the country. Intravenous this, infusion that. Everything.'

I shook my head. Loss of a hand was bad enough.

'It's like my brain's telling me that my hand's amputated but shouldn't have been. There's lots of books on the subject. If you get a chance, read one by Dr.Ramachandran. He's an authority.'

Graham started explaining the different theories as to where the pain originates and how the brain computes the absence of a limb. Understanding the problem was one thing. Resolving it quite another.

We'd reached the Dronfield turning. I thanked Graham for the lift. I couldn't thank him for the salutary experience this had been. I'd forgotten all about direction. So had he. When you live with the pain Graham described, any thought of direction was irrelevant.

The Window Systems Executive

I couldn't leave Graham behind. I carried him with me as surely as if he was packed in my rucksack. While I walked away from the lift, Graham was still living with that pain. When I travelled on, I might be in a different place. He wouldn't. And every time I raised my hand to thumb a lift, I remembered one left hand resting on the gear lever where another hand wanted to be. Joni Mitchell sang about not knowing what you've got till it's gone. Compared with Graham's experience, mine had been trifling; a prostate condition which often had me in agonies trying to find a loo in time, until one day I seized up. Now I really appreciate the freedom to pee, and the skills of a surgeon.

'Doing without' often has a flip side. Crawling out of dank caves in my twenties, I relished the pure tanginess of fresh air. I'd wolf down refreshing lungfuls as if rationing had just ended. Blasts of exhaust fumes on this hike stopped me taking fresh air for granted but, when lift-less for any length of time, I had to remind myself of the relief to follow, and the surprise company I'd keep. The thought of those compensations made waiting worthwhile. How might it feel to live with a loss that never could be redeemed?

'Doing without' had a particularly hollow ring when my next lift turned up. To date, I'd been more concerned with the mechanics of climbing on board than the make of car. But I couldn't mistake a Mercedes when it stopped. He'd be heading up the M1, the driver said, as far as Junction 35, the Chapeltown turning. Would that be OK? What?! I shuffled in and, when I handed him my card, he reciprocated. As if I needed anything to remind me of the last lift, he too was a Grahame, with an 'e', but dark-suited for a different reason. This Grahame was a window systems executive. Driving a Merc in typical pin-striped suit and tie, he presented a familiar picture. An old boss of mine took great pleasure trading in his Merc for a brand new model every year. Was Grahame anything but today's model of a successful businessman?

He fleshed out his background. At fourteen, he joined the school cadet force. That led him into the army. His five-year stint had taught him self-discipline, initiative, a respect for other people and an appreciation of life. The way he rattled them off made another point: marshalling thoughts – that's what the army had done for him.

We were passing the outskirts of Sheffield in this swish 'little box', with the relics of a past industrial age barely visible, when he told me his family mattered most. 'It's a big task, bringing up children to be well-behaved,' he said, 'especially teenagers. Mine might be bleeding me dry but I'm proud of them.'

Nothing out of the ordinary yet then, but things seemed too pat. The door panels in a Merc reach higher than most cars. The height made me feel enveloped and, with the comfort of the ride, cosseted. Could I tease out what challenged him?

'It's all about being positive,' was Grahame's reply. 'Even if it's a negative, I turn it round.' He used to have disputes with a chap whose glass was always half-empty.

I told him about the accountant I once shared an office with. Les was pessimistic with a passion. One day he brandished a letter. "Customer complaint," he said. "You've got problems with a builder. Rory's done a lousy job."

But I knew Rory had standards and asked to see the letter. "Don't know what you're talking about Les," I said. His glass was so empty he'd read 'lousy' for 'lovely'.

Grahame related to that. 'My wife once convinced herself she was pregnant, but it was all in her mind.' He took his eyes off the road for a moment and looked over. 'I read a book on the Buddha years ago. It was so positive. That's how I see things nowadays. You know the mistake people make in the way they treat kids?'

I didn't.

'If they hit their head on a table, what do you do?' He paused like a teacher waiting for a hand to go up.

I kept quiet.

'You hit the table. Bad table, you say. Naughty table. But what's that doing? Teaching kids not to have responsibility – it's never their fault. Big mistake. I've made it myself.'

'Yes,' I said, fisting the air. 'I've done it too. Why do we? I mean, always look for someone or something else to blame?' I was surprised at the force of my outburst.

'Because it's easy,' he said.

I laughed at this unexpectedly obvious revelation. Sheffield had come and gone, and the M1 was in full flow, as we schmoozed our way to the Chapeltown junction.

'I'd like to retire in the next three years and live abroad; Spain will do nicely.'

He didn't look much more than fifty to me. 'Big decision, that.'

'Oh, I always listen to the wife,' he said.

After Grahame dropped me off, I walked over to the slip road. It was still not eleven. I'd made good headway but I wasn't sure what I made of Grahame. Did he conform to my Merc-driving businessman stereotype? And hadn't I expected more of him? Possibly and yes, I started thinking.

But he hadn't talked business once. He wasn't obsessed with success, simply concerned with the quality of life. In Grahame's life, family mattered above all. That was a commonplace notion. His commitment wasn't. Nor his determination to stay positive. *Take responsibility for everything that happens to you,* he'd said in as many words. I marked them out for **Tenet Fifteen**. That attitude went for thinking too. Mine. He'd picked me up, hadn't he? It just happened to be in a Merc.

The Golfing Salesman

'At 11.02, while I was proceeding in an orderly manner down the slip road at Junction 35, a van driver swerved towards me deliberately.' I was so shocked I might well have been giving the cops a statement. I froze, and only glimpsed something about scrap metal on the rear doors before the van sped away. But I had to put the matter out of my mind; a poisonous thought I neutralised with an injection of Grahame's positive thinking.

I repositioned myself near the top of the slip road before drivers picked up speed. It worked. A quarter of an hour later I was ushered aboard by another smart suit, Peter. He could take me up the M1, skirting round Leeds and drop me off on the A58 near Scarcroft, not far from Wetherby and the A1(M).

We hit it off straightaway. I told him about the Merc. He used to hitch and still remembered his best lift; in a Rover 3½ litre V8. 'In those days, and I'm talking about twenty years ago, drivers diverted on to a slip road to look for hitchhikers.'

'Now they try to run them down,' I said and started on the threatening swerve story before I realised I was leaking bad news. 'These things happen,' I added, changing tack to tell him what I was trying to achieve.

His journey had been a bit of a diversion. He had a degree in civil engineering but couldn't afford a mortgage on the salaries offered then. Scanning a university vacancy board, he found you could earn three thousand more per annum selling paper to printers. That was twenty-one years ago and he was still doing it.

'I enjoy meeting people,' he said, 'and the freedom. But a redundancy package would suit me fine. The biggest buzz I've had in life was the birth of my kids.'

My mind flashed to Grahame. How might Peter's approach differ?

He had four of them, from ten right up to eighteen, and less risk-taking than he'd been. 'They're happier playing computer games than going out,' he said. 'I had a motorbike when I was fourteen, but I have to force them off PlayStation. Parents fear perverts outside but there's more chance of kids getting corrupted on the internet.' His older children had ambitions. The eighteen-year-old daughter fancied work in the catering trade while his sixteen-year-old wanted to become a pilot.

What about him?

'Golf,' he said. 'That's all I want to do.' On Saturday afternoons, he met up with seven of his mates. 'It's the companionship and you learn about life. The best player doesn't always win. Golf's good for self-control and thinking on your feet. Think negative and you'll have a bad shot, like as not. But don't beat yourself up about it. Smell the flowers. That's what I say. Always smell the flowers.'

'You've got to keep a positive outlook when selling, haven't you,' I said. 'Not easy on commission only, like I used to be.'

'Part and parcel of being professional, isn't it? High expectation; happy outcome. Golf teaches you that too,' Peter enthused. 'You have to expect that ball to go in the hole. If your eyes are on the target when you make the stroke, you sink the putt.' Peter didn't stop at golf; he played tennis and badminton too. 'I'd play tiddleywinks, given half a chance,' he said. What lessons would he learn from that?!

Life has its lessons too. He'd had a discussion with Mandy, his wife, on the difference between being simply pissed off and being depressed. 'I used to poke fun at people with bad backs,' he said, 'until I had one and that really pulled me down. Then Mandy reminded me what it was like giving birth.'

Peter must have been impressed by the argument. 'No excuse for any bloke getting depressed,' he said, 'when we don't have to go through that.'

Even so I could tell where Peter's real allegiance lay. 'Who's your role model then?' I asked mischievously.

'Seve Ballesteros,' he said emphatically.

Golf 1, Wife 0 then. But Mandy might score a late penalty.

Peter and I talked like old friends. Pity we couldn't have been golf buddies. But it was the end of this round. He dropped me off on a stretch of road with sweeping landscape views and a legion of dark grey clouds marching towards a towering range of snowy white cumulus. That's where I'd be heading.

The Glass Dish

It was not yet mid-day and I'd made such good progress I could afford to ease off. The theatrical sky reminded me of home. Living on the North Devon coast as we do, the unpredictable dramas staged by winds from the Atlantic are never far away and the wildness often calls round. But change soon follows. As I walked, peepholes in the sky widened, and there was warmth in the air when I sauntered through a village. The very name – Bardsey-cum-Ryton – summoned up thoughts of croquet on the lawn and cream teas, even in mid-November.

But at the bottom of a hill, on a curve, I came upon a more disturbing scene. Orange lines painted diagonally on the road gave way to muddy trenches with tyre marks cutting across the verge to the trunk of a sycamore tree. A notice that read *Incident here between 12/11 and 13/11* – only a day or two before – and *Can you help?* had me speculating. What had happened? Most telling was the tree. The bark had been stripped in a dozen or more places, but sliced cleanly, as if planed. I could make out the impression of a bumper on the trunk and the roundness of a headlight above.

A de-icer aerosol lay on the ground, along with splintered stumps of branches. A large one had been totally ripped off, leaving a long oval recess in the trunk. Within it a cluster of small, sharp cubes of glass glinted; startling freeze-frame evidence of the moment the car slammed into the tree. Its nearside would have taken the full force of the impact. That main branch had most probably speared the windscreen before snapping and showering glass over the occupants. Fragments must have shot across the bonnet into the dish shape left by the severed branch.

What astonished me was the immediacy: that a branch could

snap off and leave, in that instant, a crater to catch a cascade of fragments. The driver and any front seat passenger would have been lucky to survive. While I surveyed the aftermath, devastated relatives might well be keeping vigil at a hospital bedside. As far as I could see only one vehicle was involved. From the position of the orange lines, I guessed that the driver had been about to overtake at speed when another vehicle suddenly appeared round the bend. Cutting in fast, he may have lost control. Unfortunate, to say the least, that the tree lay in his path.

The 'between' dates on the police notice suggested a late night accident. Alcohol? But speed, recklessness and the driver's inexperience might also be in the mix, together with distractions from the other occupants. Teenagers perhaps.

The police would come to their own conclusions but I could imagine a survivor bewailing, 'Why did the tree have to be there?' I had my own questions. What circumstances put the driver on a deadly collision path with this tree? What if he had left the pub, or wherever, a few seconds earlier or later? We might look for cause and effect in the physical world, but a split second decision can play as critical a role.

Chance often mocks our efforts to organise and explain life. I wouldn't want it any other way. At home we still have the water pitcher that was toppled when a kitten jumped in and out. We never got around to mending it. The kitten has long since gone to catmint heaven, but whenever I look at the jagged rim and the broken pieces lying in the bowl, I am reminded of its playfulness.

The Stopgap Barman

I walked on with a question that reared up as abruptly as the towering faces of the cumulus mountain ahead. What part *had* chance played on this journey? I'd visited this question many times before. There was no predicting who would give me a lift. But I'd been on common ground with an incredible number of people, and experienced some amazing coincidences and connections. Was that all down to chance? Still I had no answer.

This was good walking country and I only stopped to turn round and raise a thumb when a car was within earshot. It was easy enough for any car to pull up on a road this quiet. I must have covered two or three miles before a car braked sharply. A young chap wearing an Andy Capp and a broad grin on a full-of-life face greeted me. 'I'm making for Newcastle. All right?'

'Fantastic.' I jumped in to find myself soon wrapped up in Jez's world.

'At school, I enjoyed people most; kids and teachers. Enjoyed and hated,' he amplified. 'I enjoyed the hating. That's how you bond with people; through displeasure.'

I hadn't heard that one before.

Jez explained, 'It's a bit like war, where you get on with comrades because of a common enemy. Our enemy was in relationships; teachers and pupils couldn't stand each other but we jousted verbally. That was something special.' Antipathy can be endearing, he was saying, in an ironic kind of way. He'd been to the school of hard knocks, but learned to live with them. Jez had a lot to live up to. His parents were teachers and, unlike him, his sister had finished a degree course. But he'd had ongoing problems from the time his parents adopted a young boy of his age and of mixed race, Afro-Caribbean.

'We were so naïve,' he said. 'We called each other niggers, not knowing the meaning of the word.' He felt that the adoption 'wasn't enlightened.' At middle school, he had to explain why his brother was coloured – I could imagine the jibes – and, on the day they started at high school, his brother told him he wanted to leave. When his parents moved to a multi-cultural area of Leeds it got really tough for Jez.

'We lived in a black area and I hung around with black people. To get accepted, I'd speak in their patois. Know what they call you? Wigga; a white person who wants to be black. I wanted to copy my brother – a trendy, hip guy – but people bullied me because I was white. I had to explain why I sounded black. If there was trouble, I got the blame. I got money taken off me, so I'd do the same to someone else.' He knew he had to jump off this roundabout.

I empathised with Jez's situation. My children are of mixed race – my wife is from South America – and they only spoke in their twenties of taunts at school. But their situation had been nothing like as stressful as Jez described.

Times had changed in the areas he knew. Chapeltown, in Leeds, used to be a strictly non-white zone, notorious for drugs and prostitution. 'Now it's got a dance college,' he said, 'and is multi-cultural, but there's a lot more racial tension.'

Hardly surprising after the terrorist attacks and trials.

Muslim friends were becoming more racist. 'When I was twelve or thirteen, I thought racism was disappearing. Now there's polarisation.' If he asks them to play pool, they'll say, 'We don't want to hang around with western culture.' They embraced the east more and more, insisting that an arranged marriage was the best way to have a family. 'They're disowning the west,' he said, 'and that irritates me.'

He told me how schools unwittingly strengthened the divide.

'We had counselling sessions for West Indians where the teacher spoke in patois, so that kids could identify. But they used it to get out of maths. Having special classes for blacks, at the expense of the whites, encourages segregation. And I'm dyslexic, but spent a lot of time in the corridors, punished for being loud.'

Jez's story was poignant. What is the point of trying to integrate other races into our society if you alienate the native population and overlook home-grown needs? Education, social services and the police cross a minefield of discrimination issues. Jez told me how convenient it was to play the race card: that 'you're picking on me because I'm black'. Yet, at school, it was always the black kids who were seen as 'cool'. No easy answers for racial questions either.

We were rattling along the A1(M) by now. Only when we reached Scotch Corner did I realise how far this lift was taking me. I was heartily grateful for that, but more so for the opportunity to hear how Jez's life was working out.

Jez had to tell me about his brother. 'It's weird,' he said. 'He should have got ten A's but spent the time with his girl friend. Now he's a chef with three kids; two of hers and a baby boy, his own: a breath of fresh air, so free, natural and self-confident. He's stabilised my brother.'

I was touched that his brother's wellbeing mattered so much to him. As it happened, the other charity I'd chosen to benefit from this hitchhiking trip – the Mothers' Bridge of Love – helps adopted Chinese children keep in touch with their roots while adjusting to another country's culture. Such bridge-building is vital. But what about Jez?

'I'm working in a bar as a stopgap. It's been allsorts since I left school.' He dropped out of university after three months on a social policy course and went travelling, running a bar for months and 'making friends with alcohol.' Jez sounded apologetic. He'd done timeshare stints at Majorca and Magaluf. 'But it was all a bit like Blackpool,' he said, 'and I came back to live with the girl friend, except she went to uni and we split up after a few months. My suggestion.'

Jez's was a story of our times, unsettling in many ways. But a young chap as sincere and perceptive as he was deserved to find an outlet for his talents.

'I worked for a bank for two years, the National Bank of Australia. Me in a bank! I couldn't believe it,' he laughed. 'But it took three years to pass GCSE in Maths. Then I had an offer of work in Corfu, touting timeshare again and working as a DJ. Now I'm back behind the bar, in Newcastle. Guess how many jobs I've had.'

I was wide of the mark.

'Twenty by the time I was twenty-three. Four's the norm. But I have to do what makes me happy.'

So what was left?

Well, he'd worked at a call centre not long ago, next to two seventeen-year-olds. The job palled even more when he had to ask for a toilet break. If he went back to that – 'not that I would,' he added quickly – he'd have to retrain because things changed so fast.

So what did he fancy doing?

'Travel properly. Thailand and China for starters,' he said. But Jez, at the ripe old age of twenty-five, was thinking he ought to settle down.

I felt like emitting a long 'aaaaah', not out of relief that he was seeing sense, but from the way a short passage of years had coloured his thinking. He'd narrowed his options down to three: drug and alcohol counselling, becoming a paramedic, or taking a plumbing course.

If only I was a careers adviser. What advice could I give? 'Go for what makes you most happy. Just take the first step and see how it feels.' I couldn't say more. I couldn't have said much less. It was hardly better than sticking a thumb in the air.

'I've been to the university of my life,' Jez said. 'It took me long enough to realise I had to establish my own identity. But where I go from here ...'

And then words fizzed out from me like champagne sprayed on a Formula 1 race rostrum: 'Ask for what you need. Say out loud: please show me within the next few days what direction I should go in. Be alert, watch for a sign, an indication. It will come. Believe me! There's an agency out there, waiting to help. Call it.'

Jez looked bemused as he pulled to a stop. We'd arrived and I had no chance to tell him about 'The Dean' or any of the signs that helped me find direction. If I was his age, I could see myself in the same quandary. How *did* you decide? But there was always time. It had taken me long enough to be where I was ... wherever that might be ... when he dropped me off not far from the city centre.

The Elusive Engravings

Standing on the pavement, I was full of self-reproach. I hadn't offered one word of practical advice, only an esoteric clue, as useful as a bent key without the benefit of my experiences. And where *was* I going? So involved had I been with Jez's situation that I wasn't ready to arrive. Spewed out on a city street, I couldn't begin to think what I'd do now. It wasn't as if the city was new to me. I'd been to Newcastle before – the riverside anyway – when a walk along Hadrian's Wall Path turned into my first book, *Off-the-Wall Walking*. I looked at my watch; barely half past three. Too early to look for a B & B. Without any sense of direction, I meandered towards the city centre.

What first caught my eye was a sign – no surprise there – for the Central Station. It reminded me about some engravings. Displayed on the Metro platforms, they commemorated the 150th anniversary of the notable wood engraver, Thomas Bewick. They'd been commissioned from Hilary Paynter, President of the Royal Society of Painter-Printmakers, the lady responsible for the handsome illustrations in my book.

I popped my head round the door of the station travel office to ask about the engravings. The girl in the office shook her head.

'There are lots of them,' I insisted, 'big blow-ups on the walls.'

She swore there were not and suggested I look round the main line station concourse instead. But drawing a blank, I trotted down a flight of steps to the Metro platforms. And what did I see straight in front of me, right next to the underground routes? Engravings you couldn't possibly miss: fourteen of them, from floor to head height. I took my time admiring Hilary's impressive handiwork and checked how far they stretched – twenty odd paces – before I left.

How on earth had the travel girl not spotted them? Intent on putting her wise, I headed up again, to find the office empty. But there was something so right about her disappearance that I gave up instantly and strode out of the station.

The Fortune Teller

Where now? Nothing stared me in the face. Casually I window-shopped the pubs, restaurants, cafes and shops but the windows didn't swap glances. Splendid as the curving facade of Grey Street was, it didn't speak to me, and the towering figure of Earl Grey was distinctly aloof atop his Doric column. Why? It was all up in the air.

My head was wrestling with Jez's choices. How could I have advised him? Plumbing might give him a trade and an assured income, but could Jez settle down to a life with pipes? Probably not. He was more of a people person. Drugs and alcohol counselling? Worthwhile work certainly. Jez would empathise with clients and find the job fulfilling. But he'd been fazed by his own family set-up and might get too emotionally involved. I'd seen the effect on Mike, the rehab centre tutor, when just one client relapsed.

What about a paramedic? Quick responses were called for and the immediacy of situations would stop Jez getting too hung up … as with that car hitting the tree. He wouldn't have time to dwell on the trauma and the next call-out would soon supplant thoughts of previous victims. Jez liked change but there'd be periods of hanging around waiting and … wait a minute, I'm thinking: I've missed something.

How could I be so blind? I see the aftermath of an accident, then Jez picks me up and wonders about being a paramedic! Haven't I got the message? He just *has* to be a paramedic. Then I remember the blue tit episode way back. Who gave me a lift straight after the road-kill bird? Wildlife rescuers!

It's what happens: the future's foreshadowed. *Signposts are here now, pointing to the next destination.* And, I predict, to **Tenet Sixteen**. If only I'd known this then, I could have told Jez about the accident scene. He might have realised the connection and understood its rightness. But I don't see what's right in front of me!

I'm stunned. This whole journey is slipping into one long conversation where each encounter is like a word, but only the connections between convey the message. I have to pass on this message – about being a paramedic – to Jez. Thank God I took down a telephone number. After this, it's as if a swirling fog has descended on Newcastle's city streets. I'm not taking anything in … until that is, rounding a corner, I am greeted by an incongruous sight: a gypsy caravan parked on a wide pavement.

It has an authentic look: the canvas bowed top arching over a wooden chassis, the sides and front gleaming with gold scrollwork and glimpses of a tasselled red damask tablecloth within. But, propped against some steps, a scalloped board with red and green lettering gives the game away:

ANGELINE LEE
The Welsh Gypsy

I Will Tell You
The Past, Present and Future
Of Your Life

I Have Predicted
For The Stars

If You Have Any Problems
I Can Help
Satisfy Your Mind

A notice next to the doorway reads:

> **Come Inside**
>
> **And**
>
> **Hear Your Fortune**
>
> **Only £5.00**

I stand outside debating but I need to come clean. I've consulted the *I Ching*, had tarot card readings and runes read, numerology predictions, sidereal chart calculations, something called an incarnascope, and even tea leaf strainings in the past. On that occasion there were so few tea leaves after I'd swilled out the tea that I was surprised I had any future.

It's all been in the cause of open-mindedness, fuelled by blind curiosity. But from each one I've had grains of truth. And it isn't so much that I've believed in each system, but in the synchronicity: that, because I elect to receive any reading at a given time and place, it's likely to reflect something about my state at that time. My mother always told me how appropriate it had been for a stray bomb to land at the back of the nursing home where I was born … on the 13th May 1941. Which is a tortuously long way round of saying, 'Here's a Fiver.'

Angeline sits me down at the side of the table, close to a crystal ball. She doesn't sound Welsh and isn't as showy as I expected. An ethnic cardigan has tear drops chasing each other around, but they're mopped up by a loosely knotted scarf. Pencil-thin eyebrows and pinched lips give her a taut look, though her hair could be more up together. Strands that have escaped from a bunch at the top frizz out at the sides, as if subject to some electric charge.

When she takes my left hand – it's a palm reading – I notice one gold ring on a finger. That's all. No bangles. No flashy nail varnish. She holds my left hand by the fingertips, inspecting the lines, but not that scrupulously before letting go. She doesn't bother with my right hand. It's my face she's interested in. Fixing me with the eyes, she begins. 'You're not superstitious, are you darling? But you believe in God.'

She doesn't wait for answers and I don't offer any. I'm trying to decide whether I am superstitious and how to qualify what I might mean by 'God' when she adds, 'But you don't go to church often.'

Hardly at all, I could have answered, meaning never, but I pull out my notebook. 'I've a terrible memory. Mind if I write things down?'

'You suffer a bit with anxiety, don't you.'

Yeah, about remembering things.

She pauses and I don't know whether it's because I've started scribbling, but she suggests, 'You should have been a teacher …'

Gosh. I was.

' … or a lawyer.'

No, though I did pass a very minor exam on the law in advertising, eventually.

'But you're retired now.'

I'd have guessed that. I'm keeping quiet, not wanting to give anything away and, to be fair, she hasn't invited feedback.

She smiles. Past smiles have etched curving lines into her face that arc down from the nostrils to the edge of the bottom lips. 'You give out more love than you receive.'

I can't speak for that.

'I can tell you good or bad things. It depends on your palm. You've been hurt by a lady from the past, darling. But she still loves you. You can get her back in your life if you want,' she reassures.

I'd better speak to the wife first, I'm thinking.

'Your choice is to be on your own at the moment …'

Pretty obvious, with a hefty rucksack on the floor. But does she mean right now?

' … but there's an old woman with you in spirit; someone you loved deeply.'

I can only think of my mother. But most people who've lost a mother would.

'I can tell you things that are going to happen,' she says, 'and what you think you know already. You're going to get a trip to Scotland soon.'

I'm shocked into speaking. 'Yes?'

'And it'll be successful.'

'Oh good.' Right on the button there.

'And you'll venture to America, but not this coming year.'

I've already been. A few years back.

'You've been thinking of selling a property, haven't you. Don't. Hold on to it.'

Dead right. We thought about selling two months back, but ruled it out. So far I'm feeling fairly non-committal, but 'teaching' and 'Scotland' have hit home. I'm puzzled though. How can she possibly have twigged 'Scotland' from lines on my palm? It's not a destination board. Then she comes out with another name.

'There's a man called Tony. Don't trust him.'

That rings alarm bells. 'Tony' was the one name that caused me anguish in business: a building contractor who cut corners on bases, and made a real hash of a gable end for a devious customer of mine, also called Tony. The Tony bogey cost me dearly, in peace of mind and the pocket.

'You'll meet someone called Christopher,' she says, 'in your line of work.'

What? That's staggering. Yes, I'm sure to be meeting my old self from time to time. How on earth did she dredge up my previous name? And there's something else: she's talking about things from the past as though they're still ahead.

'I'll give you two dates,' she says. '28th January and 20th August. They'll be lucky.'

Perhaps I ought to look back too.

'You need to believe in yourself,' she urges as she shuffles her feet, about to get up. I guess my fiver's running out. 'I can do a crystal ball reading if you like … only twenty-five pounds.'

'Awfully sorry,' I say quickly. 'Can't run to it now, thanks. But how d'you know all that from my palm?'

'Not just the palm, darling. I read people's brains. It's a gift we Romanies have, handed down from my mam and her mam before her.'

I'd like to ask more but I've had my money's worth. And her parting words? 'You'll write your own book and publish it. Good luck.'

I did and I would, again. This one. I could have said she'd be in it.

The Enigmatic Picture

Gypsy Lee had made her mark, and I'd have been playing a random remix of past, present and future, had I not heeded the call of a B & B. It took a while for the tourist information office to locate a vacant room. I mentioned the fortune teller. 'Did she say it would be hard finding somewhere to stay?' said the quick-witted woman behind the counter.

'No, but she didn't say it would be easy either,' I parried.

At the third attempt, she fixed me up with a single room at the Jesmond Park Hotel for a reasonable £26. I had trouble finding the hotel but two students put me right.

'Everyone's so helpful in Newcastle,' I said.

'It's the cold,' came the cheery reply. 'We have to stick together.'

The same warmth awaited me at the hotel. The manager, Malcolm, greeted me as if he were the owner. 'We work as friends that respect each other,' he said. There was pride in his voice as he introduced me to the elegance of the past: Regency striped wallpaper, glass-topped writing desk, wash basin in a curving unit with matching wardrobe, and an emerald green pillow on an emerald green bed. I could have sunk into it there and then, but for the small matter of the big void … in my stomach.

'They do an exceptionally good pizza at Francesca's,' Malcolm said.

The place was humming when I arrived, but the Italian waiter found me a corner table and served my Parmigiana with anchovy, Parmesan cheese, tomato, mushroom – and a thespian flourish of the hands. Italians know how to talk up their pizzas. Lively student chatter all round complemented the meal. 'Couldn't be better,' I said, as he cleared the stage of its props. And that would have been the end of the show, had I not glanced up on leaving.

Above a commanding stone fireplace, a large framed print took me straight back to my childhood. *The Blue Door* by Harold Harvey had been a wedding present for my parents and a constant presence in our every home. It was an extraordinary discovery. I'd last seen this scene fifty years before and still it painted an enigmatic picture.

A blue door opened on to a balustraded terrace high above a harbour, with fishing boats, a three-masted schooner and open sea beyond. A tallish woman, perhaps in her mid-thirties, wearing a long white dress under a rose-pink blouse, stood to one side of the door knitting what looked like socks. A raffish man, about the same age, sat facing inwards, playing an accordion. With deep blue roll-top sweater, a jaunty sort of trilby and cigarette dangling from the corner of his mouth, he had an easy-going bohemian look, at odds with her strait-laced appearance.

Walking back from the restaurant, I wondered how appropriate a present it had been. I could see connections: my father's name was Harold, he played the trombone, smoked, and often wore a trilby to hide his prematurely bald head. The woman in the picture might have been happy listening to the music but she hadn't shown it. Her eyes were all on the socks. Socks would never have done it for my mother. The music would.

The woman faced the musician but he was seated side-on to her, gazing straight ahead through the doorway. Neither figure made eye contact. They were two people together but, wrapped up in their own worlds, they seemed apart. And the view went begging. Was this idyllic scene tinged with sadness?

By now I was in my Regency room at the writing desk, drifting into my own shades of the past: did the picture foreshadow what happened with my parents' marriage? How close were they? When my mother died of cancer at forty-three, I was only fourteen. My impressions would be those of a teenager grappling with his own feelings. But even as young as six, I registered the worried look on my mother's face when she said, 'Your Dad's walked out. I don't know when he'll be back.' My sister was around by then, but my mother wanted another baby. Dad didn't.

Dad's harsh upbringing, and the abuse he'd suffered, made it hard to trust people and easy to look on the black side. 'Bad luck always comes in threes' he'd say and, 'Send it down, David' whenever it rained, as if agitating for more. And early on he warned me about too much sex. He assured me it led to consumption (TB, as it's now called). I couldn't disagree then but how did that odd notion affect their relationship? Linking sex with an early death strikes me as a powerful deterrent.

How little I knew the depth of their feelings. They weren't that demonstrative, and certainly not passionate. How many parents are, in front of children? But I don't recall any heated arguments. I do remember times when Mum tickled Dad, whereupon he'd curl up like a small boy and collapse into paroxysms of laughter.

For a year or more, Dad worked at Heathrow airport. Seeing him only at weekends must have put a strain on my mother. She needed company. Nearing eleven-plus exam time, I came home from school early one day and let myself in. When I went into the lounge, I was shocked to see Mum sitting close to my headmaster, so close that in my schoolboy mind she might as well have been sitting on his lap. His contact clearly went further than a progress report, but how far beyond?

She'd not mentioned about meeting him but, afterwards, confided what the headmaster told her: that his wife was frigid. 'Cold' was what I took away. Mum did talk about platonic friendship, and really I have little reason – other than my own sensitivities at the time – for thinking there was more to it than that. She was good at winkling out intimacies from people anyway. Sometime later, however, I received a gift from the headmaster: a stamp album, complete with penny reds, if not blacks, and cigarette albums. His son had apparently lost interest in them, though they were possessions that any boy prized.

But I distrust these recollections. Piecemeal memories of my parents no more reflect their relationship than stamps depict a country. Marriages have ups and downs, and theirs was no different. Feelings aren't facts: they're fluid, turbulent one moment, tranquil the next. Their union certainly had an unpredictable start: they married the day before World War Two broke out. But my viewpoint was fixed.

Did the same go for the picture? I thought the balcony couple were oblivious to each other, but perhaps my parents saw them communing: in music that sang of first love. And though my parents appeared to be in separate worlds, two very different people may have found their own meeting places. I hope so. All I can say for sure is that when Mum died, Dad was bereft. He tried to meet other women – even advertising in the personal columns – and did, but never remarried. 'No-one can ever touch your mother,' he said.

The past had caught up with me again. And I couldn't 'unsee' that picture on the wall or any other 'pop-up' picture from the past. I carried their memory as certainly as if a relay runner had thrust his baton in my hand. *Accept what you've been given to go forward*. **Tenet Seventeen** for sure. I was ready for that emerald green bed.

Day Nine

Newcastle-upon-Tyne to Burnmouth

'I want chance to challenge my thinking'

The Backpacking Mother

I woke with Newcastle on my mind. Everything had come together here: picture and fortune teller; past, present and future. If I'd stuck to my original plan – hiking up the west coast through Liverpool to Glasgow and beyond – none of that would have happened. But this path, taking lifts as they came, had led me somewhere unexpectedly right.

I swished the curtains open to let in the morning light: grey more than white. The forecast on the telly told me more: 'chilly, some showers, but mainly dry'. I could live with that. Then I caught the strains of a song from Bon Jovi: *'I just want to live when I'm alive'*. That said it. That's how life should be: lived. With an edge. No blur.

When I hit the road, the sky was still brooding. I bought a vegetable pasty and a slice of carrot cake to eat later and guessed I'd have to trudge to the outskirts of Newcastle before getting a lift. But I'd hardly stuck out my thumb beyond a roundabout when – hey – another woman driver pulled up. Peering through the open window, I only had to say who I was – with a nodded smile to the wide-eyed girl in the child seat behind – to be sitting next to the young mother, Dawn.

First lift of the day and how appropriate was that!

Dawn wasn't going far, just up the road. She'd been far enough in the past, as a backpacker. It showed in the free-and-easy outlook, sunny highlights in the hair and burnt sienna eyes that beamed earthy, go-getting miles. 'I backpacked for years – eight at least – everywhere, from the Northern Cape to Spitzbergen and the Caribbean. We sailed all the way from Piraeus to Barbados once, on a freighter. Hundred pounds, that's all it cost us. Good holiday, too. Aaaw. They were great times.' She'd gladly be living them now. 'But I'm forty this year.'

It didn't call for the usual comment. A woman who comes straight out with her age doesn't wear clichés.

'Now it's down to flyin' about here 'n there, ferryin' this little 'un around.'

Dawn didn't stop at that. She played the guitar and found time for Irish dancing. Most years the family went camping on Dartmoor, taking bikes.

Where did the pioneering spirit come from?

'My parents,' she said. 'But it's eatin' well too. We stick with organic. It's what I believe in that makes a difference and,' she added quickly when we'd reached my drop-off point, 'we're Catholics. If you don't trust in good, where are you?'

That's what I thought she said, as I climbed out. But 'good' must have been 'God'. The accent fooled me. What did it matter? Her God would be 'good'.

Goodbyes gone, it was too late to ask what she made of other gods. And no time for me to ask myself what I thought of mine. I had to keep faith with the highway. But if I didn't trust in Him or Her, or whoever my god might be, where was I?

The Racing Biker

On a slip road to the A1 was the short answer. At 10.15, with skies positively frowning, I shrugged off the rucksack and stumped it down on the verge, but thought I'd better relieve myself before thumbing. Leaving the rucksack behind, I darted behind a bridge support for a quick slash, only to hear a vehicle brake sharply, seconds later. What? A lift by proxy! I zipped up double quick, and poked my head round the support to see a bald-headed chap about to rustle the rucksack. A lightning strike. Unbelievable. 'OK, mate,' I mouthed. 'I'm all right, thanks.'

He muttered something, dropped the rucksack, scuttled back to his van and made a quick getaway. If he'd run off with it, would he have launched an enquiry into the missing owner? Not bleedin' likely. The only in-depth investigation would have been into the contents. Timing is king. Seconds either way change everything. Short pee: up ladder. Long pee: down snake. *My* god was looking after me. Good god. What the shifty man thought of his I shall never know.

It was dark enough to be evening, but not yet eleven, when another van shone a light … well, stopped. A breezy young chap but, like Dawn, possibly breaking into his forties, leaned over. 'I'm heading for Morpeth. OK?'

In I jumped, straight to an account of Kevin's hitchhiking. Past hitchhikers are all too ready to give a lift and tell their stories. Kevin's real love was biking, but he broke down in Brussels once and had to hitchhike. He was picked up by a mechanic from the GB racing team. Even better news was that the mechanic had a mobile home abroad and Kevin could have the use of it whenever he raced in the area.

That turnaround opened his eyes. Kevin's ambition was to bike round the world. 'There's more to life than working,' he said. 'People think you gotta make as much as you can, but you can get by.' A friend of his who'd been working in a kibbutz hitched from Israel to Newcastle and it only cost him 27p. Kevin hadn't had what he'd call an education. He delivered stationery now. 'I'm happy to go along with what I'm doing. *Go with the flow and good things follow,*' he said.

I nodded vigorously. 'Couldn't put it better myself.' **Tenet Eighteen** caught the tide. 'But education – putting thinking before feeling – can stop the flow,' I said. 'Sometimes you need to feel your way to what's right.' Higher education doesn't suit everyone. I told Kevin about Raymond Brown, one of the more disruptive pupils I had the displeasure of teaching. He waltzed into my class not long after leaving school at sixteen and presented me with a couple of sea bass. The fish were one catch but what else had he gained? A few months on a fishing boat netted some good sense. He spoke with a maturity he'd never shown before and I've been sold on sea bass ever since.

'I got offered a job when I left school,' Kevin said, 'and bought a house by the time I was twenty – only because I could.'

'There you are. Bit different now though,' I said.

What shook him was losing a few relatives to cancer, and young at that. 'I tell my kids – the girl's sixteen and my son's eleven – do what you can when you can.'

After Kevin said he lived at Heddon-on-the-Wall, I confessed to my own opportunism near there. 'I'd been walking Hadrian's Wall Path and my boots were killing me. I decided to knock on doors till I found someone with an old pair of sandals. But the first door I knocked was already partly open and what did I see at the bottom of the stairs? Two pairs of sandals! One knock was enough. Mind you, it took a round of drinks at the local pub to clinch a pair.'

'I enjoy listening to people who respect others,' he said.

Dry humour from Kevin? Cadging sandals off unsuspecting householders hardly qualified as respect. Perhaps the drinks did. 'Hey, Edinburgh:103 miles,' I said, as we zoomed past a sign. 'Will I make it tonight?'

'I reckon,' Kevin said. 'Good luck's catching.'

The Loss Adjustment

Back on the road, it was rethink time. Though Kevin's optimism had been contagious, I was still adjusting to my lucky break. My rucksack was a collector's item now but I had to earn my luck as much as capitalise on it. Life on the edge called for balance. I invested in some legwork. A spell of hitching mentor Matthew's swaggering did my state of mind a power of good and when the A1 downsized to a single carriageway beyond Morpeth a grassy verge put me in touch with the earth.

I had to stop when I came across a roadkill bird, dead for some time judging by its coldness. Apart from its colour, it could have passed for a kingfisher, so similar was it in size, form and type of bill. A soft blue-grey back and cap were underlined by a strident black stripe that darted all the way from the neck and across its eyes, impelling the dagger-like bill to action, if it could.

Then I remembered. I'd last seen this bird as part of a college study: a nuthatch working tree trunks and branches for insects, seeds and nuts. I admired its agility and incisiveness. I placed it back amongst the leaf litter. With its underside matching the autumnal shades of the leaves, you'd hardly have known it was there.

Stooping down, I spotted those other hallmarks of autumn: horse chestnuts. They revived childhood memories. Steeping conkers in vinegar was only one of the tactics supposed to increase one's winning chances. But seeing them as glorified coshes, what did I miss? Looking through adult eyes, I was seduced by the tortoiseshell mottling of the greeny brown husks. Prising the split in one apart, I luxuriated in the rich mahogany varnish of the conker and the white chalky dusting over the central scar. When I winkled out the conker, the husk separated into three segments, exposing the dewy white velvet of the pith bed, so delicate that one touch was enough to sully it.

Was there anything to rival the first sight of that pristine freshness, the rich gloss, or the fragile filminess? Too soon those looks would fade away and memory degrade the flush of newness. But perhaps there were compensations. Without loss, would we look afresh at what we once thought we knew? Or owned? Or loved? I toyed with another tenet. But dwelling on life's transience took me to depths too deep. I pieced together the conker and eased it into a rucksack pocket, along with two other husks, unopened.

The Would-be Jet-Skier

Looking afresh wasn't a bad idea. The sky was lifting and I'd waited at the next slip road long enough. Seeing a weasel scurry into some bushes at close to 12.30, I reckoned it was time to move on. I thumbed as I walked, flouting two of Matthew's ground rules: find a lay-by; stand still. But I did keep turning to face the traffic. When a hulking great containerised lorry shuddered to a stop by the side of the road, I snatched at the door as readily as any bet-hedging punter grabs his winnings. I'd struck lucky. The driver was going all the way to Berwick-upon-Tweed.

'Fifty miles or thereabouts,' he said.

I tried explaining what I was doing but here was a man who's just survived a long day's night, and is talking his way through to today from a white stubbly chin.

'I'm a woollyback,' he says. 'Ye heard of that? Or sheep shagger if ye like. 'S'what they call any 'un from Portsmouth.'

'Ah, right.' With such a descriptive line in self-deprecation – though he makes the nicknames sound like badges of office – Tink is a man I can respect. But the way he speaks, I'd never guess he's from the south. He ought to be Irish from the name he's given. But he doesn't 'tink' either.

He's only been working for the last five years. Before that, he was on the dole. 'Twelve years, that was. Best job I never 'ad. Been on th'oil rigs. After the army, that was. Drink driving 'uz the trouble. Got done fer it and lost me licence,' he gabbles.

I'm pretty befuddled myself till I figure it out: the army came first, the drink, then the rigs. Forward thinking is far from Tink's mind. He's into his golden years.

'Went fishing regular then. If yer after salmon, best time's August to October when them's spawnin'. Trappin' rabbits and shootin' pheasants 'uz a good life. An' I made wine. Gor. Lived like a lord, I did.' And with some lip-smacking, 'Roast pheasant in white wine sauce. Can't beat it.'

Was he better off then?

'Nah. Better now. But I've sold out to capitalism. I've sold meself.' And Tink looks troubled. 'What's in it for this mate of mine who's a schizo, with a wife and four kids. What can 'e do? Have a bet an' a couple of pints, watch telly when 'e gets home, smoke a few joints, an' what else? An' who cares? Know what I mean?'

I think I do. The situation sounds pretty hopeless. How did Tink pull things round?

'Aw. Could 'ave giv'n in. Me father 'uz alcoholic an' I might 'ave gone the same way. But no. I said, sod it an' did th'opposite.'

That must have been after the drink-driving then. I put the slight slur in Tink's speech down to hung-over habits. But he's articulate enough in his cussedness.

'I was radical in me twenties,' he says. 'BNP an' all that.'

It's still not rubbed off. He's got a low opinion of politicians.

'They go to topless clubs,' he says. 'I've seen 'em.' And he follows that up with, 'The government's taken away yer freedom of speech by givin' it. Call some 'un a nigger an' you get arrested.' He knows of a comedian in Scotland who wears a Union Jack kilt and turban, and tells jokes about Indians and Pakis. 'But if 'e was white, he'd get arrested. An' look at Sikhs. They don't 'ave to wear crash helmets, just turbans.' He has a suggestion: 'We should wear Union Jack turbans. 'Ow about that?'

Tink looks close to triumph.

But he feels sorry for Asians. 'They 'ave to duck down fer the actions of others. Know what I mean?' Then there's more revolutionary talk. He despatches Iraq with 'We should have nuked it. Poof.' His fingers explode.

A quick jerk of the head in my direction to check I'm still on board and he's quoting sources. A friend of his had worked as a bodyguard on escort duties, from the airport to Baghdad. 'Supposed to be no-go areas in Baghdad – but Moss Side ain't no different – an' good things 'appen in Iraq we don't know about. Lots o' things work. My mate: 'e 'ad no problems.'

At least he's painted the other side of the picture.

'There, look at that.' Tink is more observant than I am, sweeping a hand out to sea. 'Holy Island. Ain't that grand.' For a moment I'm lost in space till he beams me down with, 'An' bet you they ain't talking about Iraq out there. "Ow's yer bulbs doing and what's up with yer parsnips?" more like.'

If I wanted on-board entertainment, Tink knows how to supply it. But that Holy Island sighting has sent *him* somewhere else. He tells me about his taste in lobsters and how he still goes fishing. 'Perch, trout, mackerel, whiting, herring, cod.' He reels them off. 'An' there's nothing like a piece of venison. Know what I'd do if I came across a deer on the road?'

I'm well on the way to guessing.

'Make straight fer it.'

The sun rescues me from my wince. 'See that,' I say. 'It's breaking through at last.' A shaft of light is playing on the waters.

'Where I wanna be,' Tink says. 'Jet-skiing's what I really fancy. Gotta get one.'

Hard as I try to picture Tink on a jet ski I can't, but he says it with a determination that defies doubt. Everything Tink says is so emphatic that miles have missed me and suddenly Berwick's in sight. A bit late in the day I hand him my card.

He takes a quick look. 'Shelley,' he notes. 'Any relation?'

'Don't think so, or very distant.'

'That Mary Shelley dreamed up Frankenstein, didn't she: at

Whitby that was, seein' the mists roll in.' Tink sounds almost erudite. 'Now they 'ave the Dracula Experience. An' you should see the Japanese. Too scared to go in one door an' come out t'other.' Tink laughs – a sort of gruff chuckle – and the bristles on his chin twitch infectiously.

He's got it in for the Japs now, has he? But there's more to this man than prejudice. Cussedness, with anarchic relish, is taking him places. Jet-skiing? Why not? He'd certainly give the monks something else to think about when, full of revolutionary fervour, he fizzed past Holy Island.

'Not far to Edinburgh,' Tink tells me, as he drops me off. 'One and a quarter hours'll get you there.' We shake on it, like a pact.

The Sticking Point

But the first thing I do is break it. A short walk away is a Morrison's Supermarket and half an hour later my head's stuck in a cappuccino. Tink's 'sod it' comes back to me. That's how he ditched the drink … supposedly. But if 'sod it' can do the trick, why not? It's committal, a 'no' with a shovel, burying something where sods belong.

What do I want to kick? Expectations, or having to live up to them – like Edinburgh in one and a quarter hours. That target stopped me enjoying this cappuccino, even as I drank it. And, if I don't make Edinburgh in time, I'll have lost twice: this enjoyment and that satisfaction. But you can only stare at dregs so long. 'Sod it.'

I yank the rucksack back on my shoulders when a chap sitting opposite says, 'And where're you off to?'

'Edinburgh hopefully,' I say, 'hitching.'

'Ah, you want to make for Pitlochry,' he urges. 'Beautiful country. A wee bit further but worth it.' And he waxes on about the great times he's had thereabouts.

Only after I say, 'Oh yes, I must,' does the irony dawn on me: I've taken on a new expectation. I set off again with a good two hours of daylight left. The landscape is boundless as never before, virtually devoid of trees, but pervaded by the vast presence of the North Sea on my right. And a vast absence of traffic.

I can see the odd car or lorry approaching from miles away. But

I'm a tiny comma in the land of an open book to drivers. Thumb too soon and I'm a punctuating irrelevance. Thumb too late and I'm an irritating afterthought. My timing is never right. No-one stops. Too visible for too long, I've lost the element of surprise. But after twenty minutes or so solid trudging, I'm drawn to one light on the horizon: a sign, at first sight indecipherable, at second worth a wild whoop – 'Scotland Welcomes You'. Yoo-hoo! Do I welcome Scotland. I never imagined the border this close. And from that moment, I decide: no lift till I cross the line.

At 2.52 p.m. on Friday, November 17th, nine days after leaving the Lizard, I jump from England – this side of the sign, to Scotland – that side. It's an entry in my notebook but a poor substitute for a passport stamp. Others came prepared. The sign is plastered with stickers, mostly bizarre. 'Death Skateboards' terminated here. 'Hardcore Hobbies' were extremely crafty and 'Barham is the happiest place on the Murray', wherever that is.

My first experience of Scotland's welcome is not so happy. Over the crest of a hill, I'm battling with a harsh onshore wind, whipping my rucksack and whacking me sideways. With the light failing, I need somewhere to camp. There's some level grassland in the lea of a railway line but huddles of sheep have lodged claims to the best sites. Then, after a six or seven mile tramp, a promise of respite from this icy blast: a sign which reads 'Burnmouth'. And I'll take 'burn' to mean excessive warmth rather than a Scottish stream, if you don't mind.

I wrestle the wind down the road to the village, which sits in a valley leading to the sea, and latch on to the first B & B sign – White Craggs – and a mercury-rousing welcome. Maureen, the landlady, greets me with carrot and coriander soup, a huge teapot, a microwave to heat up my vegetable pasty, a gas-fired lounge with sofa and footstool, oh and a hot water bottle for later. Heaven!

From the house I can pick out Holy Island and Bamburgh Castle and, sitting down in the lounge, feet up, I dip into *The Power of Now*. Page 29 leaps out: 'Whatever the present moment contains, accept it as if you had chosen it. Always work with it; not against it. This will miraculously transform your whole life.' I'll settle for that. Edinburgh can wait. The present is working with me: White Craggs is perfect. But have I been simplistic in thinking about expectations? You have to set goals of course. I've written endless lists of things to do and be done by in the past. And I have to expect that I'll reach Dunnet Head in six days' time (there's a ferry to catch), or I wouldn't make the effort.

Maybe it's not expectations I'm railing against as much as the predictability that goes with them. I want a choice of moves: 'what if I do this?', 'what if I don't?' and 'what if I do that instead?' And I want chance to challenge my thinking. The road of reason is too often the plodding, pedestrian one. Hitchhiking's fed my taste for the unexpected. Even down to the horse chestnuts I picked up … which reminds me: I have two to prise open.

On my way to fetch them I meet Maureen. We reminisce. I recall some of the people on this trip, including the sculptor whose drowning figure so impressed me, and she recollects a visit to Ellis Island in the US where early immigrants were processed. She saw a sculpture there of a man being pulled out of the sea, symbolic of the way immigrants were helped to get a foothold in America.

Horse chestnuts seem less important after that. But opening them up in the lounge, I'm astonished. Where I thought conkers were uniform in colour, I notice darker flashes across the surface and markings like contour lines on a map. And where I'd have said that conkers were more or less round, these forms are far more varied, being flattish or dimpled in places and humped in others. Round ones were the currency in my conker-bashing days. That's what nobbled my thinking.

Accepting the present as if you had chosen it is one thing. Appreciating what's in front of you is something else. But ditching stereotypes you're hardly aware of is an awesome challenge. Sometimes you need a reason to look to realise you've never seen. Stick-on labels don't do it.

[DAY NINE]

Day Ten

Burnmouth to South Queensferry

'If chance posed the questions, perhaps it provided the answers'

The First and Last

I woke at twenty to seven. Streaks of condensation ran down the window, the telltale signs of hastily washed smalls left to dry on the radiator. What *would* Maureen think? Mopping up was one reason to jump out of bed. What really fired me up was Edinburgh: not getting there so much but what to do when I arrived. On my only previous visit I'd been impressed with the sense of pride in its architecture, culture and history. How to approach it now? Newcastle had clued me up. *Set a goal but let chance show the way.* It pointed to **Tenet Nineteen**.

My plan, if I had one, was this: see what grabbed my attention, follow it up to find what message chance conveyed. Would it tell me where to go? Something I needed to know? Or would chance be playing games? I couldn't wait.

Over breakfast Maureen told me about the fate of a local pub, the Flemington Inn. There'd been a feud between two local men, one of whom was the publican's son. His adversary took revenge on the pub. I'd seen the gutted remains. The arsonist had been caught and imprisoned but a sign still displayed the unfortunate tag: 'First and Last Inn – Scotland'.

Whether it was the mention of 'first and last' I don't know but Maureen spoke about her mother. 'She was a bit of a hypochondriac, always going on to me about her ills. But she'd be joking with others, as though nothing was the matter.' When she died, her mother's last words before slumping to one side were, 'I've got … ' What she had would never be known. How many have passed away in mid-sentence? How many others wish they hadn't started one?

A sight I didn't want to miss, after the tantalising glimpses from Tink's lorry, was Holy Island. I climbed to a vantage point behind White Craggs. The wind had dropped, leaving only the swell of the sea to stir the stillness. The sun was rising through a golden white band of sky that lined the horizon, casting shades of copper and bronze across the bank of cloud above. A tapering finger of land poked into the sea, and way in the distance a hazy sunlight suffused Holy Island like a swathe of mist. It was a sight I was loath to leave. I could only imagine how it felt to be there on this magical of mornings, with a lot more than parsnips to wax lyrical about.

The Frustrated Gardener

It was 9.15 before I wrenched myself away from Maureen's hospitality and set off with mist still in my eyes. Though it was Saturday morning I had no illusions about getting a quick lift. It took a two-mile march up the A1 for another knight of the road to come to my rescue. I felt distinctly deferential looking up to 'Sir' Tommy when he said, 'Where're ye going?'

'Making for Edinburgh. That all right?'

'Aye. We'll nae be far from there. Climb in.'

It was hard holding back a victory salute.

Tommy took the job of driving a LiDL supermarket lorry seriously, wearing the well co-ordinated look of a uniform. His cap reminded me of schooldays, though a gold cipher on the peak suggested a public school. An emerald green shirt collar lapped neatly over a Lincoln green jacket and, even if the red seat belt didn't match, it could have passed for a sash of honour.

Our conversation opened the pages of a lorry driving biography. He'd worked twenty-seven years for a local council which put him in for HGV driving initially to help with the winter gritting. When services were privatised, he switched to this job, alternating between five eight-hour shifts a week and four twelve-hour ones.

Even though there wasn't much traffic he kept checking the mirrors.

'Aye. Ye look every ten or fifteen seconds,' he said, 'what's at back and sides.' His company had taken on thirty Polish drivers. 'Ach, they'd work twenty-four hours a day if ye let 'em. Some o' the lorries been damaged 'cause of their driving. Cost fifteen thousand pounds' – he weighted the words – 'to sort out two wagons.'

It was like sitting next to a reborn Tink with Poles in the line of fire now.

The road skirted the sea as we approached a town. 'Sunny Dunbar,' Tommy said, 'Ha ha.' A solid bank of cloud had outflanked the early burst of sunshine.

I wondered what he liked to do in his spare time.

'Caravanning'd be all right,' he said, 'but it's gardening mostly.' He grew tomatoes and flowers: marigolds and begonias. 'I'd grow turnips and cabbage but it's young kids that's the trouble.' Trouble was they pulled them out. 'It's senseless,' he said. 'I wouldn'a mind if they ate 'em. They've nae respect for the police, stealing cars day after day. All they do is joyride and wreck 'em. And get awa' with it.'

The kids were the clouds over Tommy's garden.

'How would they feel?' he complained helplessly.

They wouldn't, would they. It's a sad enough comment on the way some kids are brought up that a chap can't grow his own turnips.

Tommy kept tabs on things. Like temperature: 'Minus three last night.' Visibility: 'It's nae clear enough to see the ferry.' And time: 'I'm a wee bit early' when we passed the Cockenzie Power Station. The best was distance. 'Yere nae far now,' 'Sir' Tommy said, good as his word, when he pulled up on the very outskirts of Edinburgh.

The Scottish Fiddler

I had to get my bearings, so started poring over my map on the sloping exit road from the A1. I'd just about worked out where I was – at the junction with the A720 – when a car drew up.

'Can I help?' offered the incredibly helpful girl at the wheel.

'Well, I'm just wondering about the route into Edinburgh.'

My Samaritan had a three-mile trip into the city and could drop me off anywhere en route. After I explained my reasons for hitching, she told me she played the Scottish fiddle and was studying music in the community. That made sense. I could see the musician in her: the dark, lively hair with an arpeggio of ringlets; the expressive fingers; and the name, Gica.

'I'm so lucky to be working in Portobello,' she said. 'It's a suburb of Edinburgh and very grounded.'

What did she mean?

'Well, we have activities going on for all ages. The community works together. That's important: to get everyone involved. Youth can so easily be disenfranchised.'

'Tommy's turnips,' I blurted. Before Gica could look baffled, I explained.

'Yes, it helps so much if there are plenty of things to do. Where we are, the older people keep an eye on the young and look after them. Makes such a difference.'

Gica's environment sounded so wholesome.

'It's really great. I couldn't be happier.' She played in a ceilidh band and loved it. 'I tell you what gives me a thrill: when everyone's dancing, and the musicians and dancers are as one. There's nothing to beat that feeling.'

'You've found it then?' I said. 'Your direction?'

'This is how it works,' she said. 'In finding my direction, I'm giving others direction. That's what's so satisfying.'

And stunningly self-evident. 'If only more people found theirs,' I said.

Aargh. We had to break off. Gica needed to know where to drop me. The very time she asked was probably the very time to act. 'Here,' I said suddenly. With one pull of a door handle I was on the pavement and Gica was away. The parting was cruelly abrupt, but one of the shortest lifts felt like the most profound.

The Sheepish Look

The Fates were on my side. It had only just gone eleven, Gica's insights were a great trailer for Edinburgh and the unthumbed lift heightened my sense of anticipation. Where would the next throw of the dice take me? What would catch my eye? When I came to some pedestrian lights on London Road, I decided to cross: except they were at red. A pimply-faced chap sidled up with a generously studded girl. Chance had arrived: I launched into my opening gambit.

'Excuse me. Is there anything I must do or see while I'm in Edinburgh?'

No flinching. No hesitation. Their answers were unanimous.

'Starbucks.' 'Yes, Starbucks.' And the lights changed.

But there was a beep ... beep of disbelief from me. What? Here was this great city, the Athens of the North, with a prodigious artistic reputation, formidable history, rich architectural heritage, and the main attraction: Starbucks? Ridiculous!

Where did I go from here? On this side of the road was a rank of shops. I could window-shop, couldn't I? The Art Mart had half a dozen paintings on display, ready for my next tactic. Which would I buy? Flitting over a picture of a woman looking at an old Greek monastery, I alighted on ... Highland View.

Why? What exactly *had* caught my eye? Windows opened to a stylised landscape of rolling hills, leading to distant peaks and clusters of cloud bubbles. The scene had the dreamlike quality of a Chagall. But what absorbed me most were two sheep in the foreground. One stared towards the half-open windows with a quizzical look. The other sheep was oblivious, chomping away at some grass.

Explanatory notes accompanied the picture. *Highland View* was by Jerzy Marek. Born in 1925 in Poland, he'd been a UK resident since 1948. He formed the Marek Circle in Preston, encouraging self-taught artists in the North-West. His paintings often featured animals with 'weird and enigmatic expressions'.

Intriguing: the word 'enigmatic' evoked the memory of that picture at Francesca's and the two figures on the terrace. I couldn't help comparing the scenes. Open door – open windows. Distant view of sea – distant view of hills. Two people – two sheep. The similarities didn't stop there. One sheep looked at the viewer. So had the raffish musician. The other sheep was oblivious. So too the woman, engrossed in her knitting. The two paintings were uncannily alike.

What did this tell me about chance? Had something else registered subconsciously? Tommy talked about Polish drivers: Jerzy Marek was Polish. The artist had helped others: I'd been helped by Poles. In the 60s I visited Poland, subdued then by the dead hand of communism. A warm-hearted fellow, Henryk, invited me to his Warsaw home, a small flat where I met his wife, Sofia, and two teenage sons. They insisted I stay, and sleep in the one bedroom while they made do in the living room and kitchen. The hospitality was overwhelming. The boys took me on a tour of the city and thrust a book of Canaletto's paintings in my hands. We kept in touch for many years, and the generous spirit of that family is still with me, as is that book.

What did all this mean? Well, there was no likelihood of my buying *Highland View*. Not for £975. And there wasn't much chance to my choice either. Past connections – the enigmatic picture and the Poles – predisposed me to pick *Highland View*. But I'd be heading for the Highlands. That must have had some bearing too. My choice had inevitability splashed all over it. Where *was* this game of chance leading me? To challenge the role of chance? I had no idea how random other experiences had been or how subject to pre-selection by the subconscious. But if chance posed the questions, perhaps it provided the answers.

[DAY TEN]

The Unconnected Sculptures

I carried on down London Road until I reached a roundabout. The Roman Catholic cathedral was on the far side and an alternative place of worship, the sleek, glass-fronted Omni Centre, on my left, only an 'a' short of containing everything – *omnia* – that devotees of leisure pleasure might seek, with a gym, twelve-screen cinema, comedy club and all manner of eateries and themed bars. But the incongruity of what stood outside captured my attention: two giraffes, the adult about twenty feet high, and its offspring – metal sculptures mounted on the pavement and defying connection with everything around, except each other … and my mind.

Giraffes were one big attraction on childhood visits to Bristol Zoo. But so were a bison with its monstrously huge head and the legendary gorilla, Alfred. I always wanted to know what went on behind those eyes of his.

I sauntered over to the sculptures where an inscription read:

Giraffes!
A people who live between earth and skies,
each in his own religious steeple,
keeping a lighthouse with his eyes

A being as a holy edifice: that was a thought. Perhaps the giraffes complemented the cathedral, and eyes cropping up yet again: lighthouse eyes. How might the world look from their elevated perspective? There were so many ways of looking. Even as I thought it, I realised what I hadn't seen: that the giraffes were assemblages of car and motorbike parts. Incredible: that someone could see such possibilities in scrap metal and fashion from it a giraffe's grace and elegance.

I crossed the road towards the cathedral only to be halted by a giant foot: another sculpture, this one by Eduardo Paolozzi. Rigid bands shackling the foot made me curious. A passer-by knew that Paolozzi was Scottish by birth, but of Italian parentage. He thought the shackled foot was a comment on Paolozzi's internment during World War Two. I saw it as a symbol of imprisoned souls anywhere, from the earliest victims of the slave trade to those incarcerated at Guantanamo.

I took the road which led to the Firth of Forth, and on to the Highlands, toying with two conflicting images: the 'lighthouse' of the giraffe and the 'dark house' of the imprisoned. What to make of them? Different visions, brought together. By my choice. By chance? And different possibilities, brought together. The giraffe sculptor marrying scrap metal to the giraffe and Paolozzi combining shackles with a foot to make a powerful metaphor. *Making different connections leads to new discoveries*. That was it … **Tenet Twenty**. And time to ditch the one-sided thinking that took me along the same old tracks. I had to let chance open up new choices. Like Starbucks!

The Three Choices

Sadly, I didn't pass Starbucks, but made one decision straightaway: that was the last tenet. They'd served their purpose, charting my way here. I was in new territory now, literally and metaphorically, ready to embrace chance and whatever changes of outlook lay ahead. But there are no signposts to the unexpected … unless you count the board I bumped into on Queen Street:

> a play
> a pie
> and
> a pint
> making a drama out of lunchtime

Three choices in one! Brilliant: I didn't hesitate. This was The Jam House. Trialled in Glasgow, the concept proved such a hit that lunchtime shows were launched in Edinburgh. Today's performance was *Excuse My Dust*, based on the life of Dorothy Parker, the American poet and wit. I knew next to nothing about her – all the more reason for finding out. I paid the modest ten pounds to book a seat at the informal table-and-chairs arrangement. The play started at five past one and I could collect my pie and pint just before. That left me some time.

'What can I do in forty minutes?' I asked a couple in the queue.

'Why not pop into the National Portrait Gallery,' the bespectacled man said. 'That's what we're doing. It's just down the road.'

I'd been so lost in my musings that the imposing neo-Gothic facade had escaped me. Admission was free. Great. Where would I go?

'Is this the way to the twentieth century?' I asked one attendant, then turned to the couple behind – the same ones I'd spoken to minutes before – and made some glib remark about it being hard to stay in the present, before proceeding to the first floor.

What could I see in less than forty minutes? Shortness of time concentrates the mind. After the Art Mart and sculpture experiences, I opted for a quick zip round the paintings but this time there'd be multiple choices: I'd shortlist three and see what chance would throw up. Would the subconscious play a part?

My instincts took me straight to workers in the North Sea oil industry: a set of portraits by Fiona Carlisle, painted with a raw urgency. She must have caught people between shifts. One broad-shouldered man with bristly beard and moustache stood out in a bright orange 'Total' jumpsuit. That was it! Orange had been my favourite colour ever since a friend persuaded me to buy an orange Ford Escort. 'Orange for courage,' he said. This man exuded grit and guts. The painting put a human face to a resource we take as much for granted as the risks many run in winning it from the sea-bed. I'd remember the orange man when I filled my tank.

A shadowy background and three spectral figures drew me to the second picture. Why were they treated in this rather ghostly manner? The painting – by Ken Currie – was entitled *The Oncologists*: three professors, one of whom had discovered the so-called 'guardian angel' gene that triggers the suicide of cancerous cells. One held a medical implement. Another had traces of blood on his hands. All turned round abruptly, the startled look on their faces synonymous with the fear of the unknown felt by any newly diagnosed patient. Had that triggered a memory?

My father kept my mother's cancer a secret in the eighteen months before she died. Out of an imagined kindness he might have asked doctors to keep it quiet too. This painting was in no way flattering, but the artist's frank treatment of the real subject, cancer, was as commendable as the professors' presumed acceptance of it.

Oil worker, cancer specialists, and who next? My gallery tour was like a mini hitchhike with a difference: I, or my subconscious, decided which lift to accept. Time was short. I latched on to a painting I'd glimpsed earlier. A face floated over a room, like a doubly exposed photograph. The portrait by Calum Colvin was of James McMillan, 'one of Britain's most highly regarded young composers'.

Highly regarded he might be, but his head spanned a table, his nose cut a corner and an anglepoise lamp swung across his hairline. A table leg pierced his chin. With discarded manuscript sheets strewn all over the floor, it looked as though he'd been in the act of composing. At last my subconscious hadn't dredged up any connection, I thought.

Consumed by the prospects of a pie and pint, I hurried back to The Jam House. It had filled up fast but sitting at one table were the couple who told me about the National Portrait Gallery. 'Mind if I sit here?' I said, with one hand on a spare chair. I hauled off my rucksack, joined the queue at the bar for my pint, collected a very respectable steak pie and repaired to the table. Then I slung my bulky jacket over the back of the chair, only to watch helplessly while the contents of its pockets – maps, notebook, throwaway camera, pens, postcards, money – cascaded on to the floor.

The Sideshow

Seeing me scrabbling about for my belongings, my companions must have wondered what kind of wreckage had washed up at their table. They couldn't have known about the inner turmoil. Once I'd re-composed myself and hung the jacket on the back of the chair, we were into polite introductions.

'Alex and Jocelyn.'

A shake of the hands. 'Hallo again. Delighted. I'm Laurence.'

They didn't ask what I was up to but I had to explain. I tried to invest my mission with an aura of inclusiveness. 'I've met people from all walks of life,' I said. 'Top executives to drifters, all with their own stories.' And proceeded to colour some of them in, including a blow-by-blow account of Tink's contribution.

I thought my report was entertaining, but Jocelyn looked uneasy and turned to Alex. Blotches reddened on his cheeks as their exchange of views became more animated. I was beginning to feel like last man in a Chinese whispers game when Jocelyn clarified, '*We* wouldn't pick up hitchhikers.' The words were definitive. Perhaps I should have back-pedalled a bit on my exploits. She cited some friends' experience. 'Rob and Jenny picked up one hitchhiker and he had the cheek to ask them for money.'

Well I never! I made disapproving noises and changed the subject to the Portrait Gallery, thanking them for the suggestion and broaching my short list. But they saw nothing worth singling out. We did agree on the pie though – pastry nice and crisp, good chunks of steak, and gravy not too gooey.

Jocelyn did most of the talking that came my way when I wasn't filling in the silence with sips of beer. Beneath her rather bland eau-de-nil cardigan, the collar of a wildly spotted blouse peeped out, like the first flush of spring bedding. Was there a lighter side to Jocelyn? And, while Alex was greying at the edges and receding, he did have the quiet presence of a thinking man, someone who might be keeping a secret diary, or plotting an alternative life. There was something elusive about this couple that I wanted to capture. I'd left the camera lying on the table. In a moment of unthinking madness I grabbed it and said, 'How about a photo?'

Jocelyn assumed a look of incredulity that a hardened sceptic wouldn't have disbelieved. And Alex's blotches were growing distinctly rosy when she said, with the 'whoa' of an upturned hand, 'No. No, Laurence, thank you. If you *don't* mind.'

'Not at all,' I crumbled. I wasn't so much out on a limb as falling off the branch. Thank God *Excuse My Dust* was about to start.

The scene opens in a bedroom and Dorothy Parker (actress Lesley Mackie) strolls on stage in dressing gown and slippers to a bluesy jazz number. But I'm fixated by the table: it's the same style and proportion as in the James McMillan painting. There's a bottle on it, a typewriter and dial-up phone, but a stack of books and desk lamp too. While the drama turns to the workings of Dorothy's mind, I can't detach from what's going on in mine. There's no disconnecting from connections.

Being misunderstood pains her. Most people know her only for one or two poetic witticisms, such as the famous, 'Men seldom make passes at girls who wear glasses.' There's a lot more to her than that, she tells us.

I'm thinking what little this couple have said, for me to form any opinion. Have I misjudged them?

Dorothy sprawls on the bed. We hear about her unhappy past. She lost her mother at five and loathed her father so much she didn't even attend his funeral. Having found solace in writing, she became a literary critic but hated reviewing. We see her screwing up what she's written. There's a parallel with the men in her lives. She wants love but, unsurprisingly after her childhood experience, relationships get screwed up. Only two men – one was Scott Fitzgerald – ever meant anything to her.

I wonder what brought these two together. Odd people get on, I think. She talks. He listens. One complements. One compromises. But for how long?

Next we see Dorothy getting dolled up for a romantic night out at the theatre. She loves dressing-up, the fame, the glitter. It's all on show, except that she's chosen a black ensemble – slinky black frock, black fur wrap, black shoes. The only relief is a feather hat. We guess it won't work out. It doesn't. She returns disenchanted yet again and her mood blackens, helped by a bottle of bourbon.

Are they married? Perhaps not. Or perhaps they are, but not to each other. A lunchtime tryst would suit. At a play, perfect. That's why the photo was such a no-no. Of course.

But Dorothy strikes a defiant note; there's a feeling that despite everything her spirit will win through. Even if fated in love, she talks as if she's outside herself looking in, as if that 'she' is in the past. There lies hope.

The actress does a superb job, bringing Dorothy Parker to life and getting fulsome applause for her solo performance. I'm awestruck by her memory feat: an hour's worth of lines unprompted. But it's the insight into this woman's journey that I applaud. Dorothy's witticisms stand alone – that's the irony – but, set against the sad paradox of her conflict-ridden life, they are so much more telling.

Back at the table, we collected ourselves. I had questions I couldn't ask but, in the few moments left, I wanted to hear from Alex. 'What d'you make of that then?'

'Not what I expected,' he said.

No ... but? I willed him to add to the postscript. Nothing came of it. If I hadn't been on best behaviour, I'd have laughed myself silly. What *did* he expect?

'You can't beat live theatre, can you?' I said, turning to Jocelyn. 'Have you seen anything recently that's made an impression?'

She hardly hesitated. 'Oh yes, Turandot.'

'Because …?'

'Well, the heroine looked like the back of a bus but Casanova was still after her.'

I spluttered in vain. Jocelyn's bruising humour had a killer punch and a stifled laugh sounds much more explosive when it breaks out than one that has free passage. Suitably encouraged, I turned back to Alex. 'Is there anything you've read or seen that picks itself out?'

Alex lit up. '*Weekend*: I've just read it. By William McIlvanney. His latest. It's about these characters who meet up for a weekend together. They all have objectives for the weekend and you want to see whether they achieve them or not. The character development is very good. You really get an insight into them as individuals.'

What! Where did that come from? Shock wasn't the word. It was as if Alex had suddenly opened a page of his secret diary. 'I must read it,' I said.

The Review

Heading up Queen Street, I'm amazed Alex said *that* much but still disappointed I learned so little about them both. Behaving like one of the paparazzi couldn't have helped. Perhaps I expect too much. I've come to take people's openness for granted. Cars jolt words out of lift-givers. Alex and Jocelyn weren't the sort to take risks. I had to respect that. But when I can't connect, I feel disoriented.

Edinburgh's been all about connections: the sheep painting, that composer's table, the orange car and the 'orange' man portrait, my mother's illness with the cancer picture, oh and the nostalgia trip to the zoo that the giraffes triggered off. I've been zapped by connections, but isn't that the way one makes sense of things? The more connections, the greater the meaning one tenet went, as I remember. But less meaningful if they keep taking you back. Learn from the past, yes, but move on.

And I am! I'm traipsing along Queensferry Road now, leaving Edinburgh behind step by step. But I've seen nothing of its great architecture, not even the new Parliament building. The least I can do is buy a postcard. So when I spot The Blackhall Grocery Store I try my luck.

'You've come to the right place,' the owner says, pointing to a stand.

I settle for a picture of red and yellow tulips in a cheery salute to the soaring Edinburgh Castle. 'Oh, and bananas,' I add, picking up a couple of spotty ones.

'You can 'ave 'em,' he says.

There's nothing like a small goodwill gesture for generating a huge rush of … misplaced optimism. I'm hitching again, brandishing a banana as stand-in for a thumb. The trouble is no-one takes me seriously and I polish off the bananas before they turn as rotten as the idea. Thumbing is fruitless too.

I resign myself to hiking. I want to get to the Firth of Forth tonight – about four miles on – but it's dusk by the time I've kissed Edinburgh goodbye and a sign scuppers my progress: 'Pedestrians not allowed. Please use slip road'. I don't want to be siphoned off. No time to deliberate: a bus looms out of the darkness. My hand shoots up as if spring-loaded and I run full tilt to the bus stop beyond. If this is a game, I've thrown a double six. I'm off to South Queensferry for £1.40. Chance! It's here again, like a wave from the world. Whether it helps me on the way I want to go or takes me in a totally different direction, chance keeps me guessing. But it's what I don't know that drives me on. I have Alex and Jocelyn to thank for that. And Edinburgh.

When we reach the town, I ask a woman brimming over the seat opposite about a B & B. She doesn't know, but the other passengers burst into life with the unanimous suggestion: 'go up the hill.' That's how I find myself at Priory Lodge with a plush double room and a field of flowers on the bed cover, adorned by the fluffiest companion, Lamont the Lamb. He begs to be sat outside the bedroom door if I do not require breakfast, but is baa... nishing smokers and threatening miscreants with a £25 fine for the dry cleaning bill. I wish I could blame him for the droppings on the floor, but he can do what he likes. I'm for an early night. And I don't have to count sheep. Well, one's enough.

[DAY TEN]

Day Eleven

South Queensferry to Kinross

'*After today a long life seems that much more of an achievement*'

The History Lesson

If I dreamt at all last night, one look at the clear blue sky and, more to the point, one raging hunger, blot out any memory. After yesterday's crash diet of a pie, a pint and two spotty bananas, breakfast can't come fast enough and kippers – my favourite – are on the menu. But when a know-it-all at the next table hears me ordering, he leans over. 'That's an all-day meal,' he says. 'You can still taste it at five o'clock.'

Good, I'm thinking.

Then his friend chips in. 'Yes. I avoid it. 'Snot fair on everyone else.'

'Well, as long as it just repeats on me,' I retort.

The kipper police might not have caught me but my eyes are running all over the room. Jumping down from the tartan table cloth, they criss-cross a tartan carpet and hop to a tartan wall-hanging. Dancing over some crossed swords, they vault a pair of antlers. Then it's a quick squint at a photograph of a thistle and a whip round some windpipes (small bagpipe) before the majestic sight of a baying stag – the *Monarch of the Glen* by Landseer no less – brings them to a halt. Phew! I've toured Scotland already, wall-to-wall.

But there's more. A full scale battle is being waged behind me. A mural tells in graphic detail the story of the Battle of Bannockburn

– 24th June, 1314. The Scots under Robert the Bruce were greatly outnumbered by the English army. But 'not of the kind to be overawed', they brought the English vanguard to a standstill. When the Scots counter-attacked they forced those at the front back on the troops behind. There was terrible confusion in the ranks, the battle became a rout 'and a fearful slaughter followed'. The English king Edward II was fortunate to escape with his life. It was a humiliating defeat.

But, just in case, there are reinforcements on the window sill: infantry and cavalry with swords at the ready. There's even the odd orator to impart moral authority to the proceedings. This is more of a shrine to Scottish history than a dining room. What would Robert the Bruce have said about it all? His picture's on the wall and he stares out from the twenty-pound notes in my wallet. The kippers were delicious but I hear him insisting, 'Nothing but porridge and salt, man. Put hairs on your chest.'

Battles are won and lost on a breakfast. But I don't want to feel like a tattered remnant of the English army. My exit is a strategic retreat while I prepare for any backlash and I'm in combative mood back in my room. One thing for sure: *I* won't be pinned down. I make a tactical decision. I won't even hitchhike. I'll cross the Firth of Forth Bridge on foot. That'll be a new experience. Reading about it in the bedroom, I'm surprised how recently it was completed, in 1964. At 1½ miles long and 500 feet high, it's one of the largest suspension bridges in the world. But it's not *the* Firth of Forth Bridge. The other one's alongside, carrying the railway. Completed in 1890 to a pioneering cantilever design, that was the biggest bridge of its day and considered the eighth wonder of the world. Of the 4600 men who worked on it, 57 died.

But what's all this about *the*? Both ought to be *a* Firth of Forth bridge. Where there's actually *a* choice, it's too easy to be definite: *the* way, *the* truth, *the* life. That's a trap I've fallen into. Right, decision number two: the indefinite article will have prime place in my headings from now on. That's definite. After all, an *a* turned the Omni Centre into everything. *Leave things indefinite and you extend possibilities.* Sounds like a tenet, doesn't it? But that was in the old days. It's all about being flexible now. Instead of trying to embody a belief system, I'm looking for something between belief and scepticism, a sort of – I've got it – suspension bridge!

There's a whiff of self-satisfaction as I pack up my belongings but I'm about to shut the door when I see Lamont the Lamb on top of the telly where I put him last night. Shall I sit him back on the bed? No. Far too predictable. I whisk him away and, with what I like to think is a wicked sense of humour, plonk him on the toilet.

I trot downstairs to settle up with the landlady. She suggests walking down to the town before I tackle the bridge. 'They're relaying the cobbles,' she says. 'Last done in 1996 but the heavy traffic dislodges them. They have to keep redoing it.'

If I need any stronger indication of Scottish pride, this is it. How many towns down south have had cobbles tarmacked over? I thank her for the hearty breakfast and comfy room. She hands me her card and my heart sinks to my boots. It's headed:

PRIORY LODGE
Mrs Calmyn Lamb
Proprietor

Oops. What have I done? It's not funny, but facetious. Whatever will she think ... of what I think?

The least I can do is take a look at the town. The cobbled streets invite a step back to a more leisurely characterful era. Dickens or Conan Doyle would be at home here. There are mysteries waiting to be written. Old lanterns perk upwards from wall-hung brackets and a raised walkway with iron railings lends one side of a street a more salubrious ambience than it might deserve. A glimpse of the railway bridge down a side alley surprises me with its dramatic closeness.

There's a chilly breeze and an all-pervading quietness that I don't understand until it dawns on me that this is Sunday. A man perusing a commemorative plaque seems in keeping. Except he's not so much perusing as poring over it. Why? He steps back and turns an intent, lined face towards me. 'I lost my father, a major in the Seaforth Highlanders. It hurts when I look at any losses.' He's been staying in a local pub. 'I couldn't believe it: a woman in the bar was blathering on her mobile for half an hour during the Remembrance Service.'

Of course. I've forgotten. It was only last week.

'I turned the TV up full blast so at least we'd hear the gun salute. And just look what losses there've been in this small town.'

He points out the number of families losing more than one person in the First World War: Fossetts 2, Kerrs 3, Leys 3, McArthurs 3, Marshalls 3, Sandercombes 2. A father, a son, a brother in the same family perhaps, all wiped out. And then the Second World War list: fewer multiple losses, but far too many single ones.

I can only express sympathy and walk on, realising that grief in a small town like South Queensferry has a universality that transcends all boundaries.

A Bridge Too Far

Before I reach the bridge, I'm impressed by its awesome scale but, once on it, the swaying as lorries rumble past disturbs me. Bridge design, I realise, has to allow for the weight of traffic as much as wind strength. I'm reminded of the tree that's uprooted because it doesn't 'give'. A bridge is the right place for flexibility.

The wind that blew in this morning sends yachts scudding over the water way below. I lean over the railings. Some sail with the wind, others side on, but a few circle round and round. The yachtsmen trim sails as they head into the wind. I admire their skill, so unlike my own experience: getting clunked on the head by swinging booms. But there are ways of dealing with head-on challenges – apart from knowing when to duck – and tacking, the zig-zag approach, is the yachtsman's way. That goes for me too.

Setting off again I'm jolted out of my thoughts by a man in a tracksuit speed-walking towards me. 'More bracing the other way,' he says, 'into the wind.'

'Yes, but ...' I start, before the impossibility of reconciling fitness, winds and my erratic direction persuades me to cut to, '... depends what sort of challenge you want.'

'Some drunks used to walk right to the top of the tower,' he says, upping the anti. 'For a dare p'raps. But they can't do it now. It's blocked off.'

'Just as well then,' I say, sparing a thought for madcaps everywhere.

He speed-walks off but I'm reluctant to rush. Near the middle of the bridge I stop to take in the surging expanse of water. Looking down, I swing a foot to and fro in the gap between the railings. It's wide: not far short of six inches. Couldn't a toddler's head slip through, and what about its body? Did the bridge designers think of that? And I've qualms about the railings' height: less than a metre off the ground, hardly high enough to stop someone climbing over. And then – why, oh why? – I remember a conversation with a woman, way, way back, twenty or more years before. Perhaps I need to be here to remember. I've forgotten what we talked about. All I recall is her red cheeks and the intensity of her emotions. She was on a high. Months later a friend told me she'd committed suicide, from this very bridge.

You can read reports about suicide but words count for little when you see the spot where someone you knew jumped. This is no easy escape route. Looking into these depths as I am, no-one can doubt the desperation that brings someone to this point, or the supreme act of courage needed to take this way out. Could anything I or anyone said have stopped her? Probably not. I've always been impressed by the work the Samaritans do as befrienders. Simply listening, without being judgmental, is the key to their success, as it is for the most creative conversations. But how many realise that suspending one's own opinion and granting someone the freedom to speak might shape a life-or-death decision? A suspension bridge indeed.

A Time Capsule

On the other side of the bridge, I can only look forward. I'm hoping to cover the whole of Scotland in five days. But it's not so much distance I'm anticipating as the character of Scottish people. I jot down my thoughts: dour disposition ... steely grit ... subversive humour ... clannish ... and, inspired by the landscape, a sense of the dramatic ... until I realise I'm indulging in preconceived opinions. Do I never learn? If I want to be surprised, I have to leave things open. Let experience inform me each time, *afresh*. Listen to what's being said, *now*.

I'm tested straightaway. I thought a sign said 'Welcome to Fife' but in close-up it reads like a declaration of independence: 'Welcome to the Kingdom of Fife'. Does it welcome an independent hitchhiking mind? I've hardly begun thumbing when a Highway

Maintenance van pulls up and the driver doles out the instruction: 'Don't stand in the emergency lane mate. Use a lay-by.' That says it. I give my best thumbing shots from the next one. No good. The A90 is a motorway in all but name and the sheer speed of traffic deters any driver from stopping. The longer I stand, the more frustrated I get. The decision's made: walk on, never mind how far, to the next lay-by.

Tramping on, I shift between whistled riffs, odd musings that waft around till huffed by other thoughts, and disapproving glances at the roadside rubbish. But when I see a book lying in a patch of gravel, I stop, look and laugh. Who's thrown out *Diplomatic Baggage* by Brigid Keenan? Talk about missing baggage! I guess the *Adventures of a Trailing Spouse* (the sub-title) weren't gripping enough to keep the reader on board; or the book. I'm tempted to hold on to it and decide for myself, but my own baggage is bursting at the seams.

My interest in wayside litter, though, is aroused: as a resource to be mined. I begin making an inventory of the rubbish littering this A90 stretch. Here's what I find:

> *Luminous green worker's jacket (redundant),*
> *Number plate KO5 CYB (a knockout blow?)*
> *Polythene streamer tangled on plant stalk,*
> *Benson & Hedges Gold cigarette packet*
> *Bottle top, cigarette stub, apple core,*
> *Diet Coke bottle, tail end of a scarf,*
> *Feathered remains stuck in a grill,*
> *Splinter of part-painted wood,*
> *KFC tub, black rubber glove,*
> *Blue plastic shopping bag,*
> *Stones Ginger Ale bottle,*
> *Balding dustpan brush,*
> *And some red tinsel*

… that won't be adorning a tree this Christmas.

This dustbinful hardly adds to the sum of human knowledge but there's a bonus: the distance I've travelled up the A90 hasn't dragged. What's more it's lunchtime and I've discovered the

[DAY ELEVEN]

one remaining apple from my wayside scrumping in a rucksack compartment. That's soon disposed of, along with two 'Divine' chocolates kindly donated by Priory Lodge. I lob the apple core into a bush and pocket the wrappers but sycamore seeds have been spinning down all the while. When I move off a whole new set of time capsules are lying on the ground.

A Question of Balance

Two hours from the bridge and hopes of a lift look forlorn. But my downcast eyes latch on to the many foreign cigarette packets and the universal health warnings: *Rauchen ist tödlich; Roken is dodelijk; Protégez les enfants; Schützen sie kinder*. You can't get away from warnings. Not even in the gutter. I'm thinking of the Highway Maintenance man and, way back, of the pagans too. They'd had enough of rules and regulations and planned to move abroad. But what if the rules moved with them? The 'don't do' culture is getting out of hand. Soon there'll be an epidemic of warning fatigue.

What goes on in drivers' minds as they belt along? I ought to know. As one of them I've groaned at the sight of roadworks, or cursed when an accident closes off junctions. How would I feel if a sign flashed up? – 'Be happy you're alive' or *'There* is wherever you are'. But I'd like to be challenged. Warnings continue: 'Smoking can cause a slow and painful death'; 'Smoking causes ageing of the skin'. I want to shout: 'Jump out of your skin then' and 'Living can be pretty painful.' What I come across next makes me realise it.

I probably wouldn't have noticed the grubby scrap of folded paper lying in the grass, had I not been alerted by the cigarette packets. A heading 'Social Support' tells me it's a form. I sneak a look. It's to do with re-housing the homeless, asking about their current accommodation (if any), why they need to be re-housed and where they want to live. I can't resist teasing out the faded words.

The lady concerned – I'll call her Marjorie – lived at her previous address for twenty-three years before her marriage broke up. She wants to move to Rosyth, nearer relations, and is receiving professional support from a consultant GP. A letter explaining her situation and medical condition was once attached to the form. But one box is filled in with additional information.

DUE TO MARITAL BREAK-UP HOUSE HAS SOLD TO PAY OFF DEBT. THIS HAS CAUSED DEPRESSION TO BECOME VERY SEVERE AND HAS DETERIOTED BY HER HOMELESS SITUATION AND SEPERATION FROM HER DOG WHICH IS ALL SHE FEELS SHE HAS LEFT.

The very fact this form went missing makes me fear for her. The negligence of some official is one thing. But could Marjorie have thrown the form out in a last loss of hope? The way the last comment's phrased, and the spelling, makes it clear she wrote it. One more twist in a tragic turn of events can push someone over the edge. Separation from a beloved pet could do it. No professional support can compete with the tail-wagging company of a dog and you'll never find a less judgmental listener. I hope Marjorie isn't one more addition to the saddest statistic.

It'll take more than a hint of tragedy to stop the sense-numbing thunder of the traffic. The A90 has turned into the M90 and, after another hour's trudging and begrudging, I'm stuck on it. I've passed the Dunfermline turning and, with Kinross and Perth in my sights, plan to hitch from the next slip road. But what's this? Another scrap of paper. Bizarre: a Royal Bank of Scotland cheque for £21 payable to Lorna Ruxton by Miss M.S.Burnie and dated 17th November, only two days earlier.

An open window on a windy day might explain this one too. But would a cheque be left loose in a car? I toy with a more fanciful scenario: a car full of girls and Lorna's handbag is open on the back seat when an argument breaks out about money. Spotting the cheque, her companion seizes it and taunts her. Lorna tries to grab it but the other one flings it out of the window. Melodramatic? Probably. I pocket the evidence and my next stop is at the junction with the A92, the turn-off to Glenrothes and Kirkcaldy. Three hours or more of roadside bashing and I'm ready for respite. I pitch myself well up the slip road feeding the motorway and a few thumbings later a car slams to a halt yards in front. With red chevrons all over the boot and a bright yellow background. Uhuh! The cops!

A Policeman's Lot

I look innocent. I am innocent. One of them – there are two – extends the proverbial long arm and motions me to stand in front. 'You know you're committing an offence.'

I protest my innocence. 'Uh, no. Officer.' Always a good tactic: deference. 'I thought it was all right to hitch from a slip road.'

Uh, no. It isn't. Not even to walk along a motorway verge, except in an emergency.

'Well, that's news to me,' the soul of ignorance says. It's a motorway service station or nothing in future. I'm invited into the car for the full works. They want to know where I'm going and why. That's only the start.

'Name? Spelt? D'you have a middle one? Address?' And so it goes on.

It's taking time to check me out on the Police National Computer. I'm thinking about my last speeding conviction. I've always held Vivaldi responsible: an allegro movement that had me driving in time with the music. But that was years before they knew what you were listening to.

To break the silence while we're waiting, I ingratiate myself. 'My father used to be a copper. He always found domestic incidents the most fraught,' I volunteer.

'We're crash investigators,' I'm informed.

'Ah. Right.' That wasn't the cleverest point to make. But it looks as though the database hasn't caught up with my aberrant behaviour. They've drawn a blank.

'Well, this time we'll let you off with a warning.'

'Thanks.' How welcome's a warning when it saves you a sixty quid fine.

Then there's the question of what to do with me, or what I do with myself. They can't leave me here, they say, but could drop me off at an 'A' road further on. That's when the conjuring hand in the sky reaches into an inner pocket and pulls out exhibit 'A' by its ears, flourishing it with a conviction I can hardly credit.

'I happened to find this on the road about half a mile back,' I explain. 'God knows how it got there. Anything's possible.' Some creative accounting is called for: Lorna mugged in town perhaps, handbag stolen and the useless cheque thrown from getaway car. 'I was thinking I ought to hand it in at a police station, to get it logged. Personally. In case something's been reported.'

'There's one at Kinross,' they say. 'We could drop you there.'

How fortunate: the very direction I'm going in. If only Lorna knew how valuable her cheque is. On the way to the station, we're able to speak more freely. Uniforms can depersonalise. It's Brian and Michael who've been good enough to get me on my way. They talk about the accidents they investigate. Excessive speed and not keeping a sufficient distance are often the culprits. And mobile phones still being used while driving. They spare me gory details. But not till we're nearing Kinross – about ten miles on – do they mention what must have been on their minds all the time.

'A chap walked out of hospital a couple of months ago and tried to throw himself under a lorry on that slip road.'

'God. That's awful,' I say.

'He didn't succeed that time but did later. Exactly where you were standing. We had to do the clear-up job.'

The revelation stuns me: to have been standing twice in one day at a suicide spot. But I don't mention it. I blurt out, 'There must be some sights you'll never forget.'

'Yes.' And no other comment, as if thoughts have blotted out the words. Maybe their professional ethos doesn't brook emotion. I thank them for their help as we part, and they make it clear that I'm under a different jurisdiction now, the Tayside Police.

While waiting for the duty officer I'm joined by a retired police inspector – aged 76 he tells me – checking progress on some local case. Not easy to disengage from a lifetime's policing. Having handed over the cheque, I still have a possible hour's hitchhiking but not the stomach for it. Today feels full-up. So I ply the main street looking for a B & B. I pass one house called Elderlea, the occupants seemingly as keen to declare their age as the police inspector. And why not? After today, a long life seems that much more of an achievement. But a B & B is nowhere to be seen and I'm about to resort to door-knocking when I spy another sign: 'Gallowhill Caravan & Camping Park'. That'll do.

[DAY ELEVEN]

A Deadly Night

As I walk through a neighbourhood on my way there, I'm reminded what pets mean to people. Missing cat posters are everywhere. 'Much loved family pet, never strays far from home. May have sought shelter during very wet weather. Please check garden sheds.' And further up the road I fall in step with an elderly lady walking her dog. Daisy, a flat-coated retriever, is 15½ years old and looks in as good condition as the lady, a mutual benefit Marjorie and her dog might have enjoyed.

When I reach the camping park – three-quarters of a mile up the road – the owner tells me they're shut but I can stay overnight for a nominal four pounds. I'm about to set off for the pitch when I think to ask about the name: Gallowhill.

'Oh yes,' she says. 'Two hundred years ago they hanged people here. My husband looked into the history – but he's out.' Pity.

An icy wind blows across the camping field from the Ochil Hills to the west. I select a site in the far corner sheltered by an old guard of lofty oak trees and pitch the tent with the opening flaps leeward. But trying to fix the flysheet when the wind has other ideas tests my patience.

Then it's a walk to Kinross centre for provisions. I just about hotfoot it back to the tent with breakfast goodies and a haddock and chips before the first chilling drops of rain start to fall. With the weather closing in, I have no choice but to batten down for the night. I light a candle and try to make sense of today's notes. Rain spatters down from the trees. Maybe pitching the tent here is not such a good idea. Rainfall on canvas can sound comforting, but scattergun shots are unsettling. Besides, I'm feeling the cold.

I decide to slide into the sleeping bag, trousers and all. But it's too early to sleep. Where litter counts and the like distracted me on the road, there's nothing to do here but think. And shudder. As darkness descends I can't sleep. Pitching the tent under these trees *is* a mistake. Big time. It's not just the strafing with bullets that keeps me awake but the thought of the knockout blow if a branch shears off. The wind is batting the trees and I hear every creak. From that height it won't take much more than a hefty twig to flatten the tent – the lightest I could buy – and me.

Odd memories infiltrate my rattled mind. Two birds of prey

I saw today circle overhead again, hovering in turns before one swoops for the kill. And, from yesterday, a snatch of conversation: a warning of snow the further north I go. Snow! What about full-blown storms? On a night like this, warnings turn to threats.

The wind is possessed: a petulant outburst here, a harrying surge there. Squall turns to clash, anger to rage. Before I know it a raw fury has broken out. And any lull is only a breathing space for the next onslaught. There are times when the wind tears at the fly sheet with a ferocity that can only be malevolent. And the rain slashes the tent at its command. Under attack and isolated, I don't mind admitting it: I'm cowed.

And I can't ignore the solidifying cold. My hands are forged metal, my fingers iron pipes. I pull on gloves, then a woolly hat when ears feel brittle. Rubbing feet together doesn't put them back in touch, so I tug on two pairs of socks. I've never known such cold. After piling on three … four … then five layers of clothing, I begin to appreciate how people in extreme conditions lose the will to live. And hallucinate.

My night is wracked with wraiths. Imagined or dreamt, they are real enough. The shrieks are the dying agonies of a witch torched for an unfamiliar creed. The cries are the protests of a man condemned for stealing a horse. The roars are those of an unthinking mob baying for blood. And in the short intervals when the hubbub dies down, there are wailing moans from the lost souls of the departed.

Day Twelve

Kinross to Pitlochry

*'I've little doubt that intense emotions can be transmitted
through space'*

A Fair Break

Gallowhill! By God it felt like it. The wind may still whine and
the rain pelt down but there's no peace like that of this dawn.
I've survived. After a day haunted by death, that's a privilege, set
against the injustice the poor souls here must have felt at the fate
that befell them. Did the wind and rain carry their feelings?

I recall a graveyard scene on a hillside. An imam recites from
the Koran while mourners of all faiths and none stand round, and
Joe, my dearly loved father-in-law, is laid to rest. At that moment
a solitary cloud appears from nowhere, discharging a hail of icy
fresh raindrops on the solemn group. The mood lightens and
people remark, 'a blessing'. Joe loved ceremonies and would
celebrate any special occasion by sprinkling a few drops of spirit
on the ground. He was there. We knew it.

I pick at my makeshift breakfast: a tuna bap, an apple and
rice concoction, and a lemon slice, all washed down with a tot
of orange juice. And the rain still falls, if spasmodically. I unzip
the tent flaps, expecting to see the ground strewn with branches
and twigs. But if anything was stripped it's been blown away. I
should have more faith in mighty oaks, centuries old with good
reason. Seizing a moment between downpours, I make for the
toilet shed but my first few steps squelch the grass into a muddy
morass. Everything's sodden. One trip will have to do. I stuff all

my possessions into the rucksack and bundle up the tent gear before decamping to the shed, drying out and repacking. Not till half past nine does the rain ease off enough for me to leave.

With a new day's hitching ahead, I have to leave yesterday's dramas behind. That's what I love about this life: the clean start and the chance to make new connections. Perhaps not so clean a break with the past this time. A two or three-mile tramp up the old road to Perth offers views of Loch Leven but no lift – there's hardly any traffic – and when I reach the small town of Milnathort, The Fair Break Café beckons. I'm pleased to hear from the lady in charge, namesake of the anthropologist Margaret Mead, that it's run on Fairtrade principles.

A distinctive timbre in a voice can keep you listening. It's that way with Margaret but what she says is as engaging. I've hardly stepped inside the shop before she's extolling the virtues of Fairtrade produce and 'slow food' locally sourced, home-cooked by and for local people to enjoy at their leisure. She makes me think how I've been eating. Snatching at food doesn't respect it. She's been interviewed on the radio about her wholesome philosophy. This morning's menu includes oatcakes and cheese, soup and a roll, but Margaret has some special recipes from Canada up her sleeve.

'I'm a Canadian muffin who's married a Scot,' she says, giving her accent away and settling my choice.

'Must have one of your chocolate muffins then and a Fairtrade coffee please.'

There are only the two of us in the café which already feels like a second home. Once the coffee and muffin have arrived, I broach the direction question.

Her answer's unequivocal. 'Direction in life comes from God.'

It's a reply that begs questions. Which God? What if I haven't got one? Can I trust my own direction? If I go down this road, we'll be here all week. But while I tuck into the muffin, Margaret points to a faith.

Hers came from parents. 'They were strong Catholics. That was good and bad.' It was presumed she'd be confirmed and she took her first communion 'before I was old and wise enough to decide which route to follow.' Then she fell in love with a non-Catholic.

I guess her parents didn't approve.

'No. There was pressure not to get serious and I ended up marrying a Catholic.'

'And ... ?'

'The marriage lasted a year – an affair with his secretary. After that I had to figure which way to go.'

'How rarely things work out as one expects,' I say. We're both sitting down now and I'm sipping the excellent coffee as Margaret retraces her path.

She divorced and the surprise was: she married another Catholic. 'That had to be in an Anglican church because the Catholic Church wouldn't marry a divorcee. The priest suggested it, though he wasn't supposed to.' Margaret hopes she's a little wiser now. 'I'm trying to discern what I should be doing,' she says.

I like 'discern'. It sounds informed. So she's still looking?

'Well, I've become a member of the Church of Scotland. Starting this Fairtrade place and learning how people live out their faith in the community has got me through.'

They sell secondhand books, have art exhibitions, story-telling sessions, and support a whole range of charitable projects in developing countries. Impressive what a small group of people acting in concert can achieve. Didn't her namesake have something to say about that? Changing the world comes to mind.

Margaret reflects unhappily on sexual abuses by Catholic clergy. But she has other reservations. 'There's this fixation about going to Mass on Sunday, as if that's enough. In the Church of Scotland a big group of elders support the members. It's a shame they don't have an equivalent in the Catholic Church.' There's much more to religion than observance. Margaret proves it. She suggests I hold out a destination sign to drivers, and finds the card and pens to make one. Perth feels that much closer already.

A Straightforward Farrier

You can see patterns in other people's lives so much more clearly than your own. But perhaps you have to be far enough away. When I reach the outskirts of town I realise that Margaret's story is all about finding the right relationship with religion and people, and that the search for one has parallels with the other. I like the way she thinks of it as work in progress.

Despite the sparse traffic on this minor road, the B996, I hope that flashing my destination sign will do the trick. Sadly 'Perth' is soon obliterated by sharp showers. Taking cover in a bus shelter, I pop out like an automated weatherman whenever a car approaches. But wouldn't people take pity on someone getting soaked? I abandon the shelter, pull the hood over my head and stride manfully on. It takes a succession of showers and one really heavy one before I'm drenched enough to wring the pity out of a driver.

Colin is only going three or four miles up the road to Glenfarg but I'm as appreciative as if he'd arrived by search and rescue helicopter. Probably in his early thirties, he sounds like a man on a mission. Just as well: a short, sharp lift demands straight-to-the-point questions and answers. When I ask what he wants out of life his wish list couldn't be more straightforward.

'I've been going out with a girl four years. Nice house and a family would be fine.'

'Good enough,' I say. 'Life doesn't need to be more complicated than that.'

'You've gotta keep things simple.'

He's a farrier, happy enough in the job – 'it's not rocket science' – and doing well. I pose one of those annoying QI questions that's bugged me in the past. 'How can you keep replacing horseshoes and still get a good fixing?'

'Ah, simple,' he says. 'The hooves grow downwards.'

Why didn't I think of that?

We've reached Glenfarg and, just before I get out, he tells me he's off to somewhere called Lairg later tonight. 'Got some shoeing to do up there. Keep me busy.'

'Good for you,' I say, and pointing to the heavens, 'Look, you've turned the grey skies blue.' After he's driven off I give myself one almighty kick. Lairg! I consult the map. That would have taken me straight up the A9, well beyond Inverness and only a day's hitching from Dunnet Head. All I had to do was fix a pick-up point. Curse it!

It seems I have to be far enough away to see what stared me in the face. It's one thing to talk about living in the present, but listening to what's being said and acting on it there and then is quite another. How many more lessons do I need? Perhaps something

[DAY TWELVE]

held me back: an inner doubt about a flying leap north, an intuitive 'no'. I'm not convinced. I've an inner suspicion I boobed.

A Tortuous Tale

Suspicion grows. The road starts off with straight stretches but soon meanders, then takes a turn for the worse when it enters a steeply wooded valley. Thumbing's a waste of time. The road's narrow with no stopping places to speak of or the sanctuary of a verge. As bend succeeds bend, I have to adopt a survival course: dodging from one side to the other. The sun is shining but, trapped in the treetops, little light penetrates the cheerless shade. A river in full spate flashing down the valley is some consolation but, with the trickle of traffic on this atrocious road, my slog feels like a never-ending story. Some way back a sign said nine miles to Perth. I'm beginning to think I'll be walking it.

At times like this I hope 'The Dean' or one of his agents might show up: the good Christian even, with long white beard and crooked staff. I suspect he'll tell me that The Celestial City awaits … but only if I manage to cross The Slough of Despond. When I come across The Famous Bein Inn at the foot of the valley, I'm tested. With parking places reserved for Sir Elton John and Bob Dylan, I reckon I've slipped into The Land of Wishful Thinking. And this must be The Trough of Temptation. I push on hurriedly. OK, I'll come clean: it's ten past one and I've got to make up for lost time. My only regret: I can't say I've been in The Famous Bein Inn.

Another two or three miles, and on the A912 now, I'm still liftless but the road's flat and mostly straight. With fewer trees to The Disenchanted Wood, I see light: a hint of Perth – 'The Fair City', if not yet Celestial – in the distance. At last a wide verge too, perfect for thumbing from. Twenty minutes later, I'm sitting comfortably, next to John Kyle. And he begins.

A Bender of Sticks

His once-upon-a-time was as an engineer. 'I used to work for the Coal Board but in 1990 I went offshore. Two weeks on, two weeks off, and horrendously unsafe. Give an example. We were shown round a new oil rig at night. About fifty yards up we'd have been. The chap in charge was walking along a gangway ahead of us when he stopped dead. A six-foot section was missing. Clean gone. One false step and he'd have been a gonner.'

I can paint the picture. The grit and guts 'orange' man I'd seen at Edinburgh is in it. For John this was the turning point, but epiphany too strong a word. It was more that the risks were too great. So he packed in the job and took up willow weaving.

I give him one of those 'come again' looks.

'You wouldn't think it, would you?' he says.

'It's a helluva jump.'

'I know. I met a friend of mine a fortnight ago who's an IT consultant. "You're up to your neck in high tech," I said, "while I'm bending sticks for a living." '

What exactly does he do? I can only think baskets.

'I make rustic joinery: hurdles and fencing. The season for cutting and gathering is coming up now: December to March. But living sculptures are my main interest.'

That makes me sit up. 'Living sculpture? What's that about?'

'Well, I can plant and shape willow into a dome, for instance, tying it all together with organic string. Eventually that rots away and the willow keeps growing.' He works a lot with children, making everything from tunnels, arbours and screens to giant rats and even a medieval fort. That's at Dunkeld, and still growing. The kids play a full hands-on part. 'Most of the designs are theirs,' he says modestly. 'We made a giant igloo once.' Over a willow framework, I assume. 'The kids would've happily scraped away at the snow forever.'

Hearing John talk about his work conjures up my own memories of teaching pottery to children. The excitement was as much mine as theirs and I never ceased to be surprised at the pains they took to realise their ambitious ideas. What started John off on this tack?

'A Highland Show at Edinburgh. A willow weaver from Galashiels persuaded me to have a go and said my attempt was every bit as good as his first. That spurred me on. I worked part-time at first but now it's a full-time job.'

And how's he making out?

'The money's only half what it used to be. Two weeks on, two weeks off sounds good, doesn't it. But after the first week, I was

counting the days back. It was no life: I just became a consumer.'
And now?

'Worlds apart. The compensation is working with children,'
John says with a passion. 'What's important in life is time – how
you use it. And the job satisfaction.'

He drops me on the outskirts of Perth and our chat has put me
back in touch with a life I once knew, with creativity at its heart.
The pull of the imagination had worked its magic on him as it still
does on me. And the miry swamp of thinking I was in a short time
ago is now firm ground full of possibilities, the A9. But I had to go
through that to get here, didn't I?

A Free-range Man

Do I really have to earn my lucky breaks through hardship?
'Bad luck always comes in threes,' was one of Dad's mantras.
But while we waited for the third mishap, maybe we overlooked
opportunities to cash in on any good fortune. No accounting for
the fluctuations in my fortunes. Even with all the wiles Matthew
taught me – and a few I've picked up – there's no knowing what
will prompt the next driver to stop. A friendly disposition and
having been a hitchhiker once might help. But a sudden whim or
the chance of a chat could be enough.

When a car pulls up after a brief wait at a lay-by, I find myself
sitting next to Lawrie Duncan Stewart. Long on name, he can't
be short of words. And I'm in luck: he's going to Pitlochry, some
thirty miles away, the very place I'd set my sights on. A glance
tells me the conversation could go anywhere. There's an edge to
Lawrie. He's wearing a hat with turned-up ear flaps and a brim
curving over his forehead like a visor ready to drop. The ginger-
rich stubble and probing blue eyes create a mean lumberjack look,
Scottish-style: a blue tartan collar bulges out from his black leather
jacket.

I only have to mention direction to set Lawrie off on a trumpeting
improvisation. 'I'm sorry for the working class in England,' he
says. 'I *was* British but I'm SNP now. Scotland was bought for less
than four hundred grand ye know.'

I don't get the connection. What's he saying? That the English
working class has lost political clout but the Scots haven't?

Probably true, but Lawrie's in full flow before he's half started. 'I've come back here after thirty-four years in Nottingham – capital o' crime that is – but you wouldn't a trust 'em if you see 'em, the coppers. Biggest crooks though are solicitors.' Has he had dealings? But quick as he was on to crime, we're into the Irish troubles. 'If you'd a 'W' in your name, you'd likely be killed by the IRA. But with a 'U' in it you'd be safe ... in Dublin.' The 'W' is William: I can make that much out, but the 'U' has me foxed. There's no time to dwell on it because he's suddenly gone religious.

'Used to be you couldn'a do nothin' on the Sabbath, not even hang out yeer washing. The Pope was supposed to be Antichrist, devil in the flesh an' all that nonsense. Best thing was when I went to school in Perth with Catholics. Makes you more tolerant that does.'

Guessing he spent his early years in Ireland, I make understanding noises which only prompt him to start weighing up Islam. 'It's a good religion but distorted,' is as much as I take away from his disquisition.

Lawrie's gone free-range with his opinions. The direction is anything but organic. I'm totally unprepared when his tone of voice changes as we pass a heavily wooded valley. He points to a spot deep in the trees. 'A woman drowned bairns an' herself right there. Thirty-five years ago that was. But if ye go to that place now ye can still feel the sadness yeerself.'

Most of Lawrie's observations float over me, but this one I can't discount. He's felt the feelings and remembered the thirty-five years. I have to credit him with a sensitivity I didn't think he possessed.

'Perhaps one can pick up feelings from even further back,' I say and tell him about Gallowhill.

Lawrie nods without comment as if I've touched on something he has to ponder. We're nearing Dunkeld. 'Religious capital of Scotland once,' he declares, and picks out the house his granny's aunt used to live in. I'm half expecting to hear that she haunts the place. But no. 'She was a Seton,' he says, 'an' a General Seton signed the order for the Campbells to massacre the Macdonalds.' That was at the Battle of Glencoe in 1692. The Setons haven't been in best favour since, according to Lawrie.

'I should know a lot more about Scottish history than I do,' I admit.

'Yes. Robert the Bruce was born in Worcester,' he asserts. 'They dinna tell ye that.'

'No.' I hadn't heard. I'm adjusting to Lawrie's take on the past. But what about his own story?

'Used to be a white van man in London, paid by mileage,' he says, 'an' I worked on a pipeline – water, not oil – for a bit. But I'm on benefit now. Homeless. I'd just bought a council property,' he explains, 'when the council offered me a job. Trouble was I had to put the house up for sale an' make meself homeless to get it. An' then the job fell through. But I took up an offer on the house all the same.'

That was two and a half years ago. I can't understand how he's arrived at this parlous state … until he tells me he loaned a caravan to someone who promptly sold it to some Romanies. But 'I couldn't mess with the chap who'd done it because he was a terrorist for the Orange Order.'

Lawrie seems well capable of landing himself in trouble. He goes to the job centre every day though, and logs on to the internet. But because he's fifty, there's not much on offer, and what there is goes to the Poles and the Czechs. 'I don't mind tellin' ye, I'm bitter. They take less wages, so employers make more profit. Scotland'll explode before long,' Lawrie warns. And when we reach the point where the River Tay meets the Tummel, he announces, 'We're in the heart of nationalism,' as if the forces for Scottish independence meet here too. 'Scots won't be put upon.'

History's on his side there. But how is he managing?

'I'm stayin' with a friend who's in a bad way. He's got leukaemia and diabetes. He was in 9 Para once, jumpin' out of planes. But some days he can't get out o' bed.' Lawrie helps him cope in return for a roof over his head.

He's doing me a favour, waking me up to the history all round, the pressures in society and now the landscape. 'No, that's not a Munro,' he says, about a mountain on the skyline. 'Gotta be over three thousand feet for that. Likely a Graham or Corbett. Up towards Blair Atholl you'll see Munros, an' snow on the ridges.'

Then he adopts a confiding tone. 'Have ye heard of the

Shahowian? No?' He looks at me with those eyes of his as if I'm …
well, English. 'It's a cross between a sheep an' a goat. Has special
powers they reckon. On a mystical mountain ye find it.'

Where? I want to know. There are depths to Lawrie I haven't
begun to plumb. Sadly I'm out of time: he's come to a halt at
Pitlochry. But he won't let me go before wising me up on the Battle
of Killiecrankie that took place just up the road in 1689.

'The Jacobites won then,' he says, 'but they lost at Dunkeld less
than a month later.'

Fortunes change. I hope they will for Lawrie. My own challenge
is a mere recce – to find somewhere to bed my head.

A Breaking of News

My first port of call is right where he's dropped me: at the
Backpackers Hotel. But no-one's there. A youth hostel will do but
when at last I find it – getting drenched in the process – that's
closed too. Third time lucky, I check in at the Rosehill Guest House,
persuaded by the warm greeting from the owner Jackie, and head
into town for a very slow meal. Margaret Meade would approve.

The Strathgarry Hotel fits the bill beautifully and I'm looking
forward to the steak and ale pie, complete with Dijon mustard,
seasonal veg and creamy mash. They're even going to check if the
coffee's Fairtrade. And then two young women walk in, selecting
the table alongside, a far too fortuitous decision to overlook.

'What weather,' I say. Not a novel chat-up line but it gets us
talking.

They've driven up from Middlesbrough on a 300-mile trip to
Inverness for the funeral of a treasured uncle.

'He must have been someone special for you to travel all that
distance.'

'My mother was one of sixteen,' Mel – the older, slimmer one
– tells me. 'He was her favourite brother.'

Mandy, her sister, says he had cancer and that the last time they
met had a finality about it. 'There was something about the way
we parted.'

'It's strange,' I say, 'but I keep coming up against death.' Not
wanting to dwell on it, I tell them about my journey and ask about
their lives.

Mel is a road safety officer, running cycling proficiency sessions in schools amongst other things. 'It's fulfilling,' she says, 'but not enough.' She studied psychology at university and the job doesn't offer much scope for advancement.

I'm about to ask Mandy what she does when my pie arrives, served by a young chap who'd look more at home in the second row of a rugby scrum. The steak is separated from the crust so I can see how much I'm getting – plenty.

'Oh, and the coffee is Fairtrade,' he says. The rain is still gushing down and swilling across the road as he speaks. 'Doesn't get much better,' he says. 'Awful last night, wasn't it. D'you hear the news?'

'What about?'

'The climbers. From Aberdeen.'

I shake my head.

'Two young chaps in the Cairngorms. Died last night.'

'No?' I'm aghast.

'Terrible conditions. Minus 20 they said and winds up to 120 miles an hour.'

'Unbelievable,' I say, though I have every reason to believe it.

'Yes, tragic: first fatalities this climbing season.'

The news is uncanny and I comment on the deaths to the girls. I'm back in the tent at Gallowhill, feeling that cold, hearing that wind and asking myself questions. What happened? And whose *were* the cries carried on the wind?

'I have to see the news.'

'Oh, we never watch,' Mandy replies.

'Really? Never?'

'No. Nor read the papers. Too slanted,' Mel says. 'And second-hand opinions.'

I sympathise but know I shan't be able to stop myself. We carry on talking as life goes on around us: the clearing of empty plates, the wiping down of tables, the taking of new orders. Mandy works at a call centre for a cable company but she has an ambition: to study environmental science at university. She might have to take a foundation course first. 'But I'm thirty,' she concedes.

'No age,' I say. The cliché is as vacant as the feeling I have when we part and two young women continue on their way to a treasured uncle's funeral.

A Sense of Place

Back at the guest house I remark to Jackie about the weather. She calls it 'dreich'.

'Good word for this dismal stuff,' I say.

'We've plenty more like that,' she says. 'If broccoli wasn't fresh enough, we'd say it weren't fit to build braw bodies.'

I love it. There's nothing like a snatch of the vernacular for establishing the identity of a place and a people. 'I like the way the 'wee' word is stretched,' I tell her. 'I heard someone talking about "golden oldies that have been around a wee while".'

'And then there's always the wee dram,' is Jackie's riposte.

I've dried out. I've chilled out. And I've switched on my mobile just before six for my GPS position to be relayed to the family. Good that they're in the know.

Soon it's time for the news and a report on the deaths of the climbers. They were in a party from the Aberdeen University mountaineering club, but went off on a climb by themselves. Hit by the bitterly cold, gale force winds, they struggled to get back to safety. The mountain rescue team fought through snowdrifts, to find them only a mile from a ski lift car park. But conditions were so horrendous that the students had been overwhelmed with exhaustion and hypothermia.

From my caving days I know how thin a line separates risk from recklessness and I feel a kinship with those young men. I was out in that night. I felt the force of those winds and the icy cold. I sensed the threat, albeit nothing like the one they faced. Whatever the feelings I picked up – and I'll never know how real or imagined they were – I've little doubt that intense emotions can be transmitted through space, and possibly time too. And I find that no more unlikely than that I can watch a live report from Afghanistan in my living room, or see starlight emitted thousands of years ago.

For relief I view a comedy sketch competition on BBC Scotland, hoping to tap into the Scottish sense of humour. One sketch has in-jokes played out on Inverness folk from an Aberdeen perspective. Another portrays Bonnie Prince Charlie as a superstar. But the winning sketch features a wishing-well sprite and a hard-done-by mortal invited to make the customary three wishes. Unwittingly he blurts out as his last one, 'I wish I had your job,' whereupon he's swapped with the sprite who happily trots off to Disneyland arm-in-arm with the hard-done-by's girlfriend.

A little later my mobile chirrups. It's a text ... from my son. He's had my GPS reading. *'Hi Dad. Gr8 to see ur at Pitlochry. Not far from where we got engaged. Gd Luck!'* I knew Elwyn had proposed to Lyndsey on a Scottish mountain but not exactly where. If I wanted some news to lighten my thoughts, it was this. They married only two months ago – as magical as a wedding can be – with a spirited ceilidh to get guests in the merriest of moods and a surprise firework display. A strong wind had glasses crashing to the ground, but made for striking shots of the bride's veil billowing skywards. What I can never forget is the most extraordinary coincidental link with their relationship.

They met while reading chemistry at Birmingham University and, when we celebrated Lyndsey's doctorate at her parental home, I mentioned that Bill Arkle used to live not far away. He'd been a guiding light in my twenties and his lookalike gave me a lift earlier on this trip. I'd spent countless weekends at his home, enjoying an eclectic mix of delicious curries, music, poetry, and mysticism, most evident in Bill's paintings. He had painted a mural in one particular room, the music room, featuring an idealised landscape. I was astonished to hear, first Lyndsey, then Elwyn, say they'd seen it. They'd both been in that very room. Ages after Bill and his family sold up they'd been invited to a party there. One simply couldn't mistake that room and any owner would have been foolhardy to paint over such a unique feature.

I'm not sure what I make of this coincidence. Pure chance is the most plausible answer. But my experiences on this trip change all that. If deeply felt emotions do impregnate a place – as embodied in Bill's mural – can that place exert a pull that connects a whole network of people? I have much to sleep on and off.

Day Thirteen

Pitlochry to Portsoy

'When did I last visit someone to find out why I'm there?'

A Diverting Possibility

When I wake, my mind is racing with thoughts. Why did Mel and Mandy sit next to me? Other tables were free, but with death in the air, could shared concerns have put us together? That intrigues me. A casual conversation I once had with a theatregoer next to me revealed we'd been born in the same maternity home and, at a wildlife trust AGM, the woman alongside knew a great friend of mine who lived about 80 miles away. Unless I'd spoken we'd never have found out.

Why did I speak to Mel and Mandy? OK, they were attractive young women, but it was fortuitous that they *chose* to sit where they did. The synchronicity suggested there was more to it than pure chance. Chance with a significance. Is that so fanciful? It's certainly beyond a suspension of disbelief. But open-mindedness demands more than not disbelieving. After the last two days, I'm prepared to give outlandish possibilities a shot. If we don't think beyond what we know – like John Kyle – can we go further than where we are?

What if I think this? What if I do that? Those are the questions to lead me in new directions. The tenets brought me so far. 'What ifs' take me further. *What if chance can connect us with like-minded people? What if we find ways to tap into those connections?* I have a more pressing connection question: Inverness is my next stop on the A9 and, looking at the map, my eyes have strayed to the east along the Moray Firth. I've seen the name Findhorn, the home of a spiritual community that I came across in my twenties. How has it developed? I'd like to know.

Further along the coast, I spot Portsoy: the only other place in the UK, according to Mr Casley at the Lizard, with deposits of serpentine rock. I fancy forging a geological link between England and Scotland. That would nicely counterpoint any unearthly connections between people and places. But how can I connect with Findhorn and Portsoy? With a 120-mile round detour I might miss this Friday's ferry to North Ronaldsay. It's a leap of hitchhiking faith. I'll take the next lift as a pointer. Let chance make the connections.

The day looks promising. The lightest of winds brushes past me as I head out of town. Even the grey smirches of cloud look bright in a crystal-clear blue sky. And at ten past nine I realise why one shoulder aches more than the other. It's the adjustment on the rucksack straps: lop-sided, stupid!

A Leg-pulled Boss

Woodland borders the A924 out of Pitlochry with views to the River Tummel and a ripple of hills ahead. When I rejoin the A9, dual carriageway alternates with single stretches. From time to time the road criss-crosses the river and a railway line criss-crosses the road. I feel like shouting, 'All change.' A mile or two on, the Killiecrankie sign reminds me that battles have to be won. Beyond a bend which should slow the traffic is a lay-by. The shadow of hitchhiking guru Matthew falls across my path. Perfect. I station myself at the front.

In my usual tweak of his tactics, I eyeball drivers. I've experimented with switched-on smiles, nods of the head and raised eyebrows but they've all been turn-offs. Having pulled my face in so many different directions, often at the same time, I've convinced myself that just looking human is the best strategy. That's hard enough!

At the best of hitchhiking times, the sight of any car stopping is out-of-the-ordinary. Nothing's more unreal than the car that slips into the lay-by ten minutes later: a metallic green BMW 530d. I'm greeted by an executive-suited Bob heading for Inverness airport. Geronimo! Leave the choice to chance and look what happens! Bob's lift resolves all doubts about where I'm heading. I ease myself into the front with the mindset of a lucky dip lottery winner and Bob seems almost as pleased. We exchange cards. He's the managing director of a firm supplying products such as high tech conservatory roofs. Since I used to run a small-scale conservatory business I'm interested to hear more.

Years before, his father sold the company to a national firm. Though Bob continued working for them, they weren't doing a good job with what had been a local family firm. So he and his brother used the dad's money to set up their own company. 'We're lucky to have found a unique niche in the market,' he says.

We talk about the everyday challenges of running a business and the perversity of sub-contractors. 'Some of mine knew what customers wanted better than they did,' I say, 'and that wasn't cutting corners.'

'The trouble is getting people to see the business your way,' he says. 'Attitude counts. People can get too regimented in their thinking.' Bob left school at sixteen and doesn't insist on higher education levels from those he takes on.

I wonder how he manages his workforce.

'I'm probably too easy-going, but like to think I'm on friendly terms with them all.'

I want to ask more about his background but can't ignore the striking view of a snow-capped mountain ahead. It had to be a Munro.

'Oh, you'll see a lot more and bigger,' he says.

'I'll look forward to it,' I say and mention my hopes of catching a ferry to Orkney in time for the Friday sailing to North Ronaldsay.

Without further ado, Bob stops, taps a number into his mobile and asks his office to check the ferry times and dates.

'Very kind of you,' I say, taken aback by this spontaneous gesture.

While waiting for the return call he tells me he was born in India and has the right to settle there. He respects Indian culture but is aggrieved not to have total Scottishness in his background. I'm half-expecting him to support the SNP when he confirms it, favouring full control. Then the advice comes through from his office to head for the Gills Bay ferry. It docks at St.Margaret's Hope on South Ronaldsay and there are three daily sailings.

I can't thank Bob enough.

He suggests that if I pass by a town called Lybster I call on David Mackay, a stone engraver who's had many public commissions. 'He's shaped a stone in the form of dolphins at John o' Groats and hauls huge slabs of granite around. His cottage is almost the last one on the right. Look for the porch.'

I guess Bob had a hand in its design. Though I'm intrigued by the weight-lifting tactics, the mere suggestion is enough: I'll act on his tip-off. It's another opportunity to put chance to the test. When did I last visit someone to find out why I'm there?

Bob's thoughts turn to some sad news. A month ago his friend's opposite number on an oil rig – they did alternate three-week stints – was killed in an explosion.

It hammers home the non-stop danger of oil rig work and I recount the unnerving experience that galvanised John Kyle into changing course.

Bob is happy to continue in his role for another seven or eight years, at least until he's fifty-five. 'I'm not out for world domination,' he smiles wryly, 'but you can't avoid growth.' As it is, they have twenty-three employees.

And relaxation?

He and his wife love travel 'for the weather, culture and freedom.' He has eclectic tastes in music and enjoys fishing when not preoccupied by his two teenagers. Views of the Moray Firth open up. Bob tells me that the peninsula jutting into the sea is called the Black Isle, possibly because of the black soil, or the black arts once practised there. 'The Battle of Culloden was fought near here,' he says. And yet another Jacobite rebellion put down, led by Bonnie Prince Charlie that time.

History is close at hand in this corner of Scotland but the phone cuts off our conversation. 'That was a self-made man,' Bob tells me when the call's over. 'He hopes to buy a farm that has planning permission for nine houses. Funny thing is you'd think he was a farmer. When people see him wearing overalls they ask for the owner. He doesn't look like the boss.'

Bob has a regard for the no-fuss, no-frills approach. But back at the office, does he get the respect he deserves?

He laughs. 'The Glasgow premises were broken into some time ago. Shortly after I had a phone call from my brother. He said, "There's been another break-in Bob. Your office this time." That had me really exercised, till he added, "But don't worry: we've tidied up." I hadn't had time to clear my desk.' He has to put up with some leg-pulling. But I reckon he gives as good as he gets.

Bob stops at the approach to the airport. The journey's passed in no time but I've got to know the man behind the suit. He'd never make heavy weather of exercising his authority, or need to. Even delivered with a lightness of touch, his words carry conviction. I wish I'd had the pleasure of working for such a boss.

'Watch out for the views of the Moray Firth,' he says. 'Very picturesque.' Those are his parting words: another tip-off. Thanks, Bob.

A Sprinting Spiritualist

I can't believe my luck. Bob's dropped me about eight miles beyond Inverness on the A96. At only 11.25 I'm well on the way to Findhorn. When things go wrong, I look for reasons, or hope 'The Dean' is on standby. When things go this right, I ought to accept it. But still I speculate. Was that really chance at work, or a wish granted? If so, I'm sure wishing wasn't enough. Remember the wishing-well sprite! It had to be the right wish. And I had to help things happen: put some work in (legwork), take a decision (the right place to hitch from), and be patient (wait). Talking of which, there's a junction ahead with a pull-in beyond. Ideal: I can carry on thinking while I wait for the right lift.

That takes me back: I had to find my way out of Vienna once, before I could carry on hitchhiking. A chap who wore lederhosen gave me good directions in English. But I soon forgot what came after 'first left, second right'. Other passers-by didn't speak English or suggested different routes. After half an hour's confused trudging, I gave up and waited in a shop doorway. At that exact moment, the lederhosen man reappeared. 'Keep straight on,' he said. 'You're on the right track.'

How *do* these things happen? Do you help things happen by letting things happen? But I wonder whether there's another factor. If intense emotions can be transmitted through time and space, can wishes too? *What if strongly expressed wishes can be picked up telepathically?* So-called chance events might simply be the equivalent of a wireless connection to Amazon.

When a driver suddenly pulls up and opens the door, his cap makes me feel I know him. It has a curving brim just like Lawrie's. A strong chin and bright blue eyes are all the more prominent for being framed between that brim and the neck-hugging collar of a padded polyester jacket. Perhaps he wants to feel coddled.

My luck's in: he's visiting a seventy-six-year-old aunt. That takes him past the Findhorn turning. His aunt brought him up and he has a great affection for her. He's been driving trains since 1977. 'But it's sprinters now,' he says. 'Buses on wheels. With only two or three carriages, they get away quick.' He often does the four-hour stint from Wick to Inverness, but loved the six-mile steam train run from Aviemore.

'We lived next to a train driver when I was a nipper and that's all I ever wanted to be,' I enthuse. I spent many Saturday mornings train-spotting on Temple Meads Station in Bristol, talking to drivers, glorying in the sight of flaming hot coals and itching to get a hand on the shovel. Diesels never had the same appeal.

David's on another line of thought. 'The strangest things happen. My sister died at only fifty-one. Five weeks later my mother died too at seventy-five. Then – would you believe? – my marriage broke down. I was at a really low ebb.' Looking for solace, David joined the Spiritualist Church and remembers one particular session with a medium. 'My father wanted to come in first, then mother, and sister, all vying for attention. My mother said she wasn't with me twenty-four hours a day but comes when I need her. Father said, "You've keys to a vehicle other than for pleasure." He can only have meant the train. He died before I took up train driving but knows what I'm doing now.' That was a comfort. David had other confirmations. 'I was told about a gold watch I'd inherited and the medium gave my son's birthday, 18th August.'

I recall my only meeting with a medium, a generously endowed lady, who said I should take sculpture work more seriously. When I taught ceramics, sculpture had been my passion. Then she asked whether an 'Ellinor' figured in our family. Ellinor is the name of our Swedish niece. I couldn't discount either revelation. Both were too uncommon to be hit upon by chance.

David's private readings have given him a faith in the future. 'The medium said I'll be flush with money for the first time in my life.' He goes in for the lottery much more now. And he's buying a house soon, a two-bedroom flat in the centre of Inverness. Not banking on any winnings I hope, because he'll have to keep paying the Child Support Agency £400 a month for his seventeen-year-old daughter while she's in full-time education.

What else does the future have in store for him?

'Some things are so cryptic,' he says. 'I've met this lady at the pub. She's separated. It just happens we get on fine. I'm hopeful something will come of it.'

'That's one thing no-one can predict,' I say. 'Hope it works out.'

A Spiritual Pathfinder

I was so absorbed in what David told me, I missed the views of the Moray Firth. On the long flat road to Findhorn – one and a half miles off the A96 – there are wide open vistas across scrubland and pasture, and hints of the sea in the flush of sky beyond. But I'm too absorbed in my thoughts to appreciate qualities of light. Even the roar of aircraft from RAF Kinloss fails to stem them. I might be embracing uncertainty but a kind of certainty is taking its place: that the road I'm on is exactly the right one. Leaving things to chance is working out. It's taking me where I need to go and giving this life an edge I couldn't have dreamt of.

That lift with David and talk of mediums has reopened the whole business of telepathy. The messages were surely too specific to be coincidental. Can mediums tap into the unconscious mind through some telepathic channel? An uncomfortable concept for some, but one that chance events are persuading me to consider. Didn't that fortune teller in Newcastle say she read brains?

As I approach the Findhorn Community site, I'm surprised at its nonchalant appearance. It looks to have just landed – appropriate when it's part-built on an old runway. There are caravans in assorted liveries plonked here and there, a food store and a reception building I assume, all loosely grouped round a rough track. I'm heartened by the picture this paints: of individual seekers drawn to this place who've put down roots in their own way, forming a network of relationships that hold the community together, like marram grass with sand. How far has the community come? And in the limited time available – I'm hoping to make Portsoy tonight – how do I find out?

I do what I can only do at times like this: take the next obvious step. That leads me to the Phoenix Community Stores and some eclectic survival rations: a permissive pizza slice, a new age salmon, goats' curd and cucumber bap, a life-has-to-go-on scone and an eternally tempting apple. And the next step? Find someone to answer the questions. I ask the next obvious person – at the checkout.

'Why not pop over to the visitor centre?' the obviously sensible assistant advises.

I do as I'm told, waiting patiently while a hippie-era chap, Rory, with ponytail inheritance talks to a devotee. Am I being flippant? Probably. In fact, he has a distinguished leonine look and I might well have been part of this world had I not chosen a more conventional life.

I read extensively about Findhorn in my twenties. An age before The Eden Project, the co-founders, Peter and Eileen Caddy and Dorothy Maclean, wrested a flourishing plant life and vegetable crop from an impoverished sandy soil. Enlisting the support of nature spirits, and some powerful compost, they grew legendary 40-lb cabbages in the Findhorn Garden. Sympathetic souls converged on the New Age community from all over the world. I still have drawings from one 'sensitive' that depict the spirit forms within plants. The oak deva impressed me. At a college of education in my early thirties I was sustained by regular mailings of *God's Word*, messages received by Dorothy (also known as Divina). The guidance helped me survive the arcane studies that supposedly qualified me for a career in teaching. I never got around to visiting Findhorn though. Not till now.

Rory is ready but my enquiry gets charmed by his accent. That North American twang with a tot of Scotland would bring a delicious precision to the wildest prairie and, when words sound so good, listening is a pleasure. Rory will be my guide I decide. He'll tell me *his* Findhorn story. Luckily he seems game for it.

A whole series of events brought him to Findhorn twenty-six years ago. 'I was one of the Vietnam War and Woodstock generation. Dropping out of university in the US, I started to read about comparative religion, and became attracted to an alternative way of life.'

I'm with him already. Why didn't I drop out?

'I read *At the Edge of History* by William Irwin Thompson, a professor at Massachusetts Institute of Technology. Inspired by meetings with Alan Watts – Zen Buddhism and all that – and others, Thompson formed The Lindisfarne Association: a network of people to discuss the emerging planetary consciousness.' Rory drops other names in: Richard Alpert (also known as Ram Dass) and *Be Here Now* was a formative book. Someone I've vaguely heard of, the guru Yogananda, gets a mention, so does Meister Eckhart and Aldous Huxley with *The Perennial Philosophy*.

Rory's bibliography could sound dull and dilettantish. It's not. It's a record of one man's search for the meaning he didn't find in academic studies. And it echoes mine. I read *The Perennial Philosophy*. I was the outsider in Colin Wilson's *The Outsider*. I couldn't stop reading. My education started after I left school. For a time Rory attended the Californian Esalen Institute, an alternative educational centre that fosters intellectual freedom. Finding a teacher of Chinese philosophy, he practised T'ai Chi and studied the *I Ching*. But how did he square these esoteric pursuits with the material side of life?

'It created a lot of dissonance trying to launch myself on a spiritual pad in a society which values it not at all,' he says. 'My family thought I would come to my senses and take a proper job. But I never found it easy to work in the world.'

So what did he do?

'My problem was motivation, like I was from another planet. I was not interested in amassing wealth and any job I took was steeped in exploitation: big fish eating little fish.' He did voluntary work, helping out with a youth theatre. Going for more up-the-scale posts, he was told he was too intelligent. 'In the end I settled for lower echelon jobs where I was free to be myself.'

Some of my happiest times were spent in undemanding jobs: petrol-pump attending, labelling wine bottles, and delivering bread.

'If you're on a path, things will conspire to help you,' Rory assures. 'That doesn't save you from the wilderness but, if you have a path, it's hard to despair.'

So what about this path? Who comes to Findhorn now?

'We have a waiting list of people who want to build their own ecological house. They may not give up a salary but they're keen to improve their quality of life. It's a complex society,' he says, 'evolving from the inside and responding to external pressures. The dedication of the founders has not been duplicated in anyone else, so there's some watering down. But the basic ethos has stayed the same and spread.'

And how would he describe the ethos?

Rory is unhesitating and articulate. 'To live a loving, tolerant, spiritual life, encouraging transformation.' One concept, he tells me, is that of recycling – not bottles, tins and papers – but people who may need to learn to start all over again.

I wonder how that's worked out for him.

'I was a gardener for fifteen years here, but I've spent seven years in reception.' He's called a focaliser, not a manager. It's a paid job that he really enjoys. His personal interests are art and music. He plays the clarinet and the Celtic pipes.

But how easy is it for newcomers to integrate?

'We encourage people to stay for a year and perform a role. It takes up to a year to be assimilated. An individual can decide if he or she is too uncomfortable in a position and learn new skills or deal with themselves. All rules have exceptions but a definite commitment's required. If anything we're like a workshop centre.'

Working on oneself might be more of a challenge than finding the right role I'm thinking.

Rory explains how Findhorn relates to the outside world. 'We're an educational charitable trust working within the laws of the land. We're not adversarial. Some commune people find us pretentious but others are impressed by the eco-village side of things.' They explore sustainability issues as a template for future development, liaising with Moray Council, and involving school groups. 'If you take time to design and build a sustainable system,' he says, 'you use a fraction of the energy, the draw on petrochemicals is minimal and,' he adds with relish, 'you end up with a palpably beautiful place to live.'

It sounds like a crusade. Rory may not thump the table but he's passionate about their aims. 'It takes living into the realm of art. People can express themselves and build their dream homes – all different – where creativity and caring are central.'

If only more people could get a taste of the Findhorn transformation. But those ideals can only be words, however well spoken, for the vast majority. That's a shame. I thank Rory profusely for sharing this vision.

'It's a centre for demonstrating these things,' he says. 'A refuge and a springboard. Its purpose is to go out in the world to inspire and demonstrate a different way of living, with spiritual ideals but,' he adds a little impishly, 'we question each other constantly.' I liked that. Having experienced the spirit and vitality of this place through Rory's words, and joined my journey with his for so short a time, I'm sorry to leave.

A Healing Nurse

I wish I had more time to walk round some of the twenty-five acres that Findhorn covers, to see the eco-houses, the straw bale homes and whatever else helps these idealistic people live out their dreams. I'd like to ask other residents what brought them here and what difference Findhorn has made to their lives, but I have to reach Portsoy before dusk. Heaving my rucksack on, I barely step outside the entrance before a 4 x 4 pulls up. I haven't thumbed. A young woman – mid-thirties perhaps – opens the window and leans across, ginger hints to her hair and bright blue questioning eyes.

'We saw you earlier,' she says. 'My friend thought he recognised you.'

'I'd be surprised,' I reply, 'but I've got that sort of face. Beards are beards.'

There's a moment's hesitation. We're both thinking. 'Well, can I give you a lift?'

You bet! That mile and a half back to the A96 will be a great help.

She's Liz and I'm Laurence, blessed to visit Findhorn at last and to have met Rory. I explain why I'm making for Portsoy. And what?! Liz offers to take me there: forty miles out of her way. When I try to dissuade her – what sort of insanity is that? – she insists. I must be dreaming. This is a lift I haven't worked for, a lift I've tried to decline, and a lift that only happened because I was mistaken for someone else.

I start explaining my mission when she butts in. 'You're good to throw away conventionality,' she says. Circumstances wrought a big change in Liz's life. She was a paediatric oncology nurse but found herself in 'a painful darkness'. It's like she'd been waiting to tell me this since way before we met. She doesn't elaborate and I don't feel like pressing her.

So she came to Findhorn. 'I needed a rest, the chance to heal, and found myself in a garden with beautiful people.' She worked there for five months – it was a real therapy – but wanted to make a difference in other ways. 'From tending the garden, I'm now a full-time carer for Eileen Caddy.'

I'm stunned: to think that after all these years I'm as close to one of the Findhorn founders as I possibly could be, short of meeting her. 'Eileen's a frail lady now,' Liz says, 'into her late eighties.'

What does Liz make of her change of direction?

'There's a lesson in everything,' she says. 'Every given moment we have a choice. You can choose to slow down. Just exercise choice with trust. It only requires you to trust, not in God or religion, but yourself.'

That's strangely comforting.

'I don't engage with the papers, TV or radio. I engage with myself. You may say it's anal. But we don't have to engage in fear, prejudices, jealousies. We feel safe in boxes, but no-one puts us there. That's our choice too. Life's a gift and blessings aren't boxable. They're here.' She puts a hand to her heart. Liz is pouring herself out, words tumbling over each other.

I nod vigorously or look over pointedly to meet those clear blue eyes. Or ask, as I do now, what if life stacks up problems?

'When things conspire, accept the interference. Doesn't matter what happened in the past: let it be. Appreciate you were meant to live through that time.' She's adamant. 'It gives us a sense of security holding on to what we know, good and bad. That's the trouble. We think we need to hang on, but all we have to do is be. That's more than enough. We don't need to know everything, to keep knowing. "It's just about being," Eileen says.'

This is so potent. Life can be far simpler is what she's saying, if only we let it. But what brings people to that point? Her own story tells.

'Everybody has to be ready to taste that taste, to feel invited to take that bite. It never works when things are forced. We're on a road and you have to be at the right pitch to get the message.'

What does she mean? Level of awareness? I'd like to think of it as a hitchhiking pitch. How often have I had to wait to find the right place, to be ready for the right lift and the right message? Sitting next to this overflowing stream of wisdom, I want Liz to slow down. Some hopes: the words are tossed in my direction so fast I can't take them in before she's off again.

'We only see judgement, fear, what's in it for us. But we need to know what it is to be human, to trust, to leave our bicycle out without a padlock.'

That *would* be something.

'This is all about me and my choices. It's taking responsibility for them. It's me that gives out the energy. Energy is about soul, spirit, essence. Don't arrogate it to someone else.'

She's packing so much into those words that I'm totally absorbed. Though I want to make sense of them I'm being transported into a world where not-knowingness reigns. It's the feelings behind that transcend any meaning I might try to grasp. All I do know when we reach Portsoy is that we've come a long way.

I offer to pay for the fuel. Liz won't think of it. She'll only accept a thankyou. 'For the words too,' I say, with a kiss, and ask her to thank Eileen Caddy for the guidance in my twenties that helped bring me here now. I start off down the road when she calls me back. I'd left my bag of food behind. And what else?

A Coming to Earth

My impressions of Findhorn would have been so incomplete without Liz's account. I couldn't have wished for more vivid insights. Her philosophy – choice with trust – is a remarkably succinct summary of what I've been working towards. *What if we keep making choices and trust chance to work things out?* The chance comes straightaway. Looking for somewhere to kip down, I take the 'first step' option. A chap is backing out of a shed in his front garden. Strike, first time! He works at The Boyne Hotel down the road and it's £28 a night. That's sorted. So is the location of the Portsoy Marble shop: on one side of the harbour.

After I've booked in I stroll past huddles of staunch stone-built cottages down to the waterfront. This 17th century horseshoe-shaped harbour is so authentic as to pass for a period film set. A tall three-masted schooner might well be lashed to moorings even now and sailors be whetting their whistles in the Shore Inn, full of ribaldry and sea dogs' tales. As it is, a few fishing boats ride out the swell to the age-old skirl of gulls and the salt-spiced tang of seaweed.

When I reach the marble shop, in one of the warehouses, I'm mortified. It's closed. Damn! But I can't take no for an answer. I spot a light in a workshop down a back alley and, through a dusty window, a dim figure inside. A ruddy-faced man comes to the door sporting one of those beards birds could nest in. Combat jacket aside, he ought to be at the helm of a ship. He peers at me quizzically over the top of a fully-rounded pair of specs while I peer over his shoulder, pleased to see signs of stone being worked on.

'I was hoping to buy some samples of rock.'

'Ach. We're closed now. It's only one to four this time of the year.'

I mention the connection with the serpentine from the Lizard.

'It'll be nae trouble then. I'll open up for ye.'

How lucky. If I'd arrived any later I'd have missed him. John Watson's the name of my man. He shows me models of fish, rabbits and owls along with fish pendants, marble studs, agate slices, egg-shaped stones and more. Nothing as large as the lighthouses they make at the Lizard but the choice is bewildering. I ask John about the Portsoy marble. That's what they call serpentine.

'Ye can trace the use of it back to Neolithic times,' he says, 'when it was made into querns – bowls – by grinding away with flint.' John has been working the marble for forty years. Apart from one or two secret places, red serpentine is only found here and at the Lizard. There are isolated deposits of green serpentine in Orkney and Shetland, and the white veined rock is highly prized but practically unavailable. John works the marble in small batches of the same design so he doesn't get bored.

I'm interested to know what he most enjoys making.

'Och, that'll be one of these,' he says, picking up a spherical stone, with twelve evenly rounded nodules all over its surface, like a cluster of tiny bubbles.

'And what's that about?'

'No-one knows,' John says mysteriously. 'Some think they were mace heads, others that they were symbols of power in Neolithic communities or charms against evil.'

I'm warming to this game of guesses.

'They're called Fyvies,' he says, 'from the place where the first stone ball was found,' and, sensing my interest, he looks out a press cutting. The original one was 3¼" in diameter, nearly twice as big as John's copy, and had a value of £8000 put on it. That one and others like it are believed to date from about 1000 BC.

I put John on the spot. 'So what d'you think?'

'Put it in a pot,' John says. 'When the water's boiling, it'll start dancing about and ringing, telling ye it's time to throw in the cabbages. That's my idea. And it'll make the finest soup ever, breaking up the grains and lumps.'

'Sounds plausible,' I say. Convinced by the versatile powers of this strange object, I buy one. John wraps it in tissue paper with reverence. Never mind what it's for, only he knows what's gone into the making of it.

That's one present sorted. But I want something else for my two children and their partners. 'What's this?' I say, picking up a stone with a polished recess.

'Stress relief,' John says. 'Rub yeer thumb to and fro for relaxation.'

But fresh from the Fyvie I've a better idea: a wishing stone, Portsoy's answer to Aladdin's lamp. What better present than this

[DAY THIRTEEN]

for two young couples setting out on married life with so much to wish for? My thumb has worked well. Now they can put theirs to good use.

As a parting gesture John presses a sample of red serpentine in my hand. I'll tuck it in my rucksack back at The Boyne next to the stone brooch from the Lizard: a touch presumptuous to think I'm bringing the two ends of the United Kingdom together.

After polishing off the Findhorn food in my room, I'm entertained by some banter between the regulars in the pub: 'He always gets served first: it's the aggression on his face.' I stay out of that exchange with one patient elbow parked on the bar. It mightn't be coincidence that when I pose the Fyvie's purpose to the assembled company, the unanimous view is that it's for bashing the enemy across the head.

'So what gets you going in these parts?' I say incautiously, armed only with a working pint.

'Wine, women and drink,' goes their refrain. 'What more is there to live for?'

'Can't argue with that,' I say. There must be something else. Song? Maybe not. Sometimes it pays to keep quiet.

Day Fourteen

Portsoy to Lybster

'*I couldn't be anywhere else but here*'

An Unlocked Bike

It's a bright start but a band of rain is forecast. I ought to make tracks for Inverness, except something's holding me back: ignorance. A guide book makes me realise how little I know about this place. I had no idea I'm in Banffshire. There's a living language in the north-east of Scotland I've never heard of: Doric. Folk songs are sung in it. All news to me. This is a Pictish area. I knew the Picts were a fighting force the Romans had to contend with. But not that they'd overrun the pub! Nor that a famous Scottish victory was won last night. At the breakfast table the waitress, Susan, tells me that Celtic beat Man United 1-0, and puts me wise as to what happened in her native Halifax every time England scored.

'They had girls on stilts in bikinis who'd whip their tops off in the middle of the street. We had to take the children home in a taxi. That's how bad it was.' She'd been increasingly alarmed. 'There was a porn shop in the town centre. Then they allowed a lap dancing club. There's come-and-get-me girls in night clubs with hardly anything on. Sodom and Gomorrah I call it. And they wonder why children grow up as they do.' She has a boy, fourteen years old, and a twelve-year-old girl.

I'm reminded of the schoolgirl who told me that the whole family watched blue movies. No surprise that she became a teenage pregnancy statistic. This moralising over the scrambled egg and mushrooms is a bit bizarre. But I admire Susan's determination to protect her family from the creeping licentiousness.

How easy was it for her to find work?

'It all fell into place,' she says. 'They knew me only as a guest when I came but I got the job with no checks or references. They gave me the back door keys straightaway.'

I wonder how different life is now.

'No comparison. I followed my daughter a few times when we came, just to make sure. Down there she wasn't allowed out. We had to lock gates, and get cameras installed. Here they can leave their bikes outside the front wall, unlocked.'

Hah! Amazing Susan should pick on that. She's done exactly what Liz advocated: take responsibility for her choices and trust. How well Portsoy's repaid it. Susan says she can leave her door wide open! 'I can walk down to the harbour with the dog at two in the morning, sit on the wall, and not be a bit scared. In Halifax they shut the shops at three o'clock on football days and you'd never think of going out.'

Susan's story has parallels with Liz's, spurred on to make a change when a quality of life was threatened. It takes guts to uproot a whole family. When people see no other way of resolving adverse conditions, they vote with their feet, whether it's Susan to Portsoy, that lorry driver, Dave, off to Canada or Muggy, Helen and Shy sampling Gibraltar. They all looked for a saner world to live in.

Before leaving I acquire some new words for my Scottish vocabulary, thanks to Susan. 'Loon' is how you'd describe a young male and 'quine' a girl up to late teens. Oh, and 'neep' is a turnip. I can't think for the life of me why I need to know that.

An Indignant Bus Driver

I'm heading out of Portsoy at half past nine, later than I hoped, but far less ignorant as to what it means to live here. Let's hope I make good progress to Inverness. My gamble in getting here certainly paid off. Thankfully I don't have to wait long before a bespectacled, burly-looking chap pulls up, bristly white moustache to the fore and wearing a brown leather jacket distressed enough to pass as an old schoolmaster's. He's Bob and not going far, but I'm very

228

welcome. Buoyed by my good fortune I put thoughts of direction aside and sound out his theory about The Fyvie.

'I know,' Bob says, in a boom of a voice. 'Ever heard the expression: I'll give you a bunch of fives?' He fists a hand. I reel back in mock retreat.

'Good one,' I say. His idea could be a knockout … until I remember that the name comes from where it was found, not what it might do. I don't disabuse him. Instead, I talk about Portsoy and admit my ignorance. 'I've never heard of the Doric language.'

'Ah, they've started to teach it in some schools now,' he says. 'It's similar to Gaelic.' He knows because he's a school bus driver and Bob does look out of scale with the car. He needs a bigger beast. Primary school kids and Banff Academy students are his charges. But he's bothered that you can't kick them off when they misbehave. 'You can get 'em banned. But know what 'appens then? They get picked up by car. And, if they're anti-social, it's one person, one car. At twenty-five quid a time!'

I aid and abet. 'Not giving the right message, is it?'

'But it gets worse. When some kids played truant – hardened skivers, I mean – they got well punished … with a ride in a stretch limo.'

'Bonkers,' I say. 'Wonder what those who never truant thought?' I retail one of my pet punishment-fit-the-crime solutions. 'If a kid breaks a window, they pay to replace it and putty it in. So it hits them in the pocket but they learn a useful skill too.'

He has a flashback to his heydays in the Royal Scots Dragoon Guards. Then he lets on that he's half English and half German. I know which half would dole out 'a bunch of fives'. Before we part, he enthuses about the seals he's seen; up to fifteen at a time when the tide's out at Portgordon. And how one of the ospreys' favourite fishing grounds is at Spey Bay, further down the coast. That's the sort of wildlife he's happy with. 'I'm dropping you off short of Arradoul,' he says, as if it's a stop on a bus route I should know about. Oh yes, Arradoul. Thanks. Just the stop I wanted.

A Dislocated Mountain Biker

It's too small to appear on my map. But I'm exactly where I should be. *What if we always are where we're meant to be?* This time

I couldn't be more convinced. A signpost at this junction points to 'Standalone'. I can't do anything but laugh and obey orders. I keep saying, 'I am. I am.'

Good humour opens doors! Within minutes, another car pulls up and a youngish chap looking as sparky as I feel hails me. 'Going as far as Elgin. That OK?'

'Sure is.' I'm hardly in before Callum and I are wagging chins.

'Would you believe it?' he says, smiling away. 'I dislocated the thumb of my left hand mountain biking. Lucky I'm right-handed. Off work two months and then I did it again!'

'Couldn't manage without mine,' I say. 'Or I'd be off road too.'

He works in the oil industry. 'Operations supervisor for downhill services you could say,' he laughs.

'Better watch downhill operations,' I retort. This lift's going to fly by.

Callum's spent nineteen years in the business – looks young for his age then – but since 1998 he's been working in Africa. I prick my ears up: a good opportunity to find out things first-hand.

'Nothing can prepare you for the scale of poverty,' he says. 'But they never show people begging on TV.'

'No. I'd never have believed the desperation – even faking growths on a child's neck – till I saw it in China.'

'We're utterly spoilt in the West. I've just been in Luanda, Angola. There's no social back-up. Charities do what they can. But it's not as if there's no money. There're good jobs for locals in the oil industry. Trouble is the corruption: the wealth falls into few hands. You have people getting eighty to ninety grand driving Hummers, but the rest living in tin shacks.'

Callum tells me some mates took a local guy out for a pizza and ran him back home. 'Found out he lived in a corrugated shed two steps down from the road, so it flooded when it rained. He had a wife, heavily pregnant, and a kid. And they all slept on one mattress on the floor. The chaps were so shocked – they worked with this guy – that they couldn't speak on the way back.'

Callum's worked in Nigeria and one of the poorest countries, Chad. 'There were a lot more ghettoes than what you'd call civilised places,' he says. 'The local tribal people set up camp outside any working base and muscle in on it.' Out driving one day Callum felt humbled to see a woman at the car window with river blindness while a helper did the begging.

That reminds me of a ghetto I heard about on a trip to Lisbon. 'Beggars came in from outside the city. A woman old enough to be a grandmother was trying to flog one pathetic overall. She held it up to one tourist after another. When that didn't work she uprooted plants from street planters and touted them. The vacant look on her face was pitiful.'

'They have to get by best as they can. In Africa you see kids sitting at the side of the road in their underpants playing with next to nothing, but they're happy.'

It's a picture that might be lost on the Wii generation of youngsters. What does Callum most look forward to?

'I work five weeks on, five weeks off, so it's time at home with the wife and kids.'

'Simple pleasures then.'

'And hobbies … when I'm not falling off the mountain bike.'

I can see now why he talks about a dislocated thumb with a smile – even a second time round. Callum's experiences give him an outlook not many can share. He drops me off in the middle of Elgin, but I feel disoriented.

A Change of Perspective

'Out of sight, out of mind' is a phrase that bugs me on this street corner. How can people even think about direction when it's as much as they can do to survive? The shanty town outside the big city is a metaphor: the underprivileged pushed to the edge. Simon Ruscoe's sculpture project in Devon comes to mind, representing nine-tenths of the world that live in poverty. I hope his nine monumental figures will be sited where they can't be overlooked, and help 'make poverty history'. Those little kids playing happily with next to nothing deserve more than a slogan.

I start walking to the outskirts of town when I'm stopped in my tracks by an Elgin Museum poster advertising an exhibition on the theme 'People and Place', the very connection I've been thinking about. Having made such progress towards Inverness, I can't pass up this opportunity. It's a test run for David Mackay: to find out if there's any relevance. Choice with trust again. And over to Lord Chance.

The museum's a short walk away but 'oh no': a reprise of the Portsoy marble shop experience. It's closed. Is there life within? I knock. The door's opened by a discreetly bearded chap who lets me in absent-mindedly, as if I'm half-expected. Only when I say why the theme grabbed me does he confirm that the museum's shut. But as I'm already in, I can look round.

'Well, thanks.' I shake hands on it and introduce myself.

He likewise: 'David Addison, curator.'

I laugh out loud but, in case he's disconcerted, let on that he's the namesake of a cousin whose parents gave mine the 'Blue Door' picture – the print I'd seen at Newcastle. Conditioned as I am to expect the unexpected, is this coincidence enough to justify my presence? David seems as keen to carry on talking as I am to discover what other reason there might be for this diversion.

It turns out that we share a background in advertising. He was a graphic designer, before a passion for history took over. He takes me back to beginnings. 'About three hundred million years ago the earth was one big landmass – we call it *Pangea* – which cracked up and the separate continents started to form.' That brings us to continental drift. David plots Scotland's passage: once stuck to Canada, it pushed east and south, bumping into England at the Solway. 'And still is pushing south,' he says, 'rising as it does so – one centimetre a year it's reckoned – at the same time as England's sinking.'

I can't help thinking there's a certain volition in this.

'But it doesn't stop at that. Eventually it's going to push England under France.'

The ultimate ignominy! Not much doubt about our joining the euro then … eventually. I love the way David's putting direction in this novel context. We may think we're charting our own direction but the earth might have different ideas!

David takes the long view further. 'Civilisations come and go. The last major Ice Age was ten thousand years ago and we're the latest addition to humanity. But ten million years ago there may have been another society that there's no evidence of. Every few million years the world wipes itself clean. There was a big disaster five million years ago. Let's imagine a handful of people survived. In the Atlantis story, seven people are supposed to have emerged from the sea. A small remnant of humanity like that could repeople the world.'

I can identify with the picture David's creating. 'What if' thinking stimulates my imagination. His speculations bring the history of mankind to life.

'We may look diverse but technically we're related. In Cambodia, there are people black as the ace of spades who look Chinese. We're hardly aware of our real ancestry.' David explains, 'If the toe next to your big toe is longer, chances are you've got some Roman blood in you.'

How many people know that? I make a note to examine my feet and mention how I was drawn to walk Hadrian's Wall Path some years before, a journey that evolved into my first book.

David's eyes light up. 'Well, I used to work at Birdoswald!'

'That was one of the sites I wanted to visit,' I sigh.

'I had an experience there I can't forget.'

I'm all ears.

'I was on night duty on my own. It was a summer's evening and I was looking over to the River Irthing valley. It must have been about eight o'clock when I saw a little cloud drifting over the trees. You know what it's like when you feel the hairs raising at the back of your head?'

'Yes, yes,' I say.

'Well, I felt as though someone was looking at me and turned round quickly.'

What? Who? Ghost of a Roman soldier?

'I saw piercing red eyes looking at me through the window.'

'No! You must have been spooked.'

'I was. And I knew legionaries carried two pila – javelins. The Amityville Horror flashed through my mind until I realised what the eyes were.'

'Yes?'

'Lights on the freezer.'

I burst out laughing.

He nods smugly, master of deception. But the touch of humour only makes me take him more seriously. Now that we're on a Roman theme – in Pictish country – I ask him about the Picts. I know their skirmishing tactics outwitted the Romans.

'The Romans tried to bribe 'em but it didn't work. While the Romans believed in life preservation, the Picts thought it an honour to die in battle. Painted blue all over and screaming, they'd charge downhill. That's where 'screaming blue murder' comes from. Blue being the colour of the sky, they thought themselves invisible. And they'd fight to the death. It wasn't just men the Romans had to contend with. The women followed. If you killed her man, you'd have his woman to fight off next.'

'The men sound fearsome enough.'

'There were other reasons the Romans didn't succeed in Scotland,' David adds. 'The distance was too great. And there's the sixty-three degrees north rule.'

I hadn't heard that one.

'When Ptolemy drew his map he flattened the country and the Romans went by the Greek navigation which told them that nothing existed beyond sixty-three degrees north. They thought you'd fall off the end of the Earth, or that it was godless country with devils and dragons, so cold even the gods wouldn't want it.'

'Leaving it all to the Scots. Quite right too.'

We tour the 'People and Place' exhibition spanning 1000 years of Scottish history with a Moray perspective. But I'm more than happy with his perspective and the window he's opened on the journey of mankind. The museum is the oldest independent museum in Scotland. How fortunate to have as its curator an independently-minded person whose passion for history couldn't be more alive. I needed no coincidences to justify my presence. David's enthusiasm was enough.

A Surfing Medic

I spent well over an hour in the museum and it's nearly one o'clock. No time to lose, not even to examine the length of my toes. Knowing that much of the traffic will be on round-town journeys, I make for the outskirts. Four roundabouts later I hit a more open stretch of road and just beyond a junction is a pull-in for buses: my stop.

I set myself up at the front: rucksack on the ground, thumb at the ready, eyes peeled. But my thoughts are shifting like tectonic plates between the people I've met: David, the train driver, Rory and Liz from Findhorn, John Watson and Susan at Portsoy, Bob, the bus driver, Callum, of downhill services fame, and now David, the curator. How they've enriched this stretch of the journey. And what incredible luck! But is it? The timing's been impeccable and the whole diversion feels orchestrated. To have the Portsoy shop *and* the Elgin Museum opened up for me makes the point: choice and chance acting in concert. Excellent teamwork, chaps! Keep it up.

As always, hitching brings me back to the present … and future. If I get a lift to Inverness now, I can book into a youth hostel. Then I'll need a big push to get to Dunnet Head tomorrow. I'm supposed to be dropping in on David Mackay: a tall order … but while I'm thinking ahead, I'm thumbing on auto-pilot. So it's a jolt when a car grinds to a halt. I grab the rucksack and run to the door. One of the blackest barnets I've seen complete with drop-down sideburns sets off a spirited face. A loosely-wound red scarf lends a dash of colour.

'Hi, I'm Rob. Where you going?'

'Inverness.'

'I'm off to Thurso. Jump in.'

Thurso?! God. That's way beyond Inverness and not far short of Dunnet.

No time to dwell on a miracle. Rob's mind is on one thing: fun. He's spent twenty years surfing. It took him to Australia and New Zealand before that. Rob's keen to catch the surf now. The sky's racing: the sun roof's open. Fresh air floods the car and the wind's in our sails, but I don't want to be blown off course. I talk about direction-seeking.

Rob whistles through his CV. He'd been a computer analyst in New Zealand. 'Boring office job,' he says. But a South African doctor he met in a pub said, "I can see you're not happy with your life." That had him wondering where he'd be in five years' time. His father was a doctor but Rob hadn't thought of medicine. A New Zealand passport helped him get on a four-year course in Australia and qualify. As a junior doctor now, he's happy. 'I'm doing a job I enjoy, and still surfing.'

I wondered whether any specialty appealed to him.

'Well, I've been on respiratory medicine, but fancy becoming a GP, treating people from the cat's cradle to the grave.' Seeing me scribble away, Rob observes, 'You know, everything you write will be from your paradigm.'

'Interesting. Would all my experiences follow from the way I see things? And where did this paradigm come from?'

'It starts from the time you were born.'

'A bomb was supposed to have landed nearby. That can't have helped.'

Rob's in medical mode and my flippant remark doesn't interrupt his flow. 'Conditions can be psychological as much as physical. The infant's brain has a lot of neuronal plasticity, so connections are much easier to make up to puberty.' He gives an example. 'If toddlers are kept in cots too long and get used to seeing everything through vertical bars, they don't develop the means to see horizontal lines. Vertical lines become hard-wired into the brain.'

'Extraordinary. Looking at things from other points of view must be good then. But how about correcting habits that get locked in?'

'Much harder as time goes by,' Rob says, 'especially if you don't take control. Like any muscle the brain seizes up if you don't use it and you have to work hard to reactivate it. Keeping the brain active by doing things like crosswords can stave off dementia and Alzheimer's.'

Has he had to deal with the elderly?

'Might sound strange but I quite enjoy looking after dying patients,' Rob confides. 'Making them comfortable and helping families cope is rewarding. I keep them in the picture, so everyone knows what's happening and going to happen. With illness, there's always the fear of death.'

'I know it's a bit morbid Rob, but how easy is it to die?' I remember some friends whose daughter died in her twenties from an aneurism.

'Yes. Arteries can have a bubble – a balloon-like swelling – which ruptures after some form of stress. We had a tragic case in Australia. The autopsy confirmed there'd been an aneurism in a young woman. It turned out she and her husband had been trying for a second child at the time.'

I shake my head. 'Ghastly.'

'Then again, if you stripped naked on those hills over there, you wouldn't last long.'

'I don't think I'll bother just yet.'

We'd sailed past Inverness, crossed the Black Isle and were heading up the east coast on the A9 with the thin paw of the Cromarty Firth to our right and the hills of Easter Ross ranging ever higher to a snowline on the left. But only glimpses. Rob is motoring.

So what about births? Had they been part of his training?

'Sure. Delivering a baby is always an emotional experience.' Rob's often been moved to tears. Refreshing to hear that from a professional.

He married only three months earlier. 'We had a huge wedding – two hundred and fifty guests – in my uncle's barn. And a great mix of cultures: my wife's parents are from Mauritius.'

I can appreciate the richness of such an occasion. My wife's from Guyana, so I've had my share of cultural get-togethers. But what about the other buzz he gets? 'This surfing, Rob. What grabs you? All I've done is body boarding.'

'You have to be in the right place at the right time. When you get it right, you want to keep finding that rightness. A lot of time's spent checking charts, times, tides and winds. But when it all comes together it's just perfect.'

Mischievously, I wonder how clinical his approach has been today.

'Well, the wind's from the south-east and will be around ten mph this evening; there's a fifteen-foot swell coming from the west at ten-second wave lengths; it'll be low tide by five and I need to be in the water, wetsuit on, by three-thirty. Then again beaches have different conditions. At Thurso East, where I'm heading, the waves break over a slate reef, so smoothish.'

'Wow.' I'm impressed.

'Yes. There's a poetry to surfing.'

'I wonder whether that equates with the feeling I get when I'm in the right place at the right time. Like now: a sense of belonging, as if I couldn't be anywhere else but here. That's a paradigm I'd like to live by!'

Rob sits up. 'You may find this hard to believe but, when my wife and I lived in Australia, we befriended a supermarket cashier involved with a film school. They asked us on camera where we were from, who we visited and what we liked to do when we did. Then – Jeremy it was – went to my place, visited my parents at

Epsom and did the things we said we liked to do. It'll be on the TV networks by now.'

I'm intrigued by this attempt at living a parallel life. 'I've speculated how this trip might work out if I leave on the very same day next year. *What if paradigms so govern us that the same type of experiences keep repeating?* Or might circumstances challenge the choices and chance throw up new discoveries?'

'Only one way to find out. Try it.'

I laugh. But seriously, would I take the idea on? If I'd left from the Lizard a day earlier, this journey could never have started with the Love Story. Ingrid and Snowy would have been returning from a holiday. Each time surely has its own character, its own rightness. It's important simply to *be* and *be here now*.

We've crossed over the Dornoch Firth, skirted round Loch Fleet and, with the North Sea ours for the taking, two men on two missions are breezing north. The luck that brought me this far could get me within spitting distance of Dunnet Head tonight. But Rob's going to turn towards Thurso at a place called Latheron, veering away from Lybster and David Mackay. I have to tell Rob I'm keeping my promise.

We've little time left. In a flashback I remember that one of Jez's career options was to become a paramedic. Can Rob help? 'Would the job suit him?'

'Depends. It can be quick-fix exciting but there's a lot of hanging around and unsocial hours. He'd be seeing the darker side of life – alcohol, drugs – and might get threatened, but it's rewarding when you take control.'

'Mmm. With what Jez has been through I think he could handle it and he's used to working odd hours.'

'It's how he copes with everyday life too. You can lose trust and faith in people and that might rub off on other relationships.'

'Hopefully I can put that to him. Only Jez can decide.' Then I pose a far more intractable problem: Graham and his phantom limb pain.

Rob does his best. 'An area of the brain would keep telling him a hand's still there. When a nerve ending's cut it can reform incorrectly and get attached to an adrenaline receptor.' One solution, he thinks, might be to re-train the senses so that in time the part of the brain that connects to the hand atrophies.

It sounds a long and complicated process. 'I find the whole business of the body/mind connection fascinating but in Graham's case it's an incredibly taxing situation to come to terms with.'

Rob nods. 'You might be interested in a book: *Ten Defining Moments in Medicine* by James Le Fanu. And another one I found stimulating: *Dissecting the Rainbow* I think it's called. Shows how science can be used creatively.'

We shake hands when he reaches Latheron and I pull at the door handle.

'But we can over-medicalise life,' he says as I get out.

'Good surfing,' I say and put a hand up in thanks. Rob's an inspiration. It's a wrench parting.

A Perverse Syndrome

I'm a bit concerned when I look at my watch: 3.15 already, leaving Rob precious little time to catch the incoming tide at Thurso East, but a phenomenally good time for me. This was by far the longest hitch, and could have been longer, if only. For once though I can admire the view. Pity it's scarred. Two oil rigs cast a rigid shadow over the untamed flows of the North Sea. On shore, cottages are scattered like jackstones at the fringes of fields. Maybe some oil workers live in these very cottages, and where I see unsightliness they see only the risks colleagues take day by day.

It's about three miles to Lybster but I won't hitch. I'll savour the sea air. When I reach Lybster, a road sign reads *Quatre Bras*, or Four Arms, presumably referring to the crossroads, but why in French? A woman says it's a battle in the Napoleonic wars. No doubt men from hereabouts played a vital part. Substantial stone buildings line the main street which is wide enough for a dual carriageway. This feels like a village of stature. Two B & B places are full up. I'd noticed a signboard for the Bay View Hotel – same name as the road our house sits on – but didn't take the coincidence as a gimme. Now I have to play the shot.

There's a *distrait* casualness about the place. The locals at the bar hardly notice me. But the landlady's cheerful enough and it's third time lucky. They have a spare room with three single beds for a reasonable £28. Great. Her jeans scuff the ground as she leads the way. First impressions can be misleading but they stick. When

I put the kettle on for a cup of tea and it fails to boil, I am stuck. Her husband brings a replacement kettle and returns the original one a little later. 'Only the fuse,' he says.

The landlady had explained the eccentric workings of the bathroom shower. 'You have to turn the knob to cold,' she said. 'Then it gets hot.'

I'd be the first to admit I have problems with showers. I've never understood why controls can't be more uniform. That aside, I'm convinced that showers develop minds of their own, alien intelligences infected with perversity default syndrome. I turn this one to cold as instructed. But it *is* cold. So far so bad. I turn it to hot. It gets colder: perversity to the power of two! And then the shower tray starts filling up. The drain's blocked. The floor's going to fill up too. I trip downstairs to confront the landlady. 'Sorry to trouble you again but ...' de dah, de dah, de dah.

'No trouble,' she says. I leave her to play with the controls and pump a plunger while I up-end my cuppa. 'There, that's sorted,' she reassures. 'Should be hot enough now. Shall I leave it running?'

'Please.' I step in. Wow! Hot enough? The water's roasting. I can't be bothered to call her back. Or to fiddle with the erratic knob. I work out a modus vivendi: the heat offset system. Standing to one side, I gingerly hold the flannel – by its extremities – under the flaming hot water, leave to cool off and then, dotted with gel, apply it in sweeping motions as one might stroke a cat.

I can see why cats find that so soothing ... when someone else does it. Never mind. I take my time. Sometimes I stop and hold the flannel against a shoulder or small of the back, as if to ease an imagined ache. I'm reminded of the times when my mother thought the solution to any pain, strain or swelling was a hot compress. Having covered myself in a thin veneer of gel, I have the narcissistic pleasure of massaging it all off. Now I know what it's like to feel steam-cleaned and pressed.

Another discovery: the toes. I remember to check. The toe next to the big toe on the left foot is shorter, but on the right foot slightly longer. I'd never realised. Am I half Roman? Perhaps I can call myself Romano-British! I know what it does tell me: I'm as inconsistent as a malfunctioning knob. But then, there are always ways round one's deficiencies.

Day Fifteen

Lybster to Dunnet

'Chance throws up experiences the only way it can ... randomly'

A New Path

Something hasn't quite dawned on me: this is the day for the destination, but I'm not ready to accept it. When the target's in sight, it's as if I've lost the will to aim. I know why – I'll be saying goodbye to this life of lifts. But there still is today: David Mackay to meet; Dunnet Head to reach, a mere forty miles or so away; the Gills Bay ferry to catch; and Orkney beckoning. I pad downstairs where this ragged old sweater and jeans are joined at the breakfast table by a switched-on business suit. What cards has life dealt its wearer?

Between scoops of cereal, Les Dobson rattles off his career path: mechanical engineering apprentice ... testing pressure vessels ... designing equipment ... training locals in Singapore ... all by the age of twenty-nine.

'Good going,' is as much as I – technophobe to the core – can muster.

He loved the place so much he stayed three years, and met his wife there, from Sunderland ... ran an electronics laboratory in Hong Kong ... trains quality auditors now ... and administers ISO9000, 14000 and 18000, covering quality, environmental, and health and safety standards. And *I so* appreciate a simple breakfast.

I nod approvingly, but inwardly flinch. I once had a quality control man for a customer who was so disturbed by the slightest blemishes in glass that we had to replace most of his double glazing. His wife could only go shopping in his prized red Mini on dry days. Is Les like that? I hope not. But he *is* going on. More than the moves he's made, I want to know what's moved him. 'When I stopped enjoying a job, something else always turned up,' he says. 'When I was training to be a quality assurance manager this guy walked into the class with a cut-out from a newspaper saying, "I don't fancy this job. Anyone interested?" I was and got the job.' He played his luck. 'Whenever I've made a change, it's been the right time,' he says. That's more like it. Open to opportunities, he's found direction in life: aware of destinations but awake to new paths.

One path I have to explore is the one beyond Dunnet Head, to North Ronaldsay. I need to sort out accommodation for a few days. Back in my room, I call the one owner of a cottage I have a contact number for. And good news: it's available from Saturday. 'I'll confirm,' I say, 'once I'm sure of catching the ferry from Kirkwall.'

'Why not fly?' she says. 'There's a flight every day. It's only twelve pounds return.'

I'm staggered. 'Why ... yes, of course.' And so cheap. That changes everything. I can catch the Gills ferry tomorrow. I've a day in hand. What will I do with it? 'Is there anything I ought to see in Lybster before I leave,' I ask the landlady as I settle up.

'Northlands Creative Glass,' she says and I'm whisked into a personal obsession. She attends courses and shows me some of the designer glassware in her collection: a slender sculptural flask drawn up into a delicate tapering tendril, a huge light bulb of glass and a paperweight with bands of colour floating through it like tropical fish.

Forget the drooping jeans and the aberrant shower! Like Les, this lady's in transition: a landlady today but – who knows? – the glass artist of tomorrow. Showers will always go wrong but they just wash over you. Sometimes not even that. With glass the only limits are the levels of skill and the scope of an imagination. Standards are one thing; what you live for is another. I think even Les might agree.

An Allusive Transparency

It's dreich! The band of rain's arrived and my walk's a drizzly canter. But when I reach what looks like a Victorian school building I'm greeted by sunshine – a display of dazzling studio glass inside – and by Michael, the technician, who offers to show me round. He introduces me to glass blowing in the hot workshop, but glass can also be shaped over a gas flame, called lampworking. In the cold workshop, he describes how engraving effects are achieved using a copper wheel or sandblasting technique. With a lost wax process, glass can be cast and in the kiln room, glass formed from moulds is fired.

I'm astonished by the complexity of choices and the skills required. 'We do a lot of work with children,' Michael says. 'We have outreach projects with a local high school. Groups spend whole weekends here.' Bet they love it.

Artists in residence help run these projects. 'We hope to do fantastic things with glass, but also benefit the community and Caithness,' one of them tells me. Ideas are exchanged in masterclasses with painters, sculptors, architects, designers and so on. This is an international centre of excellence, attracting glass artists from all over the world. For a small fishing village in Caithness to play host to it takes some beating. No wonder the road's so wide!

I thank Michael for the conducted tour and can't believe I've been here an hour. Taking another look at the display cabinets on the way out, I'm drawn to a group of glass forms in beguiling drifts of sea blues and greens. Perfect for flower arranging. But that would undermine the meaning in the title: *Whaligoe Women*.

This group is a community. All look as if they have cloaks drawn tight against the elements. I see them as watchers on a cliff top, fearful for their menfolk who had set off for a day's fishing before a storm blew up. Though the faces are nothing more than narrow oval openings, the voids are expressive: the wise voices of reassurance from older ones but the worries of younger women not so readily assuaged. That I can read all this into the group speaks volumes for the power of glass – and Gillian Mannings Cox, the maker – to incite the imagination.

I've loved glass ever since playing marbles in the gutter as a kid. The multi-coloured leaf shapes inside fascinated me, much as a mosquito might, trapped in amber. Glass has the 'now' factor. It shifts perceptions. The sparkle of light and lure of reflections open up windows in what otherwise might only be viewed as a vase, bottle or bowl. My quality control customer wanted to see what he expected, not blemishes that might offer a less predictable view of the world.

A Spanking Stone Engraver

While I've been wrapped up in the world of glass, it's been bucketing down outside and still is. My hooded jacket and boots keep me dry but the 'waterproof' trousers only provide proof of water as I slosh my way to the outskirts, and David Mackay. I'm on tenterhooks. When I don't have a clue what to expect – apart from some weightlifting tips – how will I unearth the unknown? But I have to find him first. One house sign catches my eye: 'Mackay 4'. I try my luck.

'Ach, there's lots of Mackays round here,' the Mackay says. 'This is Mackay country.'

That's a revelation.

'You'll be wanting the Mackay at the far end on the right.'

'With a porch?'

'Aye.'

The last house on the right is a single-storey cottage set back from the main road. I knock and hear noises. Good. Someone's in. The tall, fully bearded figure of a man comes to the door looking somewhat stern. If I didn't know this was David Mackay, stone engraver, I'd have thought Captain Mackay and saluted. I apologise for the drips and explain that Bob, the glazing systems chap, recommended I look him up. But I say nothing about what really brings me here.

'You'd better come in,' he says. I leave my soggy jacket and boots in the porch, happy to accept the offer of a coffee. When I ask why he took up stone engraving, David can't think what sparked off his interest.

'Drifted into it,' he says.

'Yes?' There must be more to it than that I'm thinking.

'It's a legacy. What I do is permanent. That has to be one reason.'

I'm still not convinced. 'What excited you as a boy then?'

He looks nonplussed. 'Learning to ride a bike?'

Better be more specific. 'Might a stone have caught your eye?'

'Well, like any kid, I collected stones from the beach, and still do. For the shape, colour, form, even crystals. Seeing my grandfather at work – he was a blacksmith – could have set me off.'

'I bet.' That jogs my memory. I tell of a time I was playing with some wooden bricks in the front garden when a passer-by asked me for one. 'Three-year-olds don't argue with adults. But I was shocked to see him whittle away at my precious brick with a knife. "There you are," he said and handed me a scooped-out boat. I reckon that's when I first learned about creativity.'

'Good,' David exclaims, 'and I've remembered. One of the first rocks I ever picked up was at North Wick. Walking along the beach, I saw this beautiful green rounded rock. Serpentine it was.'

I feel like punching the air and mention my geological link between the Lizard and Portsoy. Now I've struck a personal connection with those rocks in my rucksack.

David leads me to a corrugated hangar of a building. Monolithic slabs – up to twice the height of an average gravestone – are lined up, some ready for engraving, some nearly finished. Commissions range from a commemorative stone on a Himalayan mountain to a large circular slab for a bar floor with an elaborate geometric design.

How does he move these great weights around?

'If the Egyptians can do it, I can,' he says, 'with a little ingenuity and a home-made trolley. I call it a spanker.'

245

I laugh out loud. 'Good Scottish name, that.'

He handles weights up to three-quarters of a ton, 'spanking' slabs to a workbench before easing them up on to a carpet-strip bed. A car jack and a lift help him get some blocks to the right working height. Really heavy slabs call for a JCB. Once he took out a flagstone forty feet long and three feet wide from a Caithness quarry to make an obelisk. A slice he calls it! David isn't the sort of person to spurn a challenge.

I tell him what's spurring me on: the last lap of my hitchhike to Dunnet Head.

'Ah, you'll see my stone there,' he says. 'Marks it out as the northernmost point of mainland Britain.'

Incredible! I have to tell him what clinched the destination. 'I went into a Bideford art gallery and happened to pick up a leaflet on a papermaker, Joanne Kaar, who lives at Dunnet Head. Heaven knows what it was doing there.'

David breaks in. 'I know her' – of course he does! – 'and her father, Mick O'Donnell. He's a woodturner. Lives near there too. Pop in to see him if you get a chance.' He gives me directions. 'You'll recognise the place. There's a boat outside.'

Bizarre. I'm going from one connection to another, and David's talking as if all this is commonplace. Maybe in this neck of the woods – Mackay country and beyond – creative people are more in touch. But for this southerner to meet the man who marked my destination, and knows the woman who helped confirm it, is anything but commonplace. That 'porch' man suggests I drop in on 'boat' man is hugely entertaining. I'm playing a game of consequences on a board suspiciously like a map of Scotland. I ought to be blown away by now but David makes it a reality.

'Tell you what, I can run you to Wick if you like.'

As we motor along the coast road, past the Whaligoe of those glass women, with the North Sea's vast breaths to our right, I hear one special reason why he's taking me to Wick. In 1936 L.S.Lowry painted two scenes there: one of *The Old House* and one of *The Steps*. As a heritage project, David carved reproductions in stone of those two paintings, each of which is mounted in situ. He'd like me to see them: first *The Steps*, 'known locally as the Black Stairs,' he says. I'm taken by the names of fish in English and dialect on each step as we approach his carving. 'There's something about this that other people have not picked up on,' he says mysteriously and points to a figure. 'That's my mother.'

The way he says it makes me think it's his own private memorial. Only he would know it. I trace my fingers over its surface in appreciation. Then we walk to the second site. He tells me that his mother would have been sixteen when Lowry painted his pictures and that she was born between the sites of both paintings. How appropriate for one figure to be that of David's own mother. Lowry would have done the same. A brief look at the second reproduction, an admiring glance at the historic buildings around and it's time to move on.

'So you'll be off thumbing,' David says. 'I've picked up hitchhikers in the past – a girl once, sitting on a trash can. She was German but spoke good English and we spent a day out in a boat.'

It sounds as though he fancied her.

'I said, "How brave you are to go out with a total stranger." Her eyes flashed: the sun was in them. "You couldn't have harmed me," she said. "I'm a witch." '

I'm riveted. Am I dreaming? I've heard this before, haven't I?

'She rolled up her T-shirt. Tattooed on her shoulder was a witch on a broomstick.'

'This is too much,' I say. 'Someone's told me the same story, or something very like it.' My mind's racing to places I've been and people I've spoken to, but I can't twig where I might have heard.

'You must tell me when you find out.' David's as frustrated by my amnesia as I am.

I jot down his email address. 'So did you keep in touch?'

He shakes his head. 'Treated her to dinner after and still have photographs. That's all. But something happened on the way home. I knocked down a roe deer.'

The notion that I've been told the same story twice on this journey is too preposterous for me to take in, but the harder I try to force the memory to the surface, the more it slips away. Most likely the very time I forget about it I'll remember. Getting the next lift is enough for me to think about ... for the moment.

A Liberated Cattle Farmer

On the outskirts of Wick, I wait with thumb in the air but witless. My head's buzzing. A witch keeps shooting off to somewhere I can't pin down. I have to forget that I'm even trying to remember – that's the key. And look what happens when my mind's elsewhere: a car pulls up and a man of my vintage is going my way. He carries a natural gravitas I can only dream about and his name, Erland Flett, backs it up. He's only too keen to plot his career path.

'I used to drive heavy plant and worked my way up in oil to be a main contractor for Occidental. But I sat in the office for twenty-five years, like being in prison.'

So he had a bit of an awakening?

'Well, it wasn't what I really wanted to do.'

I laughed … to myself. How many times have I said that?

'I was farming part-time then and decided to make a proper go of it. With the help of my two sons I built things up to become the biggest beef cattle farmer in Orkney.'

The mere mention of Orkney impresses me. Makes me feel I'm almost there.

'Had my picture in the press as getting the biggest subsidy,' he says. The publicity wasn't that welcome. Semi-retired now, he's concerned about the future of farming. With half the world starving, he bemoans the fact that cows over a certain age can't be used for meat: one consequence of mad cow disease. 'But if an old cow's due to be dumped, her calf can be given to a young cow that's lost hers.'

The pragmatic cattleman's talking.

'Livelihoods have been diverted to Dounreay,' he says. 'There used to be three hundred on Stroma' – an island off the north-east tip of Scotland – 'but now, no-one.'

My mind's elsewhere too. I tell him I'm bound for North Ronaldsay. What's it like?

'Raw,' he says. He last went two years ago. 'When the rain's lashing down, the old flagstone roofs can drip on you.'

I mention that I plan to fly.

'I stay not far from the airport,' he says, 'at Holm, by the Churchill Barriers.'

'Stay? Are you lodging then?'

'No,' he smiles. 'That's what we say when we mean 'live'.'

A shake of the hands and he drops me off. I guess wherever we are, we're only staying. My stay with Erland has been like one of life's lodgings. How many other lives have I lived on this trip?

A few homesteads are dotted here and there in the wildness of open country, but I'm soaking up the expanse of sea and space. The sense of isolation makes me feel close to another sort of reality, beyond. Others might think differently about 'staying' in such remote parts. One bungalow I pass is called 'Aargh'.

A Wildly Creative Mind

The road is empty enough for me to stop and thumb whenever a car shows up. I'm happy pitching along, with the sweep of Dunnet Bay to my left and the promise of more wildness round the corner. After a two or three-mile jaunt a modest car stops and a quizzical glance from the driver prompts me to blurt out, 'I'm looking for Mick O'Donnell. He lives round here, with a boat outside.' I might have guessed: he knows and can drop me there, a few miles on, at a village called Brough.

On the way we pass the Northern Sands Hotel at Dunnet. I make a note to pop in later while Simon's telling me what he didn't want to do after qualifying as a teacher: teach history to fourteen-year-olds. He went on to architecture school but didn't fancy that career either. 'I'm on an independent creative path now,' he says – he must be in his forties – and invests the phrase with an authority the biggest beef cattle farmer in Orkney would find it hard to muster. 'I do lino cuts,' he adds. 'One-foot-square images of Greek myths: that's what I'm working on. There might be twenty odd at the finish and I've written poetry to go with them.'

Simon's enthusiasm is catching. What does he plan to do with the work?

'Show them in a gallery. They'd make a panel three feet by eight, or a book maybe. I've a huge body of work but don't know what to do with it,' he adds wistfully.

Isn't that agonizingly ironic? When you find out what you want to do, you don't know what to do with it. Simon juggles with ideas but they're still up in the air.

'We're an ingenious, dark, melancholy people here,' he says. That explains the 'Aargh'. But there's hope of financial salvation. Simon has a plan: property developing with a studio to attract artistic soul mates. Looking for what they want to do, no doubt. 'I might be interested,' I say. 'You never know.' And before I know it there's the boat. Is Mick O'Donnell in?

A Well Seasoned Woodturner

I strike lucky. Again. Mick's anything but dark and melancholy. The mere mention of his daughter Joanne, and a reference to David Mackay, is enough for me to be welcomed aboard. With bristly moustache, arching eyebrows and swept-back looks, Mick reminds me of a vintage motorcyclist.

What can I tease out this time? Sitting at a table in what must double as an office, I hear he's a man of many parts: working in nuclear fuels once, then lighthouse keeper, fisherman and farmer. Many years ago he found what he really wanted to do: woodturning. He shows me a beautifully illustrated book he's written: *Decorating Turned Wood*. Mick turns the forms and his wife Liz, who has a fine arts degree, does the decoration. What surprises me is that he works with green, unseasoned wood.

'Sycamore's the only wood I use now,' he says, 'mostly from fallen trees.'

Sycamore's a tree I have little regard for: one of the maple family but with none of the graces. However, its fine-grained wood does allow Liz free rein to decorate with inks and dyes. Mick turns it thin so it's less prone to cracking but, if a piece does split, Liz designs a bird or sea-shell around the split area. That's ingenuity for you. I have to admire the light touch to these bowls that lends a poetry to the prosaic sycamore. What if a bowl splits too badly? With Mick's expertise that can't happen too often, but if it does …?

'Simple. I cut it in half,' he says. 'Then it's out of my mind.'

I applaud. If only we could treat all mischance the same. I thank Mick and get up to go. 'Ah, but I must call on Joanne.' That was a goal I'd set myself before starting this journey. 'I'd love to see her work.'

Mick draws a sketch map, then rings Joanne. She's preparing

for an exhibition but is happy for me to look in tomorrow. 'So where're you off to now?' Mick asks.

'Got my eyes on the Northern Sands,' I say. I can't believe how soon I'm sitting down to a fillet steak with all the trimmings, after Mick runs me there.

A Forgetful Reminder

I'm told that Prince Charles's entourage stayed at this hotel a while back. No wonder the meal looks good. I've plenty to mull over as I savour it. What came of my meeting with Mick? Nothing like the David Mackay revelations for sure. I couldn't expect that. Chance throws up experience the only way it can … randomly.

I'd learned about woodturning though and the common-or-garden sycamore's earned a reprieve. I did pick up that cutting-in-half tip too. I can do without reminders from past mistakes that I might fall flat on my face. Cutting them in half mentally is one way to leave them behind.

But is it that easy to forget misfortune? That's what I'm thinking as I cut into the steak when whoa! A witch crash-lands on my plate. At last I remember: the same thing didn't happen before. It was the joke that my friend Ronald told me back in Bath: about the lorry driver who picked up a hitchhiker. When the girl warned him not to try any funny business because she was a witch he took no notice, and next thing he *turned* into a lay-by. That was it!

Now that my memory's unstuck, a dose of speculation joins the tomatoes and mushrooms on the steak plate. What are the chances of an offbeat joke becoming fact? On this border between fact and fiction the odds had to be unreal. There's a belief that, if you're able to imagine something happening, it probably can. *But what if memories buried in our unconscious make connections on some ethereal wavelength? What if the last laugh's on me?* The questions follow me upstairs and wallpaper the room while I try to imagine the pattern of tomorrow.

I'll get up early. Breakfast is booked for 7.45. Then I'll strike out for Dunnet Head, but no hitching. I want to walk the five miles there and take in the atmosphere at this northernmost tip. I'll travel light, leaving the camping stuff from my rucksack in the reception. But I have to hike the five miles back for the 12.15 bus which will get me to Gills Bay – eight miles away – in time to catch the 1.45 ferry.

That's the reality. The imagining is all about how I'm going to feel on the last lap of this journey. Exhilarated? Fulfilled? I'll have done it in 50 lifts and 16 days. Those are the bald figures. But I wallow in a sea of nostalgia, thinking about all those who made this trip possible in what feels like an unbroken chain of connections.

I start listing them until I realise I'm trying to make sense. Instead of simply letting things happen, I want to learn from experience and build on it. That's what I'm doing now: hoping I'll meet the people in the most northerly house and find out what brought them there. What am I contemplating? Yet another connection! Bed stares me in the face but, in this welter of past and future speculations, the present is no bedfellow. I can't help wondering what tricks chance might play on me tomorrow.

Day Sixteen
Dunnet Head and Beyond

'How had this all happened? By chance?'

A Last Hitch

I'm ready to leave shortly after nine, delayed by a slap-up breakfast and chats with the young woman who served it. She told me not to judge Kevin, her partner – who booked me in – by appearances. He did look and sound abrupt.

My inside and outside are at one as I set off. The wind is bowling all of me along. It's tugging at my sleeves, whipping drops from the end of my nose and slapping the loose rucksack straps against my back as if I might just win the Knacker's Yard Handicap with an extra switch of the crop. I canter past Mick's cottage, catch a glimpse of one called Hilligoe and another called Sinigoe, before stretching out my hands like sails and bellowing 'Here I go!'

Soon all habitation's behind me and nothing but moorland all round. A shaft of sunlight, breaking through the veil of cloud, flashes the russets and faded purples of heathers. As I lurch along this curving track – Matthew's swagger serves me well – grasses quiver and wavelets scud in a brackish pool. I'm only stopped on my windblown path by the sight of some Highland cattle with huge upturned handlebars of horns. There's something medieval about their presence here in a thicket of gorse. They put me in mind of clerestories, rood screens and misericords – age-old but timeless.

While I gaze, a car pulls up and three young chaps jump out, all in jeans and black jackets, cameras at the ready. They're from Thailand. But whatever brings them here?

One with a white cap acts as spokesman. 'We want to explore Scotland,' he says. 'We're taking grids on the map and covering the country, bit by bit.'

I hardly know Scotland. Huge tracts of England are foreign to me, to say nothing of Wales. Set against their grid reference precision my journey feels like a drunken stumble.

'You like a lift?' the white cap asks.

'Oh no. I couldn't,' I say, shocked at the thought, 'but hope to see you there.'

It can't be far now. As they drive off I spot the fleeting white rumps of two deer, startled by the sound of the engine. I burn up the last mile, reaching Dunnet Head by a quarter to eleven and there, at the edge of the car park, is the stone, David Mackay's stone. Some seven feet high, with a pointed peak, the stone speaks the simple, 'spanking' truth in white and gold engraved lettering:

I've waited sixteen days for this. I've done it to Dunnet. Wayhay! But I haven't a clue how to celebrate until three grinning faces emerge from a dip in the cliffside. We take photos: me of them and them of me with my camera, them of me and me of them with theirs. It's all snap-happy and jolly-good-chaps-together stuff. They are Kid – he with the white cap, Jay and Pod – the black caps, all on an MBA course at the University of Wales. I'm sitting in their car now. Kid had a job at a Thai airport. 'Strategy planning,'

he says. Jay's got the travel bug but 'not to popular places.' Kid and Jay want more of the world in their lives while Pod hankers to play football but will stay in London for a year or two selling electronic parts.

I like the asymmetry: these chaps starting their exploration as I'm coming to the end of mine. I reach for the door when Kid winkles a piece of paper from his pocket. He holds out the words like a banner: 'Love conquers all. Let us all give in to love.' They smile, and I'm staggered that such a sentiment is shared by blokeish chaps like these, let alone ones I'd met minutes before.

Kid dips into his pocket again and out comes another note – a currency note! 'For you,' he says. I look in disbelief at a Thai banknote, faced up by the King of Thailand and in a denomination of twenty, whatever that's worth. These chaps insist on giving me money when all I've done is talk ... and listen. We part with hugs and handshakes. How close I've been at this furthest point to these three, from the furthest point I could possibly have imagined. I'm so taken aback by their gesture, I don't even think of giving them anything in return.

I can't leave yet though. Who might live at the northernmost habitation and what brought them there? I try the lighthouse complex. Some of the buildings look lived in but, with no signs of life, I turn to four coastguard cottages above the car park. Not till I knock on number four do I get a response, from a puzzled-looking man. They can't get many door-to-door salesmen in these parts so I cut to the chase: 'I was hoping to meet the people who live in the lighthouse buildings. You wouldn't happen to ...'

'Ah, that'll be the Sutherlands,' he says. 'They've got a recording studio and compose too. They hold concerts here every so often – soul, jazz and country.'

'Shame I've missed them.' It looks as though this will have to do. But how did he come to live here? Richard Clack puts me wise.

'Perfect timing,' he says. 'We were touring in a campervan, saw the sale sign on the Friday and the very day we found this property, we completed the sale of our place at Southampton. By the Tuesday we agreed a price on this and in three weeks we'd moved. It was meant.'

Meant? I've heard that somewhere before. But did he like it?

'Love it,' he says. 'I enjoy the wind *and* the wet.'

There we were. End of story. Dramatic enough for him but nothing like the drama of Ingrid's love story. I drop down to the car park in a haze of thought to find the Thai chaps are about to leave. They offer to take me. 'Thanks,' I say, 'but I'm OK.' That's twice I've said no. Mentally I've renounced lifts. After they've gone I look at my watch and shake my head, trying to disown the feeble thinking inside. It's five past eleven and my bus leaves the Northern Sands Hotel – five miles away – in just over an hour! I'll have to shift. Quick. Sadly, there's no way I can call on Joanne.

I see the Thais have stopped hundreds of yards ahead. I shout and wave but not in time to catch them before they move off. Further on they stop again – this is pantomime time – but I'm too far away now to grab their attention and, even if I did, they'd probably think I was waving goodbye. Half-jogging, half-running in a constant tussle with the wind, I reach the hotel reception panting and sweating with minutes to spare. I ram the camping gear back into the rucksack ready to rush outside when Kevin, the abrupt one, says, 'it's just gone.' The bus came early. I've missed it.

A Missing Link

Am I gutted? Well, it could be one of those 'oh bother' moments. But I know what to do with this hiccup – Mick's trick: cut it up and move on. So how about hitching? There's a novel thought. The paradox of my situation hits home. I hoped I'd seen the back end of my thumb. But when I try to disconnect I can't. Yet the very connections I've hoped for have fallen flat. The people at the northernmost place weren't in. Through my own stupidity I missed out on visiting Joanne. And because the bus driver jumped the gun, I'm back on chance road. Well, here goes. Lift number 51: where are you?

The cars are few and far between on this coast road. If it was just a lift I was after, that wouldn't be so bad. But this has to be a lift with a connection! To the ferry crossing. It needs to be soon. Five, ten, fifteen minutes go by. So does the occasional car. Twenty minutes and I'm starting to worry. Half an hour and still outside the Northern Sands, I'm stuck in quicksand. I've barely an hour to make it now. If I'd set off straightaway I might have covered the eight miles in the time.

Crazy! As fast as I've put the missed bus out of my mind, I'm doubting whether I'll ever get a lift: defeatism with knobs on. How do I stay positive? I know: remember 'The Dean' and all the times things turned out for the best … when I waited.

My mind game works. Ten minutes later and I'm running towards a car that was going so slowly it hardly needed to brake. 'I'm trying to catch the Gills Bay ferry,' I burble. The glassy-eyed chap lobs a visibly indulgent look in my direction. He's bundled up in a rather shapeless fleece jacket and his cheeks could do with puffing up to help support some overbearing specs.

'I can drop you there if you like,' he says, making me think he's going out of his way and rooting me in awfully-kind-of-you mode. He's Derek and tells me he was born in Edinburgh, but there's no trace of Scotland in his speech. He used to live in Blackpool.

'I lost my mother a few months ago,' he says, as if to explain where he is now. 'She was ninety-one but could have passed for seventy. She never thought about being old.'

That's positive. I settle into the seat. There's more to come.

'Even in a wheelchair she had her wits about her. I looked after her twenty-four hours a day. The relatives never knew what I had to do. We got back from Morecambe one night after a trip in the caravanette and she was very quiet, not herself. "I'm all right," she said. But I could see how pale she was. I got hold of the NHS twenty-four-hour service and they took her in. She had pneumonia and went downhill: unconscious for the last three days. I was there to the very end.' He looks at me as if I know what he went through. Then he adds, 'And during the Second World War she used to make rubber dinghies and lifejackets.'

He wants me to know she wasn't just an invalid, and how much he tried to do. But Derek's devotion is here now and he's learnt from her example. 'I keep fit,' he assures me, 'and I eat a healthy diet with plenty of fresh veg. I'm fifty-five you know,' – well, he is doing his best – 'and never had a girlfriend up to now.'

What an admission. Why is he telling me this?

'That might change. My first real girlfriend, maybe, is coming over in April and she'll stay a couple of months.'

'Oh, great,' I say, pleased for him and intrigued.

[DAY SIXTEEN]

'She's half my age, from Thailand.'

What! Taking news like this on board ought to be second nature by now, but it comes as such a shock that I can only say, 'yes?'

'The Thais are really friendly people,' he's telling me while I'm wondering how close one can get to coincidence before breaking out in spots.

'Yes, yes. I know,' I splurge, and tell him all at once about the Dunnet Head meeting, the love banner – 'Love conquers all' – and the Thai bank note.

He explains how his meeting was set up: he got in touch with an agency in Perth. The owner had been married to a Thai lady for seventeen years. It had worked for him, so why wouldn't it work for Derek too? 'Of course,' I find myself saying but fear his expectations might be dashed. He's a kindly, caring man but not blessed with a face to conjure thoughts of romance in a young woman. They must have seen photos of each other though. And who knows what she's looking for? Derek tells me she has two boys, so perhaps it's a father figure. And a better life. There'll be big adjustments I think. On both sides.

We've arrived at Gills Bay and the ferry's in dock but I've half an hour before it leaves. We sit in the car. Derek still wants to chat. So do I.

'Is it the first time you'll have met?' I ask.

'Yes,' he says. 'I can't fly.'

'And what do you know about her?'

'I have to respect her religion – that's one thing.' But he's not sure whether she's a Buddhist or Christian. 'I have to give the parents a dowry,' he says, 'if we marry. It's their tradition. But I don't know how much.'

I try not to sound sceptical but Derek's unknowing doesn't inspire confidence.

'Thai girls are looking for clean living men. They can't find them at home. So many Thai young men are into drugs,' he says. 'That's what the agency chap said.'

My mind goes straight to the threesome at Dunnet Head. I couldn't imagine cleaner living chaps. I'm really concerned for Derek now, and the trust he's placed in what he's been told. 'How will you manage?' I ask, thinking of the costs to come.

Derek isn't working. 'I could take a PSV licence I suppose. But

I'm passionate about history,' he says. He's been to Culloden and knows all about Rob Roy's grave. 'I was at some friends' house the other day and happened to look at their stone fireplace. "Can you see?" I said. "There's a fossil in it: a fish." They'd never noticed.'

Perhaps he should be a guide, I say, if he's that observant.

I have to go but he fiddles in the glove compartment. 'There,' he says, flourishing a photograph in what appears to be a bus pass. It's of his mother. 'See how she looks.'

'Grand lady,' is all I can say. I wish him the very best of luck and make my way to the ferry. I'm pinching myself: but for the lift I turned down and the bus that came too soon, I'd have missed Derek. And at the end of my hitchhike I'd never have heard this story of a possible first love: as fitting an end as I could have wished to a journey which began with the love story of a lifetime. How had this all happened? By chance?

After Words

Orkney

'Weren't my most baffling moments the best ones?'

I couldn't get Derek out of my mind on the ferry. As we ploughed past the deserted island of Stroma into the open waters of the Pentland Firth, I had doubts about his course. Was I right? Strange chemistry can make bonds. I'd been swayed by appearances, but had I underplayed what he said? He might be fifty-five but he kept fit and healthy. Like his mother, Derek wasn't thinking old: he talked of a girlfriend, imagined a wife and family.

Was he naïve, or open-minded? Derek hadn't let thoughts of religious differences colour his attitude. When he knew more, he'd respect them. He was certainly alert. That enquiring mind of his ought to capture the enthusiasm of those two young boys. He'd love taking them to places of interest in his caravanette. Derek hadn't just given me a lift, he'd reminded me of the way to go: taking things as they come.

Past experience can be a strongbox of presumptions. But the present comes with a pocketful of change: opening up to chance can do it; you can invite change as Derek had done; or change can be forced on you. That's what prompted me to visit North Ronaldsay. I had a date with some adaptable sheep.

I cadged a lift to Kirkwall from someone on the boat and loaded up on provisions before tracking down a B & B near the airport. The owner ran me there for the first flight of the day and, sat beside the pilot of the Islander plane, I had the best possible view of Orkney's many islands. The flight took barely twenty minutes and that included a touchdown at Sanday.

I was unprepared for the reception. A chap on the airstrip asked, 'Are you Les Cowan?' He'd mistaken me for the Baptist pastor due to conduct the Sunday service. I was sorry to disappoint him. I suppose I felt flattered to be thought a man of the cloth. When I said that I planned to walk the two and a half miles to Dennishill Cottage, he offered to take my rucksack and leave it inside the door. Locked doors were obviously a novel concept on North Ronaldsay, but not generous gestures.

I had directions to the cottage – not far from the lighthouse – but I only needed to spot my rucksack inside to be sure I'd found my new home. Three days to myself would be a tonic after a non-stop conversation with the rest of humanity. Once I settled in, thoughts of the last sixteen days went out of the window. My journey had ended but I was in some curious vacuum, between breaths, waiting for a fresh inrush of air. Orkney would do that all right.

I'd glimpsed some sheep on my way to the cottage. Now I wanted a closer look. It wasn't easy. They were confined to the rocky foreshore by a long dry-stone wall. As soon as I showed my face, they scuttled off in a tumble of dark grey, buff, brown and creamy white fleece. These were no ordinary sheep and this no ordinary island. Shortly before I left home I happened to catch a TV slot on the North Ronaldsay sheep. Back in the 1830s, the laird wanted to introduce bigger, more profitable sheep. To prevent interbreeding he banished the native breed to the foreshore, building a twelve-mile-long wall to encircle the island. Left to themselves, the sheep survived by feeding on kelp and other seaweeds. That was a change in diet I'd never have thought possible and a remarkable example of adaptation that I had to see.

Could there be any finer role model for someone challenged to change a routine, let alone the habits of a lifetime? But now that time was my own, how would I adapt? Would chance get a look-in?

I spent the rest of the day exploring this northernmost tip of the island. A group of cormorants fanning their wings in the morning sun put me in mind of primeval times. Did pterodactyls do the same? I exchanged greetings with a wide-eyed seal out at sea before stumbling across one on the shore with patches of puppy fluff. It snorted a warning as I approached. I tried to get close to the sheep but, though I skulked behind a rowing boat and a stone shelter, vigilant sentries soon tipped off the others. I did spot one sheep nibbling a frond of kelp, but there was no front seat for this hitchhiker. I could only be a bystander.

As I walked round, laser-like streams of sunlight played on the sea and an inland lake reflected the immensity of the skies. There are no trees on the island which is largely flat. Apart from odd cottages, only the two lighthouse towers – the operative one and an old beacon – broke up the panoramic view. I rotated. Not a soul in sight. Where else had I felt so insignificant, yet so open to the boundless space of possibilities?

Having catalogued my lifts the night before, I slept soundly until a glare at the window woke me at 5.15: the intermittent flash from the lighthouse. Over a breakfast of tinned sardines I read that this, Britain's tallest land-based lighthouse, was designed by Robert Louis Stevenson's grandfather. Visits by the writer to such remote lighthouses are thought to have inspired *Kidnapped* and *Treasure Island*.

Knowing that the seaweed diet of the sheep lent a highly prized taste to the meat, I planned to visit the only café, at the bird observatory. Its speciality of North Ronaldsay roast mutton was a gourmet treat. Having the use of a bicycle, I rode back across the long neck of land to the main body of the island where the multifaceted roof of the observatory stood out from the simple gables of the island's cottages.

'So you're the hitchhiker,' the waiter said as he served the Cullen Skink starter – a creamy, smoked haddock soup. Word spreads fast round a community of some sixty people. He interrupted the drift of our conversation to remark on some stray sheep in a field. 'Must be a breach in the wall. Not so bad this time of the year but in summer they'll be after the crops.' The sheep's adaptability knows no bounds.

While I sipped my soup, four other people – a couple and two women – were chatting two tables away. I caught snatches:

'remember you're fifty, not fifteen ... never mind what I fancied, it was sandwiches or toast.' One of the women was from Fair Isle, about twenty-five miles away, though her accent sounded terribly English against the sing-song quality of the Orkney tongue.

I'd have liked to join in but couldn't force an entrance. I thought I'd relish some silence on the island but I hadn't adapted. Perhaps a cough would get me noticed. It didn't. *What if I said something provocative, had a fit, feigned death?* I was getting that desperate when the arrival of the sheep put a stop to my plotting. The slowest-roasted lamb in red wine with rosemary sauce could never rival the distinctive taste of that mutton and no garnish conjure up a life lived on the seashore like this did. Ironic that this was the way I got closest to the sheep.

The departure of the two women gave me an opportunity to air my hitchhiking credentials and ask what brought this couple here.

'I'm the Baptist pastor,' he said.

What? 'You must be Les Cowan,' I said, explaining how I'd been mistaken for him. Not so much of a coincidence on a small island. But why did I think to mention Simon Ruscoe's sculptures representing the poverty-stricken world? 'They might be sited in a lake,' I said, 'as if drowning.' I remembered the B & B lady at Burnmouth telling me that immigrants used to be processed at Ellis Island in the US where a symbolic sculpture of one figure is helped out of the water by another.

Fiona, his wife, piped up, 'That's how we met.'

'How do you mean?' I said.

'Les pulled me out of the water twenty-seven years ago and saved me from drowning. We've been married twenty-five years now.'

'Extraordinary,' I said. No escape from chance meetings.

Les told me about the inter-faith co-operation here. When a Church of Scotland minister was overstretched, Les stepped in to cover services, and vice versa, even if there were only half a dozen in the congregation, as there had been that morning. 'Worship has moved with the times,' he said. 'Now it's often accompanied with modern music played on guitars. Then we might have forty-five minutes of teachings, but that can be shared experience and interpretations.' How refreshing.

I cycled back to the cottage, reminding myself to write postcards home. 'Wish you were here' would hardly do. But a thought flashed. *What if, like Les, I had to address a congregation?* How would I share my experiences and interpret them?

I could tell my parishioners about the great wave of humanity that gave me lifts: from bricklayer to bookkeeper, drifter to doctor, barman to managing director, willow-weaver to woodturner. I could say how they'd found their directions in life. Or were still looking. Or weren't.

I could laud my discoveries: the sweetest taste of a badly blemished apple; the velvety softness in a horse chestnut husk; the exotic plumage of a blue tit. But I'd have to mention the shards of glass lodged in the trunk of a tree. And what had I learned about the state of society? I'd gleaned a pretty good idea of the prevailing mood from the cross-section of voices. There was hope and vision for sure, but the unease and discontent were loud enough to concern any congregation.

Back in the cottage, dunking the last of my digestive biscuits, what I'd had to unlearn – the preconceptions – kept coming back to me. I'd had lifts from six lone women drivers, a good number from young men, and at least four from people I hadn't even thumbed. And the re-thinking I'd had to do! The chips that made me change my tune about the transport café for one, never mind all the other misjudgements. Should I tell my congregation about those?

What about beliefs? There was no gospel for me to hang on to: I'd left 'The Hitchhiker's Way' behind. It served a purpose but I'd had to embrace 'What ifs?' and let the unpredictable have its way. Look where it led: to Findhorn, Portsoy, then on to David Mackay, the Thai people, Derek and maybe the start of another love story.

I had no idea how these, and so many other meetings materialised. But weren't my most baffling moments the best ones? I had chance to thank for them. Of course. *That's* what I'd talk about: chance. And how would I explain it? Pure coincidence, divine intervention or the doings of 'The Dean'? I might speculate that fate played a part. Often chance encounters seemed to carry a meaning, as if to point me in the right direction. But maybe I read too much into the purely random.

How much had my mindset contributed? Perhaps my

expectations acted as a trigger and my subconscious helped make connections. Might extra-sensory perception have been involved? Questions. Questions. And where did they take me? Into the unknown! If this journey had any lesson it was a paradoxical one: that the closer I came to my destination, the further I drifted away from conclusions.

Back to something I *could* deal with: the postcards. I'd have to catch the post tomorrow, my last full day.

The wind and rain were spoiling for a fight when I woke. I decided on one last walk round the headland. Would I find the young seal again? The faintest trace remained: a few strands of fur stuck in a crevice. The cormorants were still there, balancing on the outermost slabs of rock, wings tight. And the sheep were huddled, hugging the stone wall. I would miss them. Theirs was a wild self-possession that I admired intensely. They had inheritance rights. But, rattled by the wind and stung by icy fusillades, I was losing my hold.

I battled my way to the post office at the other end of the island and wrestled with the door to be greeted by Sandra, a plumpish woman my sort of age, wafting confidence. A generous head of jet black hair left no room for doubt.

'Fierce, isn't it,' I said.

'This is mild,' she countered. 'Often it's force eleven or twelve.'

The post office seemed to double as an off-licence, but wore other hats too – a whole assortment lined up on a shelf – Sandra's own woolly hat sideline. 'Runics' she called them, knitted in the native sheep's wool, of course.

'How d'you come to live here?' I asked. She didn't sound like a local.

I could hardly credit what she told me. She and her husband used to run a jewellery and goldsmith business but their lives had been rooted in the land, farming on the Yorkshire moors. 'We had great security,' she said, 'but gates to open and close on the way out. That's what made us vulnerable. A gang lay in wait, attacking from behind and kidnapping us.'

They took them to the farmhouse, then to the shop. In total the gang made off with a million poundsworth of gold, silver and jewellery, but not before stringing them both upside down from beams. Horrific! The graphic way Sandra related all this I might have been watching a *Crimewatch* reconstruction.

They managed to struggle free but the whole experience shattered them. Even more unnerving, the gang was never caught. The trauma was devastating: enough to make them desperate for a new life. No wonder. They toyed with America, New Zealand and Australia. Nothing gelled until one day Sandra popped into the newsagent to collect her Sunday paper.

'But I picked up the wrong one by mistake,' she said, 'and tucked inside the *News of the World* was an *Exchange & Mart*. When I saw this post office business advertised I couldn't believe it. I phoned up straightaway. Then I took a cup of coffee up to my husband – still in bed – and said, "You're in for a bit of a shock. I've bought a place in Orkney." ' They'd been here eleven years. Her husband's Postman Pat and they love the life.

Surrender! I felt like waving a white flag. Back at the cottage I packed my stuff but couldn't tidy up my thoughts. How *could* I talk about chance? And explain it? Impossible. Chance had given Sandra and so many others direction. It's what brought me here and what blows me away. But I couldn't pin it down. Nor did I want to. Chance would speak for itself.

After plane, bus and boat, the coach trip home was an eighteen-hour stint through the night and early morning. I hardly spoke to anyone or took anything in. But my lasting memory is that of a Scotsman behind, engaged in a non-stop chat with a mate. And the only word I ever made out was 'Aye ... aye ... aye ... aye ... aye.' I'd go along with that.

The faces of my fellow travellers

A small sample of the incredible people who gave me lifts and without whose generosity this book could never have been written. Those pictured have not been identified to protect their privacy.

Appendix One

THE HITCHHIKER'S WAY – The Twenty Tenets

1. There are many routes to a destination.
2. The more connections, the greater the meaning.
3. Direction can come from avoiding destinations, and fixed ideas.
4. Watch out for signs and learn how to read them.
5. Keep following the unfamiliar to go further.
6. Out of stillness come new insights and directions.
7. Doing what you love doing transports others.
8. Letting come, letting go makes it so much easier to move on.
9. Let what you feel passionate about lead you on.
10. Difficulties are the route march to discoveries.
11. Change yourself if you want to change where you are.
12. Signals from one's surroundings help one make sense of situations.
13. Challenges to a routine are the springboards for change.
14. Knock on enough doors to open up opportunity.
15. Take responsibility for everything that happens to you.
16. Signposts are here now, pointing to the next destination.
17. Accept what you've been given to go forward.
18. Go with the flow and good things follow.
19. Set a goal but let chance show the way.
20. Making different connections leads to new discoveries.

Index to Lift-givers

A Note from the Author

At the end of any book, writers usually contribute a few choice notes about themselves. But readers will have learned quite enough about me from the text. The effect this journey had on my attitudes may well be of more interest. In any case it raised so many issues – about the sort of society we've created, the quality of lives we lead and the role of chance in influencing directions – that readers might want to discuss them further.

I end the book with a comment that one can't explain chance. This is not a cop-out but a recognition that random factors and calculations of probability may not be enough to account for so-called coincidences. One can certainly speculate, as I do, on what else might be involved. You may have had experiences that you wish to share. Please feel free to contribute them and any other comments to my blog: *http://onchanceroad.blogspot.com*